KABBALAH

KABBALAH

Secrecy, Scandal and the Soul

HARRY FREEDMAN

BLOOMSBURY CONTINUUM
LONDON · NEW YORK · OXFORD · NEW DELHI · SYDNEY

BLOOMSBURY CONTINUUM
Bloomsbury Publishing Plc
50 Bedford Square, London, WC1B 3DP, UK

BLOOMSBURY, BLOOMSBURY CONTINUUM and the Diana logo are trademarks of
Bloomsbury Publishing Plc

First published in Great Britain 2019

A catalogue record for this book is available from the British Library

Library of Congress Cataloguing-in-Publication data has been applied for

ISBN: HB: 978-1-4729-5098-7; ePDF: 978-1-4729-5096-3; ePub: 978-1-4729-5097-0

2 4 6 8 10 9 7 5 3

Typeset by Newgen KnowledgeWorks Pvt. Ltd., Chennai, India
Printed and bound in the United States by Berryville Graphics Inc.

To find out more about our authors and books visit www.bloomsbury.com
and sign up for our newsletters

Dedicated to the memory of

Louis Freedman 1921–2017
Joan Freedman 1926–2018

For the winter is past, the rain has gone. The buds have appeared on the earth, the time for song has arrived and the voice of the dove is heard in our land.

Contents

List of Illustrations

Preface

Next time you meet a Hollywood celebrity, take a look at their left wrist. See if they have a knotted red string tied around it. If they do, the chances are they have visited a Kabbalah Centre, where red string can be bought for as little as $26 a length and small bottles of Kabbalah water for only $4 each.

The Kabbalah Centre used to say that their water was subjected to a process that restructured its intermolecular binding. After a BBC documentary challenged their assertion they dropped it from their website. In reality, Kabbalah water doesn't seem to be any different from the ordinary variety. Yet the claims made for its healing powers are outrageous. It is beneficial to soak one's feet in it, while meditating on letters from the Hebrew alphabet. It can, apparently, even cure cancer. Madonna, the most prominent of all the Kabbalah Centre's devotees, planned to fill her swimming pool with it.

Red string bracelets are said to protect against the evil eye. Whatever its power, it didn't help David Beckham at the Euros in 2004; he wore the string, missed a penalty and England were out of the competition.

Neither red string nor Kabbalah water seems to offer much protection against calumny and scandal, if events surrounding the international network of Kabbalah Centres are anything to go by. Set up in the 1980s by an enterprising former insurance salesman and his wife, the Kabbalah Centre proved astonishingly successful in attracting wealthy celebrities, as well as selling string and water. At the peak of their popularity, which occurred perhaps not coincidentally around the turn of the millennium, their VIP visitors included Ashton Kutcher, Demi Moore, Lindsay Lohan, Elizabeth Taylor and Sandra Bernhard. Mick Jagger, Princess Eugenie of York, Kylie Minogue and Britney Spears are just some of those seen wearing the red bracelet.

But as the glamour years subsided, fraud and sex scandals began dogging the Centre's reputation. Its leaders were accused of running a cult. Sandra Bernhard, who had first introduced Madonna to the Kabbalah Centre, summed it up: 'The wheels started to fall off ... Unfortunately, money corrupts everything, even spirituality.'

By its very nature celebrity attention is ephemeral. It was bound to pass. Perhaps for the rock stars and movie icons Kabbalah was nothing more than a passing fad, a whimsy by which public lives could attempt to reconnect with their inner being. But there is nothing faddish about the philosophers, scientists and intellectual giants who have been drawn to Kabbalah. C. G. Jung, the founder of analytical psychology, brought the subject to the attention of post-war Europe's intelligentsia, maintaining as he did that Kabbalah's portrayal of the cosmos reflected the structure of the human psyche. Gottfried Wilhelm Leibniz, the philosopher who claimed to have discovered the principles of mathematical calculus, dabbled in Kabbalah, while his great rival Isaac Newton studied and repudiated it. John Locke, the founder of modern political liberalism, the poet John Milton and maybe even William Shakespeare were familiar with Kabbalah. Today, scientists of a mystical bent point to the astonishing similarity between the fifteenth-century Kabbalistic description of the creation of the universe and the modern theory of the Big Bang.

Critics of Kabbalah – and there have been many – will point to the so-called cranks and social misfits whose Kabbalistic dabblings enabled them to impress, influence and often manipulate their more gullible followers. Aleister Crowley invariably tops this list, followed by Eliphas Lévi and a host of lesser-known occultists, of whom the most interesting is probably the obscure Dr Falcon, known as the Ba'al Shem of London. Centuries earlier, Kabbalah's weird and wonderful cast list had included Heinrich Cornelius Agrippa, immortalised in literature as Dr Faustus, the magician John Dee, Emperor Rudolf II of Prague and, as legend would have it, the golem who terrorised the streets of his city.

History is full of the names of those drawn to the mysteries of Kabbalah, some immersing themselves deeply, others barely scratching the surface. Yet, for the different ages in which they lived, and for the great variety of their lifestyles, they all had one thing in common. They all consumed Kabbalah as if they were plucking from a tree laden with ripe fruit. They barely gave a thought to how its theories were devised, how its cosmology had developed or how its mysteries had been revealed. That Kabbalah was a mysticism immersed in the Jewish tradition, with roots going back two thousand years, meant very little to them They knew nothing of the years of study, the self-abnegation and ascetic rigour which had enabled the classical Jewish kabbalists in Provence, Spain and finally Galilee to perfect their art.

And nor need they have known. For the most part the philosophers, magicians and scientists were drawing not on the Jewish tradition of Kabbalah, but on its Christian reformulation, conceived during the Renaissance by men like Pico della Mirandola and Johannes Reuchlin, Christian scholars of the Hebrew mysteries.

Arguably it was the divergence of Christian Cabala from its Jewish progenitor which paved the way for other Kabbalistic strands that emerged through the ages. Again arguably, it is the existence of these diverse strands that make it impossible for anyone today, even the classical kabbalists, to claim that theirs is the sole, legitimate expression of Kabbalah. That at least is the argument of this book.

Kabbalah today is more popular than it has ever been. In its classical Jewish incarnation it is practised and studied by mystically inclined Pietists in inward-looking communities. A world away, those seeking to overcome the stresses and conflicts of modern life take courses, read books and attend lectures on Kabbalah's contemporary manifestation. These two Kabbalahs speak to wholly different cultures, but they share the same story. It is the story I hope to tell.[1]

Introduction

Kabbalah was never meant to be fashionable. Its earliest exponents, deeply mystical, other-worldly Jews, studying in closed, secretive groups in twelfth-century Provence, would have been amazed, probably horrified, to hear how far and wide their doctrine has spread and how universal it has become.

The recent interest in Kabbalah emerged out of the hippy movement's fascination with mysticism and meditation in the 1960s. It became particularly popular with the advent of New Age spirituality in the late twentieth century, when it was feted as a powerful technique for personal development. This was not Kabbalah as it had been practised in the twelfth or thirteenth centuries. But Kabbalah has always evolved, changed and bifurcated into different strands. The twentieth century was by no means the first time that Kabbalah had broken away from its early, exclusively Jewish confines.

Christian Cabala (note the different spelling) was conceived at the high point of the Renaissance, in Lorenzo de' Medici's Florence. As the sixteenth century progressed it became allied to magic, alchemy and Hermeticism. Kabbalah contributed to the scientific revolution and played a central part in the nineteenth-century occult revival. Meanwhile, enigmatic new Kabbalistic practices and beliefs were becoming ever more closely embedded into mainstream Jewish life. Kabbalah is a rare example of a spiritual philosophy open to people of all creeds, yet one that does not detract from their faith. Today it is studied by more people, of all religions and none, than ever before.

The essence of Kabbalah is the quest to understand how the divine will conceived, created and maintains the universe, to use that understanding to draw closer to the unknowable source of all, and ultimately to restore the flawed cosmos to its original perfection. But, of course, it's far more complicated than that.

This book tells the story of Kabbalah's origins, its development and spread, from its earliest beginnings until the present day. Exactly when those earliest beginnings were is not so easy to pinpoint.

Our story begins in the first centuries of the Common Era with a group of Jewish mystics whose curiosity about the nature of heaven inspired them to embark on mystical voyages of discovery. We do not know the names of these people, nor where they lived, but we do have some of the literature they left behind. Sunk deep into meditative trances, they constructed elaborate travelogues of their visits to heaven, describing in detail the architecture and layout of the empyrean palaces and halls, cataloguing the dangers waiting to entrap the unwary traveller and extolling the delights awaiting those who deserve them. They knew the names of the angels, categorised them according their various ranks and hierarchies, brought back tales about their complaints and rebellions and learned to sing their songs and adulations. The heaven they described, its awesome majesty and teeming host, appears little different from the court of an ancient oriental potentate. Heaven in their imagination was the idealised paradigm of an earthly seat of power, splendour and glory.

The heavenly voyagers hewed pathways along which the initiate might travel to experience celestial bliss. But for later generations, experiences rhapsodised by enchanted minds were not enough. It was illuminating to know that through the use of meditations, incantations and body contortions one could experience the sublime: that through the use of such techniques one might attain mystical communion with God and his angels. But utopian delight is not intellectually satisfying. Human curiosity demands more.

The intellectual component arrived, in the form of a book that set out in complex and impenetrable detail the numinous tools and techniques used by the Almighty to create the world. Written in Hebrew, the Book of Formation is a strange, terse, almost haunting work, impossible to understand when read literally. It created a mystical vocabulary for the first time, and a quasi-scientific, interconnected way of understanding how, in the eyes of its unknown author, the cosmos was formed. It was all to do with language, and numbers.

The Book of Formation's laconic hints were developed and expanded by different schools of mystics, philosophers and putative scientists over the succeeding centuries. By the time the threads were drawn together in twelfth-century Provence, the principles of Kabbalah were established.

One only has to read the first chapter of Genesis to know that God commanded the world into being. 'Let there be light' is the first thing he said, and sure enough 'There was light'.[1] The world was created through God's speech. Hebrew speech, for that is the language of the book of Genesis. Speech is composed of words, and words are made from letters. Letters, specifically Hebrew letters, are therefore the basic tools of creation. The discovery that the alphabet is the foundation of the material world was as important to mystics at the end of the first millennium as was the discovery of DNA's centrality to life for scientists a thousand years later.

Letters are the building blocks of the cosmos. And, like all building blocks, letters can be arranged, jumbled up and rearranged. When they are arranged in a certain order they appear as the text of the Bible. Within this text, the mysteries of the world's creation are all encoded. By manipulating and rearranging the letters of Scripture, Kabbalah aims to decode and make clear the divine mysteries.

By the end of the tenth century or thereabouts, the Jewish mystical tradition had discovered how to travel to heaven, the means of communication with the angels and the principles of decoding the Bible to reveal the secrets of the greatest of all powers, the power to create worlds. The focus of Kabbalah now became putting this knowledge together into a coherent, if mystically fuzzy, system. And then to learn how to make use of this knowledge to draw down heavenly bounty that bestows benefit upon individuals, humankind and the world.

Armed with this knowledge, Kabbalah no longer needed to simply gaze at the heavens. Understanding how the cosmos was created brings with it the ability to manipulate creation, to transfigure the physical world. Even before the first kabbalists had finished setting out their doctrine, some of those who possessed mystical knowledge discovered how to use it to change the natural order of things. Far more successful than the magicians of old, the things they could now do were amazing. They outwitted demons, annulled spells, procured wealth, induced fertility and cured illnesses. Kabbalah is not magic. It is much more powerful than that. Ever since Kabbalah was discovered, magic has always ridden in its slipstream.

The word Kabbalah means reception, in the sense of a received tradition. This tradition, according to the kabbalists, was handed down through the generations by word of mouth, beginning with Moses, who received it directly from God. It was eventually set down in writing, according to these same kabbalists, by a second-century rabbi in the Land of Israel. His name was Shimon bar Yoḥai. A member of the fraternity who laid the foundations for modern Judaism, he is quoted frequently in the early rabbinic literature. However, there is no mention in this literature of the book he is supposed to have written, in which he explicated Moses's oral tradition. This book was lost, or deliberately concealed, for over a thousand years. It eventually surfaced in the thirteenth century, bearing the name Zohar, in the Castile region of Spain.

The mystery of what happened to the Zohar during its years of concealment is, to historians and rationalists, no mystery at all. They believe it only 'appeared' in the thirteenth century, because that is when it was written. They believe it was attributed to Shimon bar Yoḥai by its medieval authors, in order to provide it with a venerable prestige.

Of all the many Kabbalistic books, the Zohar is by far the most important. The questions of who wrote it, where it came from and whether it really is the product of an ancient revealed tradition are all secondary to the impact that the book has had on the development of Kabbalah.

The Zohar is a gigantic tome that meanders between stories, parables, metaphors, mystical allusions and metaphysical speculation. It is a compelling, if lengthy, book to read. Yet beneath the captivating romance of its narrative lie the mystical outlines of Kabbalah, ideas which were elaborated upon and systematised by devotees over succeeding decades. As time went by Kabbalah became more intricate, its concepts more abstruse, its terminology more complex, its allusions more daring.

The world of the Zohar and its kabbalists was small and secluded. It stayed that way for over 200 years. Then, in the space of just five years, two unconnected events took place, after which Kabbalah could never be the same again. In 1492, the closed world of the kabbalists was ruptured when the Jews were expelled from Spain together with their Kabbalah. Around the same time, in Renaissance Florence, Giovanni Pico della Mirandola extracted Kabbalah from its Jewish context, proclaiming it a universal science whose true importance was not to Judaism but to Christianity. Pico's scholarship marked the beginning of Christian Cabala.

From that moment, Kabbalah dwelt in two distinct, disconnected worlds. In Christian Europe it became the source of arcane hints designed to support the principles of Christianity. Later, Christian Cabala was utilised to buttress new, emerging systems of thought. As a putative natural science it contributed to Enlightenment philosophy, its occult nature underpinned the dissident beliefs of nineteenth-century supernaturalists and as a tool for self-development it fuelled much of the esotericism of the twenty-first-century New Age.

Christian Cabala influenced the scientific outlook of men like Gottfried Wilhelm Leibniz and Isaac Newton, albeit negatively in the latter case. Its symbols and motifs found their way into the literature of Spenser, Marlowe and perhaps even Shakespeare.[2] The angelic ranks and demonic hierarchies of Milton's *Paradise Lost* are drawn directly from its mythology; John Locke investigated it when formulating his political philosophy. Most spectacularly, Christian Cabala became allied with magic, Hermeticism, alchemy and lesser arts within the occult galaxy, to inspire devout, misunderstood magicians like Cornelius Agrippa and John Dee. Controversially, Kabbalah and the concealed arts strode side by side into the twentieth century, at the heels of the infamous Aleister Crowley.

While Christian Cabala was forging new paths, Jewish mystical fraternities in the northern Israel city of Safed were pushing at classical Kabbalah's boundaries, seeking a theology to explain their nation's traumatic exile. Scarred by the Spanish expulsion yet with their cultural horizons expanded through sojourns in Turkey, North Africa and the European Mediterranean, the Safed kabbalists embarked on a reappraisal of their mystical doctrine. Their work reached its peak in the thought of Isaac Luria, who saw earthly exile as merely a consequence of a far greater dislocation that had taken place in the divine realms above. This dislocation, the drama of heavenly exile in Luria's theory, was a necessary act, essential for the creation of the world. Isaac Luria became as important to the future of Jewish Kabbalah as Pico della Mirandola had been to its Christian offspring. Significantly, or not, both men died at a very young age.

The approach of modernity did nothing to lessen Kabbalah's appeal to the dreams and fantasies of the masses, or to diminish its disruptive potential. A messianic crisis rooted in Kabbalah rocked the Jewish world in the seventeenth century. Its repercussions could be felt across Europe; they still reverberate today. A hundred years later Kabbalah was instrumental in creating Hasidism, the most vibrant, yet anti-modern of all Jewish religious movements.

Kabbalah became fashionable in the late twentieth century. The Kabbalah Centre, famous in its heyday for its celebrity devotees, formulated Kabbalistic responses and techniques to address the aspirations, stresses and traumas of modern life. Buffeted by accusations of cultism, sexual offences and financial misdemeanours, its short history has been rocky. It has won praise and criticism in roughly equal measure; as has all Kabbalah throughout its history.

Today, Kabbalah exists in many incarnations, and is taught from many perspectives. Its story is far from over. I have tried in this book to provide a flavour of its history so far.

A vast amount has been written on the Kabbalah. There are many guides aimed at lay people, the best of which offer an accessible introduction to the principles and theory of Kabbalah. Yet the great majority of the literature is highly specialised and technical, inaccessible to a general readership, frequently mystifying even to those who have immersed themselves in the subject for years.

A critical approach to Kabbalah is taken by the academic community. Scholarly researchers come at the subject from many different angles. Some look at how particular ideas developed by examining their historical setting or external influences. Others explore the social structure of Kabbalistic communities, and the environments in which they flourished. Still others seek to identify previously unknown mystical circles, investigate the literary structure of Kabbalist texts or review how Kabbalah has influenced the life and thought of those beyond its borders.

I have taken a slightly different approach. Rather than being a book about what Kabbalah is or how different variants and theories emerged, I have chosen to discuss what happened to Kabbalah, looking at milestones in Kabbalah's history and its key interactions with the external world. I have written it for anyone who thinks that the history of Kabbalah might be interesting, interesting enough at least to spend a few hours reading about it. It is an unusual history, and one well worth pondering.

Although the academic study of Kabbalah is as much a part of its history as everything else, I have not devoted a separate chapter to the subject's many scholars. This book is based, in large measure, on the research, theories and conclusions of the academic community, as referenced in the footnotes and bibliography. I hope that conveying their insights to the best of my ability is the most appropriate way of expressing their contribution to Kabbalah's history. I have frequently had to choose between competing academic theories, but I trust that for the most part I have remained close to whatever consensus may be said to prevail among the scholarly community. All errors and infelicities in the text are, of course, mine.

Kabbalah's popularity today was never a foregone conclusion. It has always had opponents who ridiculed and vilified it. Even today there are many who look with suspicion upon what they term pop-Kabbalah or Kabbalah-lite, who mock the mystically absorbed, closed world of the devout religious kabbalists, or who scorn the whole subject as superstition. Such views might indeed be correct: it is not the purpose of this book to persuade you otherwise. Like all religious beliefs, Kabbalah may be irrational; it is certainly not an empirically validated science. But the bigger point surely isn't whether or not Kabbalah is superstition, but whether it works for those who practise it. Provided, of course, it is not used to exploit the vulnerable or to justify unethical practices, a charge which has been levelled against some practitioners of the art in recent times.

Kabbalah today is practised on many levels. There are those for whom it is a real, everyday part of their highly devout lives. There are others who live contemporary lifestyles, yet at times of crisis or moments of life-changing significance may go to one of these devout kabbalists for an amulet or a blessing. Many people who read and study Kabbalah regard it as a tool that helps them to successfully navigate life in the twenty-first century. Kabbalah in the contemporary world can be approached in so many different ways that nobody, even the most conventional of classical kabbalists, can claim their perspective is the real thing, that they have sole rights to Kabbalah's genuine expression. As this book tries to make clear, there have been so many different incarnations of Kabbalah, existing side by side for so long, that it is meaningless to speak of authenticity.

Even before I began to write this book it was clear that the field of Kabbalah is so wide, and that its history has included so many personalities of note, that it would not be possible to include everything and everyone within the overview I was planning. As a result, many significant kabbalists do not get a mention at all; others only receive a few words. Of course, every thinker makes their mark. But unless that mark has moved the story of Kabbalah forward in some significant way, the chances are that, for reasons of space and readability, I have not been able to include them. If your favourite Kabbalist does not receive a mention in the text I can only apologise. Even deeply profound insights, however uniquely expressed, do not always result in significant historical development.

One of the problems when writing about a subject heavily rooted in a foreign language, as Kabbalah is in Hebrew, is how to deal with the technical jargon. I have tried wherever possible to use English equivalents for Hebrew concepts, names and even book titles. But, remarkably, some ideas are more intelligible when expressed in their original Hebrew than in an English translation. The *sefirot* – a fundamental principle of Kabbalistic theory – are a good example. There is no English word which even comes close to providing an adequate translation. So I have included a glossary for easy reference when a translation has appeared to be inadequate.

Using words in their original language gives rise to the problem of transliteration, how to deal with letters in the original language that have no equivalent in the target tongue. There are two letters in Hebrew which sound like the 'ch' in the Scottish word loch. One is softer than the other and neither is satisfactorily rendered by the letters 'ch', usually pronounced as in cheese. I have chosen to follow a convention that renders the harder pronunciation by 'ch' and the softer by 'ḥ', i.e. with a dot under the 'h'. Unless, that is, the word is commonly used in English, in which case I have followed the usual spelling. For example, Hasid and not Ḥasid.

All Kabbalistic systems are complex and I have not discussed them in any greater detail than is necessary to get across the historic points. Nevertheless, there are times when it has been necessary to refer to basic Kabbalistic ideas, otherwise the topic might make no sense at all. I have therefore included a very short appendix outlining the key principles of the theory of the *sefirot*, the most fundamental of all Kabbalistic principles. This is not designed to replace any of the excellent guides to Kabbalah that already exist – it is far too short and incomplete. But it may be of some use in understanding some of the discussions in the book.

The Origins of Kabbalah

A story is told of four men who entered the *Pardes*. Nobody knows for sure what the *Pardes* was, but the word in Persian means a garden. The story, however, is not about a visit to a garden; it is an account of a mystical journey to the heavenly spheres. The word *Pardes* is the origin of our word Paradise.

The four men lived at the end of the first century. The most famous was Akiva, best known of all the rabbis of the Talmud, the great Jewish compendium of law and ethics. His companions were ben Azzai, ben Zoma and Elisha ben Abuya. Ben is not a name, it means 'the son of'.

When they entered the *Pardes*, ben Azzai looked (at what, we do not know) and died. Ben Zoma looked and was 'afflicted'. Elisha ben Abuya looked and 'cut the shoots', meaning he abandoned his faith.[1] Only Akiva entered in peace and came out in peace.[2] It is a very short story.

It's likely that Akiva had made the trip before, and that his three companions were novices. He was the only one who took care not to look, and in one version of the story he even warned the others against it. His warning, however, was too opaque: 'When you get to the stones of pure marble,' he said, 'do not cry "water, water", for one who speaks falsehood will not endure[3]'. Clearly his companions didn't understand what he meant.

This tale is well known because it is one of a very small number of episodes in early mainstream Jewish literature that deal with the occult. Death and madness befalling travellers in a mysterious place give it a sort of malign appeal, a fascination not unlike that of a ghost story told around the campfire. The story appears in the Talmud as a justification for the religious ban on occult speculation.[4] It is a cautionary tale, to warn people of the dangers of dabbling in things they don't understand.

Akiva's warning 'do not cry "water, water"' is puzzling. The Talmud doesn't explain it, but there is no reason why it should; it is only reciting the story as a cautionary tale. But Akiva's exclamation starts to make sense when we step away from the Talmud and examine alternative versions of the legend that appear elsewhere. Notably, in a collection of little-known, often incomprehensible and frequently confused mystical texts which discuss the very things the Talmud is warning against.

Composed between the third and ninth centuries, these texts describe the experiences of Jewish mystics trying to undertake journeys to the palaces of heaven. We don't know what sort of people these mystics were, nor are we ever told why they were prepared to go through the rigorous mental training and physical deprivation necessary for these journeys of the soul. What we are told is that once they are temporarily freed from the constraints of their physical bodies, they become endowed with profound, prophetic insight; an insight which disappears when they return to their natural state. Prompted by curiosity, their journeys are a quest for understanding what lies beyond. And a scientific experiment to test the powers of the human soul.

Invariably men and always anonymous, the voyagers' only memorial is contained in these texts, many of which were hidden away and lay undiscovered for over a thousand years. In one document we read that when a seeker arrives at the gate to the sixth heavenly palace – there are seven altogether – he is deluged by an overpowering sensation, as if thousands, millions and billions of waves of water are crashing into him, submerging him, sweeping him away. Yet in reality there is not even one drop of liquid there.

It's all an illusion caused by the shimmering, shining marble slabs with which the palace is tiled. Crystal-clear and shimmering to the point of fluidity, the marble has the appearance of rushing water.[5] Yet, as Akiva warns, don't be fooled; the slabs are not water. Falsehood, even when just the result of a misunderstanding, cannot endure in heaven, where all is Truth.

THE WORK OF THE CHARIOT

The texts containing these accounts of heavenward voyages are known today as *hechalot*, or Palace, literature. They are a hotchpotch of many different texts, composed over several centuries, many of which have only survived in incomplete or even garbled form. They are Jewish mystical texts, but they are not yet what we would call Kabbalah; it will be several centuries before that name comes into use. Neither are they the earliest example of Jewish mystical writing; starting in the third century BCE seers had composed descriptions of heaven and hell, terrified their readers with apocalyptic visions and forewarned them of the events due to take place at the end of time. The book of Revelation in the New Testament, although a Christian text, is among the last of the genre, and, of course, the best known.

Although the Palace texts are not Kabbalah, they are the beginning of its history, marking the first significant step in the three-thousand-year evolution of Kabbalistic thought. Up to this point, from the earliest books of the Bible onwards, all mystical revelations had been granted by God and the angels to humans of their choosing, even if they hadn't asked to be chosen. The Palace literature marks the moment when people stopped hoping for a revelation from above and set out for themselves to snatch a glimpse of heaven. It signals the moment they began constructing esoteric rituals, often involving severe ascetic deprivation, with the intention of discovering what goes on within the celestial spheres.[6]

It is in the Bible, of course, that the first divine visions are granted. The early books of the Old Testament frequently speak of encounters between people and God. Adam and Eve, Cain,

Noah, Abraham, Moses and many others have conversations with their Creator. Even the serpent in the Garden of Eden is spoken to, though considering the punishment he received he would probably rather have been ignored. Still, he was no ordinary snake, as the later Kabbalah will make clear. But for all the visions, and the many descriptions of God, the Bible is remarkably coy about where, if anywhere, he dwells. Yes, it tells us that there is a place called heaven, and that it is in the sky. The builders of the Tower of Babel try unsuccessfully to reach it. Moses ascends the mountain to meet God, who has descended from above towards him. Together with the elders, Moses sees a sapphire pavement beneath the Almighty's feet.[7] But neither Moses nor indeed anyone else in the early parts of the Bible gets a look inside heaven; or at least they don't tell us if they do.

The first descriptions of heaven occur in the books of the Prophets. Isaiah, who lived some time before the destruction of the Jerusalem Temple in 586 BCE, has a vision of God sitting on a throne, dressed apparently in a flowing robe, the train of which 'filled the Temple'. Six-winged, fiery angels, known as seraphim, stood in attendance; when they proclaimed God's holiness their voices were so loud that the doorposts shook and the building filled with smoke.[8]

Isaiah's description of his vision was the earliest recorded glimpse of what the inside of heaven looked like. But it was the later prophet Ezekiel who provided much more detail of what a visitor was likely to see upon arrival at the heavenly gates.

Unlike Isaiah, Ezekiel lived after the Babylonians had destroyed Jerusalem and its Temple. With his compatriots he lived as a refugee by the rivers of Babylon, where they dreamed of their return to Zion and the reconstruction of their Temple. The latter part of Ezekiel's book is taken up with a detailed description of what he believed the rebuilt Temple would look like. His blueprint for the building was based upon what he saw in prophetic visions. In the very first chapter of his book he tells us that while he was sitting by the river, the skies opened, a whirlwind raged from the north and in the midst of cloud, flame and lightning, heaven appeared.

Ezekiel saw four winged creatures, flashing with fire and crackling with ionic charge. Each creature had four faces: of a human, an ox, an eagle and a lion. The creatures moved on wheels turning within other wheels, the circumference of their rims studded with eyes. The whole construction was joined together as one piece; its life force was in its wheels and whichever direction it proceeded, it was always heading forwards. When it moved, the beat of the creatures' wings sounded like a tempest of rushing waters, like the tumult of an army swelling to an almighty crescendo. When it paused, the wings subsided. Linked by their wings, the four creatures and their wheels formed the base of a sapphire throne, or Chariot, above which Ezekiel perceived an indescribable presence that he called Divine Glory.[9]

Later, Ezekiel had another vision. This time God lifted him up by his hair, suspended him between earth and heaven, and showed him the Jerusalem Temple in a state of desecration. Ezekiel referred to the Temple by the name *hechal*, the same word that Isaiah used for the heavenly palace in his vision. Isaiah's vision of heaven and Ezekiel's of the desecrated Jerusalem Temple are connected by the word *hechal*, or palace. The idea of a heavenly Jerusalem, or of the Temple as a representation of heaven on earth, which figures so prominently in later Christian and Jewish thought, begins in the prophecies of Isaiah and Ezekiel.

Although we might consider it odd to associate heaven with a mere palace or even a temple, with all their physical limitations and architectural peculiarities, in the ancient world such a description made complete sense. In ancient times some gods were regarded as little more than superhuman kings; in several cases kings even became gods. Ezekiel quotes the Egyptian Pharaoh, an earthly king if ever there was one, as claiming to have created the river Nile.[10] Neither Isaiah nor Ezekiel thought of Israel's God in this way. But it was natural for them to speak of him in royal terms.

The Jerusalem Temple was soon rebuilt, though Ezekiel did not live to see it. It survived for half a millennium, until the year 70 CE, when once again it was reduced to rubble, on this occasion by the Romans. This time it was not speedily rebuilt. All that remained of it for the Jews was a yearning, a longing for its restoration at some unspecified time in the future.

Most people expressed their yearning through prayer and repentance. But some went further. Yearning with as much passion as anyone else, they metaphorically rebuilt the Jerusalem Temple. Since circumstances demanded that it could no longer be built on earth, and as they were familiar by now with the idea of a heavenly Temple, they thrust the Jerusalem Sanctuary, so to speak, into the skies and subsumed it into its ineffable counterpart. Unable to make a pilgrimage to the Temple on earth, the mystically inclined sought a route by which they could ascend to its heavenly paradigm.

Ezekiel's experience provided the impetus for their journey to heaven. Although the indescribable, divine presence which the prophet saw in his vision was beyond all contemplation, what captured the imagination of those aspiring to ascend to the empyrean regions was his vision of the heavenly Chariot. The *hechalot* texts repeatedly describe attempted ascents to the Chariot. But, as if to protect themselves from the malign attention of evil spirits, who are always on the lookout for unsuspecting, questing travellers, those who tried to reach the Chariot never called it an ascent. The upwards journey to the heavenly Chariot is always referred to as a descent. Demons, as we all know, can be fooled by the simplest of tricks.

Descent to the Chariot could only be achieved in a state of the utmost purity. One text prescribes a regime far beyond anything we are likely to want to try today. The adept was required to fast for 40 days (perhaps eating at night, this isn't made clear). Each day he immersed himself 24 times in a river, lake or ritual bath. For all this time he was to sit in a dark house and not look at a woman.[11] Only when he had been through all that was he ready to lay his head between his knees, as Elijah had done when conjuring up rain,[12] and recite the incantations that would allow him to pass through the seven heavens that lay between him and the Chariot.

The journey was fraught with danger; it was never taken in isolation. Before a voyager attempted a mystical ascent, his colleagues would attend his physical body, to record his experiences and haul him back to safety if something went wrong. On one occasion a well-travelled voyager was giving an account to his students of the perils that may befall those who were not worthy. But he was unable to explain why some travellers were attacked and not others. The students implored him to call back his own teacher, the venerable sage Nehunyah ben Hakannah, who was at the time on his own journey to the Chariot, so that he could throw light on the matter.

They brought Nehunyah back by the simple device of exposing his body to a ritually unclean rag, making him too impure to remain in heaven. Such a technique may well have been used as a safety net for anyone whose introspection had gone on dangerously long. On his return Nehunyah told them that an attack may happen to a worthy traveller if his entourage, the scribes and companions who sat by him to record his experiences, was not of an acceptable standard. It seems that, rather like an astronaut today, travellers to the Chariot needed a home-based support team of worthy people.

But even with the best backup in place, passing through the heavens was never easy. Every heavenly palace was zealously guarded by gatekeepers, charged with keeping out unworthy intruders. To get past each gatekeeper, the voyager needed to present the appropriate set of magical seals. Constructed from secret names and stacked, like pillars of fire, at the base of the Chariot, the seals could only be acquired by a voyager who, before setting off on his travels, had familiarised himself with the multiplicity of divine and angelic names. When hoping to obtain a seal, the mystic had to recite the correct names for the one he wanted, interspersing his recitation with the corresponding incantations and hymns.

These angelic names, which occur in endless lists in the Palace literature, are often unpronounceable. Sometimes they look like meaningless, random strings of consonants. But they were packed with meaning for the mystical initiate. Every letter in the Hebrew alphabet has a numerical value and the complex names bear some sort of mathematical relationship to the occult power to which they relate. The nature of these relationships and their associated powers would have been obvious to a heavenly wayfarer, even if they are completely opaque to us.

Collecting the seals consumed a vast amount of spiritual energy, a commodity which the voyager had amassed during his weeks of mental preparation, but which was rapidly consumed as the journey progressed. As the journey proceeded, so the required energy increased. The route became increasingly dangerous. It was all too easy to fail. We have already seen what happened to Akiva's companions who mistook marble for water at the gateway to the sixth heaven. The entrance to the seventh palace was even more terrifying:

> And at the door of the seventh palace arise and stand angry all
> the warriors, strong, mighty, powerful, harsh, fearful, terrifying,
> taller than mountains and sharper than hills. Their bows
> are ready and aimed; swords sharpened and in their hands.
> Lightning flashes and streams from the balls of their eyes, and
> balls of fire from their nostrils and torches of burning coals
> from their mouths. They are girded with helmets and armour,
> and javelins and spears are hung upon their arms. Their horses
> are horses of darkness, horses of the shadow of death, horses of
> deep gloom, horses of fire, horses of hail, horses of iron, horses
> of fog ...[13]

This passage comes from *Hechalot Rabbati*, or Great Palaces, a book written in the fifth or sixth century, which describes a series of journeys through the seven heavens. Its principal hero is the second-century Rabbi Ishmael. *Hechalot Rabbati* makes constant use of his name, but in fact the book has nothing to do with him. One of the most frustrating aspects of ancient Near Eastern literature is that its authors often concealed their identity, and that of their heroes. Instead they attributed their works and deeds to well-known, but long-dead, personalities. They may have done so from modesty, or perhaps to enhance the prestige or credibility of their new composition, or simply because that was what an author was expected to do. The result is that we can never be certain who the authors of the early Chariot texts were, nor do we know anything about the actual people who undertook these perilous, supernatural (or, depending on how you look at it, hallucinatory) adventures. We are fortunate that some of their texts have survived. However, the true identities and lives of those who descended to the Chariot are a complete mystery to us. This is particularly unusual because in many other respects we are fairly well informed about Jewish life during the first 500 years of the Common Era.

Hiding their identities behind earlier rabbinic giants, and leaving only their language and style as a clue to the provenance of their texts, means that we cannot even say with certainty whether these mystics were active members of mainstream society, or whether they had withdrawn into obscure, isolated sects, the sort of oddball communities with which the history of all religions is dotted. All we can say is that, despite being unknown for several hundred years, eventually Chariot mysticism broke out of its shell. The ninth-century Aharon of Baghdad, of whom we shall hear more shortly, was familiar with it, as was the tenth-century historian Sherira Gaon.[14] We can push the dates back even earlier; some of the Jewish liturgical poetry composed in the seventh and eighth centuries contains motifs which are clearly drawn from the Chariot texts.[15] By the end of the first millennium, people in the principal centres of Jewish life had certainly heard of Chariot mysticism. But it is mentioned so infrequently in the wider religious literature of the time that it was almost certainly a minority activity. As mysticism has always been.

The principal heroes of the Palace literature are two of the Talmud's most prominent rabbis, Ishmael and Akiva. They both lived centuries before the Palace texts were composed and there is no clear indication from their own time that they really did engage in ecstatic adventuring. Even the story about Akiva's entry into the *Pardes* was first written down a century after his death. There must have been something about Akiva's personality that encouraged later generations to treat him as a mystical role model. But, at this distance, it is not easy to explain what that was.

Ishmael's presence in the Palace legends is just as hard to explain. Some sources confuse him with another Ishmael, a High Priest who did have mystical experiences.[16] It is this confusion which led our Ishmael to be regarded as a mystical voyager par excellence. But there is no contemporaneous evidence at all that Ishmael of the Talmud, Akiva's colleague, had mystical proclivities.

Indeed, far from regarding them as mystical companions, the Talmud presents Akiva and Ishmael as intellectual opponents. They differed markedly regarding the nature of the Torah. As far as Akiva was concerned, every word, letter, jot and tittle in the sacred text is of religious significance; no ink of holy writ was ever wasted. This expansive view allowed him to read far more into the text than the less romantic Ishmael, whose mantra was 'the Torah speaks in human language'.[17] Akiva was a visionary idealist, Ishmael a common-sense realist. Notwithstanding the *Pardes* story, neither appears in the Talmud as a mystic; their trade was the application of logical principles to biblical interpretation. A time would come, many centuries later, when there would be no conflict between logic and mysticism; when a Talmudic sage could switch between rational analysis and mystical speculation with little more than a tug of his beard. But at this early stage, the chances are that their presence in the Palace literature is mythical. In legend even the rationalist can be transformed into a mystic.

Hechalot Rabbati, the text that contains most of the Akiva and Ishmael legends, is a very obscure book, known only to devotees of ancient mysticism. But one passage from it has surfaced in contemporary discography. It is the original version of 'Who By Fire', the song made famous by Leonard Cohen, the great Canadian songwriter-poet who died in 2016. Cohen didn't base his song directly on *Hechalot Rabbati*; his is a rewrite of a later version, a synagogue hymn that anticipates the coming New Year. *Who will live*, asks the hymn, *and who will die? Who in their due time and who not in their due time? Who by water and who by fire? …* The poem continues in this vein, ending with the couplet *Who will be brought low, and who will be made high?*

Hechalot Rabbati's older version, which Leonard Cohen may also have known, begins with the couplet that concluded the hymn. *Who will be brought low, and who will be made high?* The book's author, pretending to be Rabbi Ishmael, continues, *Who will be weakened and who will be strong? Who will be impoverished and who will be rich?* … His final pair of opposites is *Who will inherit Torah, and to whom will be given Wisdom?* Wisdom, according to this view, is the elite property of the mystic. Torah, meaning religious study, which traditionally is considered the highest form of learning, comes a poor second. For the author of *Hechalot Rabbati* the acquisition of Wisdom is the only fitting consequence of the difficult and dangerous journey through the seven heavens to the Chariot.

THE PRINCE OF THE PRESENCE

Of the numerous angelic names recorded in the various books of Palace literature, the best known was that of Metatron. Prince of the Divine Presence, he was the senior angel in the entire empyrean constellation and of a wholly different nature from all his colleagues. For, uniquely among the divine beings, Metatron had once been human. His earthly name had been Enoch; he is recorded in the book of Genesis as the son of Jared and the father of Methuselah, the man famous in the Bible for living longer than anyone else. Unlike his father and his son, however, Enoch did not die. The Bible says as much: 'Enoch walked with God and was not, for God took him[18]'. This intriguing sentence was enough to spawn dozens of myths and legends about the immortal Enoch. It even gave rise to its own genre of literature. At least three books ascribed to (but not actually composed by) Enoch were written between the second century BCE and the sixth CE. The third book, naturally entitled 3 Enoch, is a classic of the Palace literature.

The angels grumbled when Enoch was brought into heaven and transformed into Metatron. According to 3 Enoch, Metatron himself told Rabbi Ishmael that Prince Anapiel had been sent to fetch him from the midst of humanity. When he was still 3,650 million parasangs[19] away from heaven (about ten million miles), the heavenly beings smelled his odour. 'What is this smell of one born of woman?' they demanded. 'Why does a white drop[20] ascend on high and serve amongst those who cleave amongst the flames?'

God pacified the rebellion. 'Do not be displeased at this,' he commanded, 'for all mankind has rejected me and my great kingdom and gone off and worshipped idols. This one whom I have removed from them is the choicest of them all. This one whom I have taken is my sole reward from my whole world under heaven.'[21] The legend is concise and direct. Enoch, to whom the Hebrew Bible devotes just nine words, and of whose actions it says nothing, has been transformed into the most righteous of all people, by sole virtue of the fact that he 'walked with God and God took him'. This tendency to mythologise, to construct narratives behind the façade of people long departed, or who perhaps never lived at all, is an indispensable feature of Chariot mysticism.

Metatron's role in heaven was to act as an intermediary between God and humanity. Like all heavenly beings he has many names and titles, depending upon the particular power he is tasked with using.

Huge chunks of the Palace literature are taken up with dialogues between Rabbi Ishmael and Metatron, in one of his various guises. In one encounter, in which Metatron is ministering under the name Suriyel, Ishmael complains that the Romans had sentenced ten leading rabbis to death and were holding four others for ransom. (Confusingly, Ishmael himself is listed as one of the four hostages.) Suriyel hears Ishmael's complaint and reassures him that the Almighty has decreed vengeance against Rome; clouds will overhang the city, infecting the inhabitants with a variety of unpleasant skin diseases: scabs, leprosy, pox and scalls. Then, when the plague has fully run its course, the city's ruler Lupinus Caesar (an emperor only known to the Jewish mystical literature) will be destroyed, together with his palace and all the city's inhabitants.[22]

The story goes on. On the evening before the rabbis are due to be executed, Suriyel snatched Emperor Lupinus from his bed and put him to sleep in a pigsty. He then took one of the condemned rabbis and placed him in Lupinus's bed. He swapped their appearances so that the emperor, still in his pigsty, looked like the rabbi. When the time set for the execution arrived, the emperor's servants, unaware of the switch, walked into the pigsty, grabbed their master and executed him instead of the rabbi.[23]

The Metatron myth is more than just the product of a fertile imagination. Concealed beneath the surface are traces of a foreign, Dualist influence that found its way into early Jewish mysticism. In the simplest version of this belief, the universe was created by a supreme god who then handed over executive control to a minor deity.

Some Dualists believed that the minor deity had actually seized power from the supreme god, and used it to introduce evil into the world. These Dualists, whom we call *gnostics*, saw their task as gaining the mystical knowledge, or *gnosis*, that would defeat the lesser god and restore the Supreme Being to his pre-eminent status. Some scholars, notably Gershom Scholem, the outstanding twentieth-century pioneer of Kabbalah studies, suggest a close connection between Gnosticism and ancient Jewish mysticism.

The Dualist influence shows itself clearly in this passage from *Hechalot Rabbati*.

> Said Rabbi Akiva: I heard a voice issuing from beneath the
> Throne of Glory. And what did it say? 'I have recognised him,
> I have taken him, I have appointed him – this is Enoch son of
> Jared whose name is Metatron. I have taken him from among
> the children of men, and I made a throne for him opposite my
> throne. And what is the size of that throne? 40,000 myriads of
> parasangs of fire. I handed him seventy angels, corresponding
> to the seventy nations, and I put him in charge of all my
> servants in the world above and all my servants in the world
> below, and I called him the Lesser Lord[24]'.

Rationalists are horrified by passages like this. The idea that Metatron had been elevated beyond any conventional angelic rank, to a dangerously high, quasi-divine status, reeks of Dualism. It lends credence to Scholem's theory.

To hedge against the possibility that Metatron might be considered a divine being, the Talmudic rabbis constructed a counter-narrative. They composed a postscript to the story about the four who entered the *Pardes*. It was just as fanciful as the vision attributed to Rabbi Akiva, but it served to put Metatron in his place.

The postscript concerns Elisha ben Abuya, one of Akiva's companions on the journey to the *Pardes*. As he wandered through the heavenly halls Elisha saw Metatron, in all his archangelic glory, sitting and writing. Like all rabbinic scholars, Elisha was familiar with the long-held belief that angels did not sit; to do so would be unseemly in the divine presence. Since this radiant being was sitting, it could only mean, to Elisha's mind, that Metatron was a sovereign of far greater importance than a mere angel. Perhaps, he thought, there are two divinities in heaven.

Even to contemplate this Dualist possibility was untarnished heresy. But in the eyes of the heavenly host the guilty party was not Elisha. By allowing himself to be seen sitting in heaven, Metatron had committed a cardinal offence: he had caused Elisha to stumble in error. The heavenly militia seized Metatron. 'Why did you not stand when you saw him?' they demanded. They flayed him with 60 lashes of fire.[25] Metatron, like everybody else in the divine retinue, was obliged to play by heaven's rules; he too was a servant. The rationalist rabbis who composed the story could just about tolerate his presence in heaven. They could never allow him to acquire quasi-divine status.

THE DIVINE BODY

Those mystics who descended to the Chariot assumed that heaven was a physical place. They had no difficulty in thinking of God as having an actual body. After all, the Bible referred to God in corporeal terms; time and again in biblical narratives God saw, spoke and heard, he even stretched out his arm or smote with his finger. His right hand was 'mighty in power'.[26] Rabbinic literature from the same era as the Palace texts described God physically, although generally suggesting that such descriptions were metaphors and not to be taken literally.[27]

Not everyone was comfortable with these physical descriptions. In one strand of the tradition, the insistence that God had no physical form began taking root as early as the second century; the Aramaic translations of the Bible always found alternative, non-physical ways of expressing terms such as 'God spoke'.[28] By the end of the fifth century Augustine had all but won the battle in Christianity against anthropomorphic belief. In Judaism the dispute rumbled on for another 700 years. Even in the twelfth century, the talmudist Moses of Taku was still insisting that biblical descriptions of God's body should be taken literally.[29] In the opposing camp, Moses Maimonides, the outstanding Jewish philosopher of the Middle Ages, ruled in his legal code that anyone who believed God had a body or a form was a heretic.[30] And although his ceaseless critic, Abraham ben David, complained that Maimonides had no right to call such a person a heretic, since greater and better people than he had genuinely held anthropomorphic views, over the course of time Maimonides's view prevailed. Belief in God's corporeality was eliminated from Jewish thought.[31] But it always remained something of an issue in mystical speculation.

The Palace literature of the fifth to seventh centuries certainly had no misgivings about the physicality of heaven, or of God. Akiva heard a voice announce that Metatron had been given a throne as large as 70,000 parasangs of fire. A parasang is the distance that a person can walk in an hour. Presumably, a parasang of fire is the distance that a conflagration will travel in the same time, a concept similar to that of a light year. The speed that fire travels on earth depends on what is burning, and in what circumstances, but in heaven such considerations do not apply. Heavenly fire is bound to be fast and a celestial parasang will be far further than a person might walk. Metatron's throne occupies billions, perhaps even trillions of miles.

Big numbers occur frequently in the ancient world. The seventy thousand myriads of Metatron's throne is small fry compared to some of the numbers in Vedic, Mahayana and even Greek computations, which at times exceed 10 to the power of 80, the number of atoms in the universe.[32] It is also small compared to some of the numbers in one of the strangest books in the corpus of early Jewish mystical literature. Known as the *Shiur Komah*, or the Measure of Stature, the book describes the dimensions and proportions of God's body.

Like nearly all mystical literature of the period, *Shiur Komah* has not been preserved in a single authoritative version. Manuscripts, in the age before printing, were copied and recopied. Each time a manuscript was copied, errors and inaccuracies crept in. Sometimes the scribe was clumsy and missed out bits, or was careless and jumbled up the order of sentences and paragraphs. Sometimes manuscripts were 'corrected' by people who thought they knew better, or had their own ideas they wanted to add; these 'corrections' might then be inadvertently included as part of the main text in subsequent copies. At other times, readers might scribble notes in the margins; these, too, could be mistaken by a later scribe as part of the text. For one reason or another, the various texts of *Shiur Komah* differ considerably from each other and, although it has been suggested that a particular manuscript in the British Library represents the original text,[33] the only thing about which we can be certain is that, whichever version we look at, *Shiur Komah* is not a scintillating read.

The book presents itself as a revelation from Metatron. At times he addresses Ishmael, on other occasions he speaks to Akiva. Metatron announces the secret, mystical names for each of God's limbs and gives colossal measurements for each one. The names are obscure, unpronounceable and incomprehensible. The measurements, expressed in millions and billions of divine parasangs, which, as we have seen, are themselves impossibly larger than human parasangs, suggest divine limbs far exceeding the size of the universe. In one text the soles of God's feet alone are thirty million parasangs high and one parasang is described as ninety thousand times as large as the world.[34] Clearly, one is not expected even to contemplate these dimensions. God's height, according to one *Shiur Komah* text, is 236 thousand million parasangs, a number based on the numerical value of the words 'great in strength' in Psalm 147.5.[35]

It has been suggested that the purpose of *Shiur Komah* may be to obfuscate a passage in the biblical book Song of Songs, in which the heroine describes her lover in affectionate terms: *His head is as the finest gold, his locks are curled, and black as a raven … His cheeks are as a bed of spices, as banks of sweet herbs; his lips are as lilies, dropping with flowing myrrh.*[36] In both Jewish and Christian tradition, the erotic Song of Songs is regarded as an allegory for the love between God and his worshippers. Joseph Dan argues that *Shiur Komah* may well be a rebuke against those who understand the physical description in this allegory too literally;[37] don't try to think of God as a beautiful young man, implies the book's author, think of him as an unimaginable being of impossibly large size with an incomprehensible shape and limbs.

Another view is that *Shiur Komah* is not an extraordinary text at all; it simply reflects a trend in ancient Near Eastern literature to aggrandise mystical visions by adducing mathematical data. Howard Jackson quotes an assertion by the fourth-century Syrian philosopher Iamblichus that the size of a divine being is in direct proportion to its power: the bigger it is, the greater its authority. The Alexandrian poet Callimachus, commenting on the size of the statue of Zeus at Olympia, remarks that the size of the god is five cubits higher than the seat of his throne. The author of *Shiur Komah* may well have been influenced by similar ways of thinking. Like Callimachus he is interested in overall height, for this conveys the impression of divine grandeur.[38]

Whatever its origins, *Shiur Komah* has proved to be the most controversial of all Jewish mystical texts. It is not just that it projects God as a physical being: it has the temerity to reduce his physicality to a set of numbers and seemingly meaningless names. Maimonides regarded it as a Greek forgery, an idolatrous work which should be destroyed and forgotten. Moses of Taku strongly disagreed.[39] With hindsight, they were probably both wrong, although, when all is said and done, it is a bizarre document. But at least we understand what it is trying to tell us, even if we don't know why. Which cannot be said with certainty about another early Jewish mystical book, perhaps the oldest of them all. This one is known as the *Sefer Yetsirah*, or Book of Formation.

THE WORK OF CREATION

Ezekiel's vision of the heavenly throne was the inspiration for those who craved an ecstatic, mystical experience. Here was biblical proof, validated by the words of a prophet, that a human soul could ascend to the ultimate spiritual heights. But, of course, such activity could only be accomplished by souls of profound spiritual status; voyagers to the *merkavah* may not have been prophets of the calibre of Ezekiel, but necessarily they were persons of deep piety and profound sanctity. The heavenly palaces were surely open only to a very few.

Another route was open to those who sought truth but eschewed ascetic discipline. Subject to different passions, they did not yearn for ecstasy. Rather, they were looking for answers. Today we would call them scientists. What captured their imagination was how the world worked and the manner of its formation. The biblical passage that fascinated them was the very first chapter of Genesis, the story of creation. And whereas the vast majority of Jewish mystical texts during the first millennium concentrated on what the Talmud calls the Work of the Chariot, just one document, the *Sefer Yetsirah*, or Book of Formation, focused esoterically on the Work of Creation. It has left people scratching their heads ever since.

A passing remark in the Babylonian Talmud states that two rabbis created and ate a three-year-old calf.[40] They did this by studying the *Sefer Yetsirah*. One might wonder why, having gone to the trouble of performing such a feat, the two rabbis simply ate the calf. But the Talmud tells us nothing more about it.

This brief reference is the earliest mention of *Sefer Yetsirah*. Several hundred years were to pass before it was mentioned again. When it did resurface, in the tenth century, it was presented by its commentators as a scientific treatise on the creation of the world. Joseph Dan calls it 'the most important work of Hebrew language and cosmology of the High Middle Ages, influencing centuries of scientists, philosophers and mystics'.[41]

There is little agreement on when the book was written. The *Sefer Yetsirah* mentioned in the Talmud may not be the same as the one which appeared in the tenth century. The book's style is so unique that it does not slot neatly into any other known genre. Its concepts and terminology were adapted and expanded upon by later Kabbalah, but whether or not it can be classed as a mystical book is largely a question of definition.

Opinions on the date of the book's authorship range from the first century to the tenth, with most authorities placing it at the beginning of that range. There are no scholarly views on who wrote it. The only thing that the academics agree on is that traditionalists, who attribute it to Abraham, are incorrect. But traditionalists will argue that the book itself says that Abraham referred to it, and that academics have been wrong before.

The book starts with an explanation of how the world was created, in which it expands the biblical narrative. In the biblical account of creation, in the book of Genesis, God commanded things into existence. Each time he spoke something new was created. The first creation was light, the tenth was humanity. The whole of creation was accomplished in ten acts of speech. We still regard speech as a creative activity; the magical invocation *abracadabra*, a word of Aramaic origin, means 'I create as I speak'.

Speech is the instrument that creates, but speech is made up of words and words are comprised of letters. Letters therefore are the building blocks of creation. The Hebrew alphabet, the biblical language of creation, contains 22 letters. So the world was created through 22 letters and ten acts of speech, 32 elements altogether. The *Sefer Yetsirah* calls each element a path of wisdom. Most of the book is devoted to explaining, in enigmatic language, how these different paths of wisdom combine to ensure the proper functioning of the universe.

Crucially the book makes no distinction between words and numbers. This is because numbers and letters in the Hebrew alphabet are represented by the same symbol. The symbol for the first letter is also the symbol for the number one, the tenth letter represents number ten. The subsequent letters represent 20 to 90; the count then ascends in hundreds. Every letter has a numerical value, each word aggregates to the sum of its letters and one can perform arithmetical calculations with words, just as with numbers.

The ten commands that God issues at creation are given a special identity in the *Sefer Yetsirah*. Rather than calling them commands or sayings, it calls them 'countings'. Speaking and counting are connected in English, too; the word recount means to count again, or to tell. Someone who counts money in a bank is called a teller.

The Hebrew word that *Sefer Yetsirah* uses for 'counting' is *sefira*, plural *sefirot*. It is a word we will come across a lot in this book, as it will eventually become a key term in later Kabbalah, although it will refer to concepts apparently very different from acts of divine speech. But that is for a later chapter. The *Sefer Yetsirah* just wants us to contemplate the idea of *sefirot* as verbal and mathematical commands issued by God to bring the world into being. Not that it provides clear instructions, or makes our task easy:

> Ten *sefirot* without substance,[42] ten and not nine, ten and not eleven, understand in wisdom and be wise in understanding, examine within them and search in them and place each word upon its base and set the Creator on his foundation.[43]

Understanding these *sefirot* with wisdom, or being wise in them with understanding, is no mean challenge:

> Ten *sefirot* without substance, their end is pierced into their beginning and their beginning into their end, as a flame is connected to a coal, for the Master is singular, and he has no second, and before One what can you say?[44]

Later in the book the author introduces the secret properties of each letter, variously attributing powers to them. These powers encompass the whole of the physical and metaphysical worlds, from the planets in the sky to the orifices of the human face, from the passage of time to human emotion.

> He made the letter *Resh* king over Peace and bound a crown
> to it and joined them one to another, and with them formed
> Saturn in the universe, Friday in the year and the left nostril in
> the soul, male and female.[45]

Sefer Yetsirah is completely different from any other Jewish mystical work known to us from the first millennium. The Palace literature is devoted exclusively to ecstatic adventuring, describing journeys through the seven heavens to the divine Chariot, experiencing the mysteries of the heavens and explaining historical events in cosmic terms. In contrast, *Sefer Yetsirah* concerned itself with the mechanics of the creation, how the universe was brought into being. It foreshadowed later Kabbalah, which took over many of its concepts, redefining them as it did so. For, although the quest to experience the mysteries of heaven never fully disappeared, increasingly mystics began to concern themselves with the 'how' rather than the 'what' of the cosmos. In Jewish mysticism, *Sefer Yetsirah* represents the first step on this journey.

One man in particular stands out in this journey. We know very little about him, for he left no great mystical or philosophical works behind. If he had descendants, history has forgotten who they were. He may not even have existed, he may just be a legend. But that doesn't matter, the point is that he *could* have been real. His importance lies in the fact that he was considered to be a transmitter of traditions, a link in the chain. But a supremely significant one as far as the future history of Kabbalah is concerned. His name was Aaron of Baghdad, *Abu Aharon* to his friends.

Out of the East

AARON OF BAGHDAD

As far as anyone is aware, Aaron of Baghdad left behind no testament to his existence.[1] If he did, it is yet to be discovered. But others wrote about him, and although much of what was written is fanciful, the main facts appear consistent.

Abu Aharon journeyed from Baghdad to the Italian port of Gaeta, 60 miles north of Naples, in about 870 CE. At that time Baghdad was the most vibrant city in the Jewish world. The reasons why he left are unclear but the two main sources that mention him suggest that he had been expelled.

The more fanciful of the sources, written about 200 years after his arrival in Italy, attributes his expulsion to a quarrel with his father, Samuel. A miller by trade, Samuel had left the youthful Aaron in charge of the donkey turning his grindstone. Bored and restless, Aaron wandered off somewhere, leaving the poor animal unattended. When he came back, he found a lion calmly gnawing its way through the remains of the ass. Quick as a flash Aaron seized the lion (how, we are not told) and harnessed it to the mill wheel, in place of the donkey. He expected a rebuke from his father for losing the donkey, but at least to be praised for overpowering the lion. He received neither. Instead, Samuel berated the boy. 'What have you done? You have humiliated a lion. The Almighty made it a king among beasts, upright and proud, and you have turned it into your servant, obedient to your will!' His father, according to the story, exiled him from the family home for three years.

This legend appears in the *Chronicle of Ahima'atz*. Written in 1054, the *Chronicle* is a poetic history, exaggerated but rooted in fact, which records the exploits of a prominent Jewish family, descendants of a certain Rabbi Amitai, in southern Italy and North Africa. Aaron was not a member of the family, but he established the community in Oria, in southern Italy, whence the family hailed, and he taught them his mystical secrets. In return the family invested him with a semi-mythical status. Taming the lion is just the first of several legends about Aaron that the *Chronicle* records. The legends introduce a magical theme which runs all the way through the *Chronicle*.

Thrown out by his father, Abu Aharon travelled to the port of Jaffa. There he boarded a ship bound for Gaeta. On his arrival he got chatting with a Jew from Spain, whom he invited to share his Sabbath meal. Even though there is a religious obligation to treat the Sabbath as a festive occasion, the man refused to eat. Aaron, naturally disappointed, pressed his companion for a reason for his abstinence. He discovered that the Spaniard was in a state of considerable distress over the disappearance of his son. Aaron was nonplussed. 'Eat with me and if your son is alive I will find him for you.'

The next day the two of them went to a house they knew the Spaniard's son had regularly frequented. The house was occupied by a sorceress, and in her yard was a donkey tethered to a millstone. Aaron, possessed as he was with mystical insight, perceived that the donkey was in fact the Spaniard's bewitched son. Uttering a magical formula, Abu Aharon released the young man from the spell and restored him to his father.[2]

Not all Aaron's legends are about donkeys. Journeying from Gaeta to Benevento, he entered a synagogue, only to discover that the supplications recited by the prayer leader were not being accepted on high. Abu Aharon quickly diagnosed the cause; the prayer leader, although appearing to be healthy, was in fact dead. On quizzing the living corpse, Aaron discovered that as a young man the unfortunate soul had fallen ill. Knowing the grief that his death would cause his mother, an elderly sage had inserted a magic amulet beneath his skin. The amulet, inscribed with the divine name, was designed to keep him in a state of waking death. Now, many years later, he yearned for nothing more than to die in peace. Unfortunately, the incision the sage had made in his skin had long healed and nobody knew exactly where in his flesh the amulet had been placed. Aaron, of course, found it, extracted it from beneath the skin and the zombie went peacefully to his rest.

Further on in the book the author writes about his ancestor Shefatiah, whose magical prowess and poetic skills came to the attention of the emir Sawdan. Both Shefatiah and Sawdan are historical personages. Between the years 857 and 871 approximately, Sawdan ruled over Bari, a small Muslim province in the midst of Christian Italy.[3] Shefatiah wrote Hebrew liturgical poetry, some of which is still in use.

Sawdan, who was captivated by Shefatiah's poetical prowess, brought him into his palace as an intellectual companion, bard and confidant. On one particular Friday Shefatiah wanted to return home from the emir's court in time for the Sabbath. Travel after sunset on the Sabbath eve is forbidden, so Shefatiah was in a hurry to get away. But Sawdan, whether out of mischief or malice, delayed him. 'It is too late now,' mocked the emir. 'You will not arrive before the Sabbath begins.' Despite Shefatiah's pleas Sawdan continued to find ways of delaying him. Finally, when he was certain that it would be impossible for Shefatiah to make the journey in time, he let him go. The emir, though, had failed to reckon with Shefatiah's magical powers. The poet inscribed the secret name of God on the hooves of his horse, the earth concertinaed up beneath him and he accomplished the journey in a twinkling of an eye.

Ancient Jewish folklore maintains that the patriarch Jacob benefited from a similar contraction of the earth, just before he saw his vision of a ladder stretching to heaven. In Jacob's case, it was a miracle,[4] whereas Shefatiah accomplished the same feat by magic. But no ordinary magic. The secret name of God which Shefatiah used was that known only to those versed in the ancient esoteric secrets that permitted voyaging to the Chariot.

The *Chronicle of Ahima'atz* is suffused with this mystical magic. God's secret name was no secret to the chronicler's family. They inscribed it on amulets, on pieces of paper, even, as we have seen, on horses' hooves. Once another family member, Hananel, prevented the body of his deceased brother from decomposing by writing a variant of the ineffable name on paper and placing it in the corpse's mouth. The body remained intact until his other siblings arrived for the funeral.

Medieval magical stories of this nature are not remarkable. The only reason why the *Chronicle of Ahima'atz* features in the pre-history of Kabbalah is that the family's mystical-magical powers made use of the techniques associated with Chariot mysticism. Ahima'atz tells us as much; in his introduction he states that his ancestors 'understood secrets … knew the mysteries … and gazed into the secrets of the Chariot'.[5] It is an important statement, marking the first mention in a European document of the mysteries of the Chariot and the first allusion to ecstatic, *merkavah* practices.

The *Chronicle* is also the earliest European source to be aware of the ancient literature describing Chariot voyaging. Shefatiah, we are told, made regular use of a 'book of the Chariot'. After his death the book passed to his son, who was something of a reprobate, far less devout than his father. The book was treated with disrespect in the son's household, resulting in a plague breaking out in the family. Many died. Fortunately, as the plague raged, a wise man in the town seized the book, placed it in a lead casket and took it to the sea. The sea fled when it saw what was about to happen, but the sage pursued it and thrust the casket into the brine. The writing on the book's pages dissolved, the waters returned and the plague abated.

Aaron and his magic connect the Jews of southern Italy with the ancient mystical voyages to Heaven. Based on folklore, it is not a historically valid link, and certainly not enough to prove definitively that Aaron even existed, let alone that he introduced Chariot mysticism into Europe. Fortunately, there is another, much more reliable source, written more than a century after the *Chronicle of Ahima'atz*, which offers a more sober assessment of the legendary Abu Aharon's impact on the history of Kabbalah.

The source hails from the city of Worms in Germany. Its author, Eleazar of Worms, is unlikely to have known the legendary accounts in the Italian *Chronicle of Ahima'atz*. Even if he had known them, his was not the sort of fanciful imagination that would have paid much attention to them.

Born around 1176 and dying in 1238, Eleazar was a member of the Kalonymus family, an eminent pedigree of rabbis and poets who traced their lineage back to southern Italy in the ninth century, the very time that Abu Aharon is said to have arrived from Baghdad. A family tradition, recorded by Eleazar, was that they had been transplanted into Germany by the Holy Roman Emperor Charlemagne in the ninth century. This would make them among the first Jews in northern Europe and the founding fathers of contemporary Ashkenazi Jewry.[6]

Eleazar writes that his family inherited the secrets of Chariot mysticism from their ancestor, Moses, son of Kalonymus, a resident of Lucca in Tuscany. Moses received them from Aaron of Baghdad, who had travelled to Lucca to reveal them. The *Chronicle of Ahima'atz* says nothing about this; in fact, it states that Aaron returned home to Baghdad after his sojourn in southern Italy.

The antiquity of the sources that mention Aaron, and their legendary nature, make speculation on Aaron's Italian exploits pointless. But they are the only information we have, and there is little reason to doubt that an historical character, an Aaron of Baghdad, was responsible to some extent for the transmission of Chariot mysticism from the East to Europe.

And it was in Europe, in German cities along the Rhine, that Jewish mysticism went through yet another iteration. Still not Kabbalah. But getting closer.

ELEAZAR OF WORMS

Moses son of Kalonymus left Lucca versed in the esoteric traditions that Aaron of Baghdad is said to have taught him. He and his family settled, according to Eleazar, in the German city of Mainz.

Generations later, in the spring of 1096, the Jews of the city were attacked by a Crusader army. Fired by religious zeal and inflamed with the desire to liberate Jerusalem from Muslim rule, the Crusaders took frenzied retribution against those whom they blamed for the death of Christ. Over the previous three weeks they had massacred the neighbouring Jewish communities in Speyer and Worms. Now it was the turn of Mainz to suffer a similar fate. Kalonymus son of Meshullam, the current scion of the family which had emigrated from Lucca, called the Jews to arms. Weakened by prayer and fasting, and untrained in warfare, they were powerless against the fury of the Crusader army. More than a thousand were massacred. The mob moved on to Cologne, where they raped and murdered still more Jews.

Eleazar describes this event in his family chronology. He calls it the 'Wrath of the Lord'. It was a wrath he knew only too well. One hundred years after the Mainz massacre, and three days before the festival of Hannukah in 1196, two Crusaders broke into his house. They slew his two daughters, Hannah aged 6 and Belet aged 13, his son Judah and his wife. They also murdered his students.

Composing liturgical poetry was the family tradition. It provided an outlet, however self-reproachful, for Eleazar's grief:

Woe is mine for my pious wife, woe is mine for my son and daughters, I lament;
The Judge who has judged me is faithful, for my sins and iniquities, he has humbled me.
Righteousness is yours, oh Lord, and mine is the shame,
The Lord is righteous and mine is the trespass and wrongdoing ...[7]

Eleazar's acceptance of personal responsibility for his family's tragic slaughter was not false piety. Nor was it an attempt to make sense, through personal guilt, of an inexplicable tragedy. Rather, it was an expression of what Joseph Dan suggests may have been the most deeply pessimistic world view ever developed in Jewish theology.[8] A view which considered human existence as a device for sorting the righteous from the wicked. Only the most pious could withstand life's trials. The people who developed this theology are known today as the German Pietists.

This world view, a response to the harsh realities of their existence, was based on a radical reinterpretation of the ancient *Sefer Yetsirah*, or Book of Formation. The German Pietists were the first people to regard the obscure and complex Book of Formation as a mystical treatise rather than a scientific one.[9]

The Book of Formation had explained the creation of the world as a complex orchestration of God's ten utterances in the first chapter of Genesis and the 22 letters of the Hebrew alphabet that formed the words he spoke. It was a precise, balanced interaction that led to a world in perfect harmony. That harmony had been disrupted by the problems and tribulations of the world. The German Pietists believed their task was to respond to this disruption in such a way as to restore the original equilibrium. They developed an idea the rationalist philosopher Saadia Gaon had come up with 200 years earlier, when he was studying the *Sefer Yetsirah*. Saadia had suggested that divine influence reached the world through a unique manifestation which had already been alluded to in Scripture.

In the Bible, the name of this manifestation is *kavod*. In English it is usually translated as Glory. 'Glory' is an inadequate translation of a word which Scripture uses to designate something akin to God's presence. When God gave the Ten Commandments to Moses, the book of Exodus said that God's *kavod*, his 'Glory', dwelt on the mountain.[10] And when Ezekiel had a vision of heaven he saw the *kavod*, or 'Glory' of God, standing there.[11]

Elsewhere the Bible uses the word *kavod* in human terms, to imply honour, praise or loftiness.[12] But the German Pietists believed that, when it is applied to God, the word refers to a divine quality which serves as the vehicle of communication between heaven and earth. It bestows beneficial influences upon the earth, flowing through channels which can be accessed through correct, pious behaviour. This behaviour requires scrupulous observance of the commandments, correct and accurate recitation of the prayers and ascetic submission to suffering. Living one's life in this way accords with the harmonious description of creation in the *Sefer Yetsirah*. The Pietist's life may be one of deprivation suffused with tragedy. But, as long as he cultivates a saintly, humble life, provided he is scrupulous with his daily behaviour, he has no need of despair.

Personal behaviour mattered; far less important was the form of mysticism one practised. It could be a descent to the Chariot; there are indications that a few Pietists in Eleazar's day still practised the old *merkavah* mysticism. Others achieved transcendent experiences through the power of words, by combining and reciting the hidden, esoteric names of God. Numerology and wordplay helped discern the secret meanings of the prayers and the divine rhythms they concealed. Some Pietists occupied themselves investigating the nature of the heavenly powers and the process of emanation which connected heaven to earth. But no matter what one's mystical proclivities, the starting point was the same. Only through a life of piety and humility, characterised by the love and fear of God together with strict observance of the commandments, would one be ready to venture beyond the trials and tribulations of life in bleak thirteenth-century Germany. To contemplate and experience an empyrean world, of which earthly existence was but a darkened, miserable reflection.[13]

The insistence on correct, religiously sanctioned behaviour explains why Eleazar's best-known book has nothing at all to do with mysticism. His magnum opus is a work known as *Rokeach*, a title which translates as *Perfumer*. It is not a book about perfume. Nor does it concern the manufacture and sale of scents or spices. It is a compendium of Talmudic law. Eleazar called the book *Rokeach* because the numerical value of that word in Hebrew is 308, the same as his own name.[14] And the reason why the book has a title which merely hints at the author's name, rather than spelling it out, is that publicising one's own name, in the eyes of the German Pietists, makes the heart proud.[15]

Such reticence was not Eleazar's idea. He'd inherited it from his relative and teacher, Judah the Pious, who in turn had no doubt acquired it from someone further up the family line. Like Eleazar, Judah is known to us primarily through his writings. For one book in particular, in which he sets out his vision for the ideal life. Known as the Book of the Pious, it is hardly a work of mysticism. But it is full of mystical beings and supernatural events. It explains why the German Pietist movement became an important link between the Chariot mystics of the first millennium and early Kabbalah.

THE BOOK OF THE PIOUS

Written in the first quarter of the thirteenth century, *Sefer Hasidim*, the Book of the Pious, is a manual for the Good Life. It outlines ethical ways of responding to the dilemmas its readers are likely to encounter. The author, Judah the *Hasid*, or Pious, had an austere view of the world. He imposed severe demands upon his audience and made a virtue out of rigorous, ascetic and penitential behaviour.

The book seems to have been written for the members of an exclusive, elite community who, due to their devout nature and other-worldliness, found themselves in constant conflict with the majority of their co-religionists. Bizarrely, however, there is no evidence that this community or one anything like it ever existed. Joseph Dan suggests that the book was written as a blueprint for a social programme which never came to fruition, perhaps because it was rejected by the very people for whom it was intended. It may have been 'a radical dream denied even by the closest disciples of the great teacher'.[16]

Because it is a thirteenth-century book, grounded in all the superstition of that age, it is little surprise to discover that the pages of the Book of the Pious are crowded with grim, other-worldly beings. The living dead, shades, genii, demons, malevolent spirits and the reborn all jostle for the reader's attention. Many of the tales are borrowed from the surrounding German folk culture. Like the ill witch who could only cure herself by sucking the blood from a healthy woman. Or the man who beat off a cat which attacked him, and was approached the next day by a woman who was wounded in the same place. But although its cast of characters and tales would not be out of place in any collection of medieval folk literature, they are merely incidental to the underlying theme of the book, which exhorts the Pietist to act in accordance with the requirements of the Divine Will.

In one cautionary tale a man decides to make a musical instrument from a piece of wood that had been set aside for a coffin. The corpse for whom the coffin was intended appeared to him in a dream, warning him to desist. The man paid no attention, he made the instrument and fell ill. The tale's moral is spelled out by the author of *Sefer Hasidim* who quotes a line from the book of Proverbs: 'He who mocks the poor [i.e. the dead] insults his Maker.'[17] Unusually for *Sefer Hasidim*, this tale does have a happy ending. His son took another musical instrument, shattered and burned it, then sprinkled its ashes over the corpse's grave. His father recovered.

Judah the *Hasid* and his pupil Eleazar of Worms were the most important, but also the last major figures in the German Pietist school. Indeed, school is probably too extravagant a word. The actual number of German Pietists may have been very few, punching above their weight in the eyes of history. The documents that have survived suggest it was a very small, fragmented movement comprising various groups and circles, perhaps no more than 20 active scholars across all the circles at any one time.[18]

The documents may not tell the full story. Other mystical circles at the time made a point of transmitting everything by word of mouth, on the basis that esoteric lore was too dangerous to be committed to writing. People like Elhanan ben Yakar of London and his pupil Ezra of Moncontour, who are said to have studied the Book of Formation and the Chariot literature, but who left no written legacy behind them. There is no way of knowing how large or small these circles were, or for how long they may have existed.

The German Pietist movement probably came to an end because of the carnage unleashed by the Crusaders on the local Jewish community, of which Eleazar's family had been such tragic victims. Eleazar suggests as much. In one of the passages in which he lists the genealogy of the Kalonymus family, he refers to the crusade a century before his time: 'We were cut down, all of us perished, except a few of our kindred.'[19] By the time Eleazar passed away the German Pietist movement was almost at an end. But Kabbalah proper was just beginning.

The Beginning of Kabbalah

HERESY, UNREST AND MYSTICAL LEGEND

Even after nearly one thousand years, the twelfth-century Cathar rebellion remains one of the most intriguing episodes in European history. Like many social protests, before and after, it was fuelled by poverty and a sense of resentment at the power and wealth of the governing classes, in this case the bishops and clerics of the papal church. But unlike other social protests it did not start out as a rebellion against authority. Instead, its origins lay in a radically different conception of the nature of God. It also, coincidentally, seems to have created the conditions for the first exposition of Kabbalistic theory. Not yet a particularly coherent exposition, but an important step on the way.

The Cathars practised a Dualist religion: they believed in two divine powers, one good and one evil. They saw existence as a struggle between the two. They maintained that Evil had wrested control of the world from Good, to a point at which even the Church had fallen into its malevolent clutches. Jesus's teachings derived from the benevolent deity, but Rome's preoccupation with wealth and power had led the Church to abandon the true message of the Gospels.

The Cathars were devout, but they were not willing to subscribe to the Church's doctrines. They denied that priests were necessary for communion with God. They regarded veneration of the cross as idolatry and eschewed the need for baptism.

The Church's initial reaction was to reason with the Cathars. Public disputations were held, large crowds of peasants and landowners flocking into the market places and great halls to listen to the oratory of each side, prepared to be persuaded. The Cathars preached a literal message, quoting from the Bible in the local vernacular, the *langue d'oc*. It was a winning move. The vast majority of people knew nothing of the words of the Bible; its Latin was unintelligible to those who had no education. The Church preachers, who refused to quote the Bible in anything other than Latin, were at an immediate disadvantage.

On the face of it there was nothing particularly unusual about the Cathars' theological opposition to the Church; Dualism, the belief in two powers, was not a new idea – its roots stretch back long before Christianity. The Cathars were not the only people of their time to hold such beliefs; their theological allies included the Bogomils in the Bulgarian Empire and the remnants of the Paulicians in Asia Minor. But in twelfth-century Western Europe, in a world in which the Roman Church was both spiritually and materially all-powerful, Catharism lit a fuse that threatened to reach the heart of Rome itself. What began as a theological challenge became the engine for a social revolution that, if left unchecked, would have destabilised the entire hierarchy of the Catholic Church.

As Michael Thomsett has pointed out, the Cathar upheaval was far more than a dissenting interpretation of the Bible. It was a social movement that responded to the clergy's exploitation of the peasantry, inspired by the 'glaring differences between the clergy and the people, not to mention the greater likelihood of a peasant being accused of heresy and imprisoned or executed'.[1] If Catharism had been just a heresy, the Church would have found a way to overcome it. As a social revolution, it posed a far greater danger.

The Cathar movement became hugely popular. In its heartland, the Languedoc region of southern France, perhaps as many as four million people regarded themselves as Cathars. They had their own schools and churches; they spurned the spiritual leadership and religious hierarchy of Rome.[2] They certainly weren't prepared to pay the tithes and taxes that allowed the Catholic clergy and their bishops to maintain their offensively luxurious lifestyle. Nor were they prepared to defer to Church preachers. For the first time since Christianity had become the default faith of Europe, ordinary people had the opportunity to make a religious choice, even if most of them probably did so for reasons of social convention, rather than theological conviction.

Catharism was not a soft option. The Cathar church was run by an elect inner circle known as Parfaits. Those admitted into the circle were obliged to renounce all contact with the opposite sex, to forgo meat and every luxury. The Parfaits preached and ministered to their communities but were still obliged to work at mundane jobs for a living. Life was hardly any easier for the members of their congregations, the ordinary believers. Particularly when Rome embarked on a policy of repression and things started to turn nasty.

In 1208 Pope Innocent III declared the Cathar town of Toulouse 'the most infamous centre of heretical corruption'. He sent his emissary Peter of Castelnau to quell the heresy. Peter's first task was to deal with Raymund VI, the Count of Toulouse, who was opposed to Roman interference in his land. Peter's solution was to excommunicate Raymund and seize his property. It was a tactic that went horribly wrong. Peter was murdered and in revenge the Pope proclaimed a crusade.

The barons of northern France rallied to the Pope's call; over a 20-year period the population of the Languedoc was systematically and cruelly slaughtered. Nobody knows for certain how many died; estimates range from tens to hundreds of thousands. As the persecution neared its natural end – when there was nobody left to slaughter – a group of survivors took refuge in the de facto Cathar headquarters at Montségur, a fortress atop an isolated 500-foot Pyrenean peak. They held out there for ten years, until the papal forces mounted a siege against the stronghold. The besieging troops spent a further nine months trying to find a way into the fortress. When they finally managed to gain entry they ordered its inhabitants to renounce their faith, upon pain of death. Two hundred and forty Cathars refused to do so. They were burned alive.

Catholics and Cathars were not the only inhabitants of the region. Scattered across the Languedoc and neighbouring Provence, largely unnoticed by the belligerents, were a few dozen small Jewish communities. Supporting neither side and doing their best to become invisible, the Jews were not caught up in the religious bellicosity. Even so, it was impossible for them to remain oblivious to a social and religious crisis of such magnitude.

The rabbis in Provence had no interest in the Dualist theology of the Cathars, or in the mystical piety of people like Eleazar of Worms. The esoteric asceticism of the German Jewish Pietists, which was beginning to exude its dark pessimism at just this time, was to make no impression south of its Rhineland cocoon. Like their co-religionists to the north and east the Provençal rabbis focused their scholarly skills almost exclusively on detailed analysis of the Talmud, the great compendium of religious law, ethics and ideas.

But change was afoot.

The catalyst was the sudden and unexpected appearance in Provence of a book which has gone down in history as the first truly Kabbalistic text. Known as the *Bahir*, from a word meaning 'light' in its opening quotation, the newly arrived slender volume gave the impression of being little more than a patchwork of loosely connected ideas. Like the earlier Chariot texts, it claimed to be a record of the deeds and utterances of sages who lived in the second century. And, like those earlier Chariot texts, even the most basic analysis of its language and content shows that it was written long after the passing of those personalities whose voices it claimed to project.

The *Bahir* set the agenda for everything that was to follow in the development of Kabbalah. Without saying so explicitly it made four key assumptions. First, that behind the physical, revealed universe lies a world of concealment. That human speech is simply a manifestation of an infinitely more powerful, hidden, divine language. That deeper, secret meanings are concealed beneath the revealed words of the Bible. And, finally, that our earthly lives, which are limited in time and space, are merely a pale reflection of an eternal life unconstrained by such limits.[3] The new mysticism hinted at by *Bahir* offered a window through which these concealed realities could be perceived.

Unlike a modern book, *Bahir* was not written from beginning to end, by a single author. A compilation, not a treatise, it is less than 15,000 words in sum, containing material drawn from several sources and spanning three centuries, all of which has been knitted together by one or more anonymous editors into a not particularly coherent whole.[4] Its earliest content was imported, with some modification, from a tract called *Raza Raba*, or the 'Great Mystery'. *Raza Raba* can be traced back to the ninth century, to a Jewish-Babylonian community, similar to that in which Abu Aharon is imagined to have spent his childhood. Belonging to the same genre as those which describe the descent to the heavenly Chariot, it contains much more magical material than its earlier predecessors.[5]

How *Raza Raba* found its way from the Orient to Provence is something of a mystery. It may have journeyed through Italy and Germany, perhaps secreted within Abu Aharon's portfolio of mystical teachings. Or it could have arrived in southern France directly from the East, maybe carried by a tenth-century Talmudic student returning from his studies in the once vibrant but now declining academies of Baghdad. Other texts may have been woven into it before its arrival in Provence, so that *Bahir* was already well on its way to its final version before its ultimate editor added supplementary material of his own. Of only one thing can we be nearly certain: it did not arrive in Provence fully formed. Its language and content are Provençal in character; most contemporary researchers are confident that Provence is where it was ultimately redacted.[6]

There is no obvious explanation as to why the *Bahir* suddenly popped up in a Talmudic environment not renowned for its interest in mysticism. Nor do we have any idea of how it was received once it arrived. It doesn't seem to have been greeted with any great interest. Indeed, it would take the best part of a century before the *Bahir* was deemed sufficiently important to provoke controversy. Its unfashionable mystical character suggests it came from the fringes rather than the mainstream community, perhaps as a consequence of the great Cathar upheaval reverberating through the region at the time. Researchers have noted similarities between some of the myths in *Bahir* and those in the Cathar scriptures, and the two systems share comparable approaches' to fundamental theological questions, such as the nature of evil. But these hints at commonality are countered by the big differences between *Bahir*'s mysticism and Catharism. Not the least of which is that *Bahir* is a Jewish text, founded on the concept of one God, while the Cathars believed in the existence of two divine powers, one good, the other bad.[7]

There is not enough similarity between the *Bahir* and Catharism to suggest that scholars from each school sat down and compared notes. In any event a collaboration of that nature is unlikely given the exclusivist nature of both the Jewish and Cathar faiths. Nevertheless, the boundaries between the two systems were sufficiently blurred for one of the early kabbalists, Asher ben David, to complain that some of those who studied the *Bahir* gave the impression of believing in two divinities, an idea rooted firmly in Cathar belief; and on the other hand for Lucas, Bishop of Tuy in the thirteenth century, to accuse the Cathars of 'Jewish perfidy'.[8]

The most probable explanation for similarities in approach is that both the Jews and Cathars were independently influenced by legends and ideas swirling around in the febrile religious atmosphere of the time. Before the violence set in, when religious choice was still an option and not a social compulsion, Catholic and Cathar preachers would have vied with each other in the streets and market places, seeking to win the loyalty of those torn between the competing faiths. Jews may have listened with interest to some of the new stories and ideas. Equally, the architects of Catharism, whose beliefs were influenced by Dualist sects in the East, may have encountered oriental texts and traditions not too different from those which had found their way into earlier layers of the *Bahir*. At least one line of Cathar thought bears a striking resemblance to an idea in *Bahir*; an idea which would eventually become a defining concept of Kabbalah.

PILLARS AND CHANNELS

In his *Book of the Two Principles*, John of Lugio, an Italian Cathar who lived in the first half of the twelfth century, argues that God needs people to serve him in order that he can fulfil his will.[9] Human deeds, he maintains, are essential in bringing the divine plan to fruition. The *Bahir* expresses the same idea, using the image of a pillar stretching from earth to heaven. The pillar is called *Tsaddik*, meaning 'righteous'.

> There is a single pillar extending from heaven to earth, and its name is *Tsaddik*. This pillar is named after the righteous. When there are righteous people in the world, then it becomes strong, and when there are not, it becomes weak. It supports the entire world, as it is written, 'And Righteous (*Tsaddik*) is the foundation of the world' (Proverbs 10.25). If it becomes weak, then the world cannot endure. Therefore, even if there is only one righteous person in the world, it is they who supports the world.[10]

This passage solved a problem left hanging by the *Sefer Yetsirah*, the ancient Book of Formation. *Sefer Yetsirah* had declared that God created the world by speaking. But it didn't explain how this happened, how commands issued in heaven made things exist on earth. Commands, after all, are just words. Like any speech, once the command is uttered, it disappears. The problem that *Sefer Yetsirah* posed was how to understand the mechanism that conducted the command from heaven to earth, and connected cause to effect.

The *Bahir's* description of the pillar named *Tsaddik* is the first attempt to describe the connection. It links cause and effect through a mystical relationship in which a conduit, in the shape of a pillar, descends from heaven to earth. God's commands at creation were conducted through this pillar. Then, once humanity was created, it was handed to them to maintain. When the world is full of righteous people, the pillar is strengthened; when the righteous are absent, the pillar weakens. This mystical, dynamic relationship between heaven and earth is the first step towards what will become the classical Kabbalistic theory of the *sefirot*, the channels of divine energy that sustain creation by flowing back and forth between the created and concealed worlds. *Bahir* is where classical Kabbalah begins.

Bahir is rich in symbols and metaphors. It introduces the theory of the *sefirot* by mentioning Aaron the High Priest, who raised his hands to bless the Israelites. *Bahir* explains that Aaron's ten fingers represented the channels that conducted his blessing from heaven to earth. His fingers become symbols for the *sefirot*:

> 'Aaron raised up his hands to bless the people' (Leviticus 9.22). What is the meaning of this raising of hands? … It is because the hands have ten fingers, alluding to the ten *sefirot*, with which heaven and earth were sealed.[11]

The *sefirot* connect to each other in shapes that reflect the natural world. One image that *Bahir* uses is of a tree, another is of the human body. The metaphor seems straightforward. Until *Bahir* explains the complex, geometric structure of the tree, leaving us in no doubt about the complexity of the underlying idea. (It is not an easy passage to follow; it can easily be skipped without losing the thread.)

> The Holy One has a single Tree, and it has twelve diagonal boundaries … They are the arms of the world. On the inside of them is the Tree. Paralleling these diagonals there are twelve Officers. Inside the Sphere there are also twelve Officers. Including the diagonals themselves, this makes a total of 36 Officers … These are twelve, twelve, twelve, and they are the Officers in the Axis, the Sphere, and the Heart. Their total is 36. The power of each of these 36 is in every other one. Even though there are twelve in each of the three, they are all attached to each other. Therefore, all 36 Powers are in the first one, which is the Axis. And if you seek them in the Sphere, you will find the very same ones. And if you seek them in the Heart, you will again find the very same ones. Each one therefore has 36. All of

them do not have more than 36 forms. All of them complete
the Heart [which has a numerical value of 32]. Four are then left
over. Add 32 to 32 and the sum is 64. These are the 64 Forms ...
eight less than the 72 names of the Holy One. These are alluded
to in the verse, 'there are higher ones above them,' and they are
the seven days of the week. But one is still missing ... This is the
place from which the earth was graven.[12]

We can see why *Bahir* failed to capture the popular imagination.
It was too obscure and enigmatic. It left its readers no clearer
about the essence of the mysticism it was trying to explain. But its
contribution to the future of Kabbalah was immeasurable. For the
first time the mystics had a written text. It gave their mysticism a
foundation on which they could build.

One family in the Provençal town of Vauvert, known in those
days as Posquières, took responsibility for developing *Bahir*'s ideas.
A family of early kabbalists, of whom it is said no mystical word
ever escaped their lips.

A FALSE TURN

Rabbi Abraham ben David of Posquières, or *Rabad*, to give him the
acronym by which he is commonly known, was part of a small, elite
circle of Provençal mystics, almost certainly the first such group in
southern France. The founder of a Talmudic college which attracted
the cream of rabbinic students, *Rabad*'s reputation was such that
he could claim that his authority extended throughout the Jewish
community in twelfth-century Provence. 'Our colleagues agreed
with us,' he wrote of himself, 'and did not challenge our rulings.'[13]
He is best known for his incisive and occasionally withering
annotations to the code of Jewish law written by the intellectual
giant Moses Maimonides,[14] a man who at first sight has nothing at
all to do with our story, yet whose name crops up time and again.

Maimonides authored magisterial works on law, philosophy
and rabbinic commentary. The de facto leader of Egyptian Jewry
and physician to the Sultan's court, he is universally acclaimed as

the outstanding Jewish thinker of the post-Talmudic era. As an out-and-out rationalist, Maimonides is peripheral to the history of Kabbalah.[15] But both *Rabad* and he play walk-on roles, due in both cases to the interests and endeavours of their sons.

Rabad's son Isaac was the man responsible for early Jewish mysticism's migration from Christian Europe to Muslim Spain. It was an obscure, fringe doctrine when it arrived on Spanish soil. By the time it departed, expelled with Spain's Jews nearly 300 years later, it had not only acquired the name Kabbalah, it had blossomed into a mystical philosophy unlike anything previously known. A philosophy which according to one's point of view either contains secrets accessible only to the most profound, holy and mystically orientated minds, or is nothing more than superstitious gobbledygook.

Maimonides's son Abraham, on the other hand, very nearly killed off the whole Kabbalah enterprise before it had even begun by joining a Jewish Pietistic movement based on Sufism, the Islamic mystical system.

In 1204 Abraham Maimonides succeeded his father as the leader of Egyptian Jewry. A fringe mystical movement had already started to make an impression on the community, in much the same way as the Pietists had done in Germany. Half a continent apart, the two mystical disciplines were very different. The German Pietists were a pessimistic, penitent bunch, whose practices reflected the austere mood of their neighbouring Christian monasteries. In contrast, the Egyptian circle was an exuberant cult, one which expressed itself through ecstatic singing and dancing, practices it had copied from Islamic Sufis. At least, that is how it looked on the outside. But beneath the euphoric exterior the Jewish Egyptian mystics practised a form of Sufi asceticism little different from that of the Pietists of Germany, fasting frequently and remaining awake all night. They mimicked visible aspects of Islamic mosque rituals, performing ablutions before prayer and kneeling in straight rows.

This was not the first time that Jewish thinkers had made use of Sufi ideas. The eleventh-century Spanish poet-philosopher Ibn

Gabirol had drawn on Sufi imagery, as had his slightly younger contemporary Bahya ibn Pakuda.[16] But there was close intellectual contact between the Jews and Muslims in eleventh-century Spain, ideas flowing freely between the poets, philosophers and grammarians of each culture. The connection between the two faiths was not so pronounced in thirteenth-century Egypt, and the Jewish Sufism movement turned out to be controversial. Many of Egypt's Jews decried what they saw as a dilution of their ancient faith.

The Sufi movement remained on the fringes of the community for the best part of a century until Abraham Maimonides joined. He established a circle in his own academy and led the movement into the closest thing it ever had to a heyday. He eulogised the religion from which Sufism had emerged, seeing Islam as an outstanding example of unadulterated faith, an aspirational model that Jews should strive to replicate. In a tract written round about 1220, he complained that the mystical treasure which should have belonged to the Jews had been denied to them and given instead to Islam. As Gershom Scholem notes, had he known about the Kabbalah he might not have felt so bereft.[17]

Opposition within the Egyptian community led to Jewish Sufism's decline and eventual disappearance. But by then word was reaching Egypt of new mystical ideas being taught in Spain; the Provençal mysticism of *Rabad* and his circle had found its way across the Pyrenees. Knowledge of the *Bahir* was spreading, helped on its way by the activities of *Rabad*'s son, the evocatively named Isaac the Blind. Kabbalah was in the ascendancy. Isaac was none too happy about it.

ABUNDANCE OF LIGHT

Rabad died in 1198, 20 years or so after *Bahir* first made an appearance. He shows no sign of having known the book. But his son Isaac the Blind not only knew and quoted from the *Bahir*, he also claimed that his father, and indeed his grandfather, were familiar with its lore. 'Yet,' reports Isaac the Blind, 'no word on this subject ever escaped their lips and they conducted themselves [with the uninitiated] as with people not versed in the Wisdom …'[18]

This isn't strictly so. Some of *Rabad*'s publicly available writings contain mystical allusions, even though he wasn't explicit about what he meant. Later kabbalists also refer to *Rabad* as a link in the Provençal chain of mystical tradition. According to these writers, the mystics in the Provençal elite had first received their knowledge from the prophet Elijah.

Elijah, who bestrides much of the biblical book of Kings, is the only person in ancient Israel not to die, or at least not in the same way as everybody else does. Instead, he is carried to heaven in a chariot of fire. This has led him to be regarded in Jewish legend as an immortal, an old man for ever wandering the earth, who reveals himself to selected people at appropriate moments. In the future he will proclaim the coming of the Messiah. In the meantime, so they say, he may be that old beggar you ignored who is now preying on your conscience. Or, as guardian of the heavenly mysteries, he may throw out a remark as he crosses your path that gives you pause and sets your life on a new course. When poets and mystics claim to be inspired by Elijah, we can take it to mean that their ideas came to them through inspiration, rather than inheriting ancient teachings brought to them by someone like Abu Aharon.

Nevertheless, how *Rabad* acquired his mystical knowledge, and the extent to which he did or not display it, is not the main point. As far as Isaac the Blind was concerned, esoteric knowledge was a family tradition, which they preserved strictly within their own four walls. It was Isaac himself who released this knowledge into the public domain through his writings, safe in the assumption that, even among the small number of people who had the skills to read, very few would be able to understand him. Despite earning himself the title 'father of the Kabbalah', Isaac held fast to the tradition, still observed today, that the most profound Kabbalistic secrets were neither to be disclosed to the uninitiated nor studied by those who had not undergone rigorous preparation. As we shall see, in his old age he fulminated against his students when he felt that they were spreading Kabbalistic teachings too widely.

According to tradition, Isaac was born blind. He was known by the name *Sagi Nahor*, meaning 'abundance of light'. It is a euphemism designed to fool the evil eye, in much the same way as the early mystics who, when ascending to the heavenly Chariot, called it a descent. There is no point in giving too much information to malign forces if you can possibly help it; they will only use it against you. But just how visually impaired Isaac really was is a matter of debate. He refers often to colours in his writings and occasionally writes that he has found something in a manuscript, all of which suggests that he only became blind later in life.

Unlike his father, Isaac the Blind was a Kabbalist through and through. He didn't write Talmudic commentaries, or engage in discussions about ritual practices or the finer points of religious law. His literary output was devoted exclusively to esoteric matters. Indeed, Isaac the Blind is the first person we know of who can confidently be termed a true Kabbalist. He introduced much of the terminology that framed future Kabbalistic discussion, and he pioneered the symbolism through which Kabbalistic ideas are communicated. He was the first Jewish mystic to come up with a coherent explanation for the problem of how God can make things happen in the material world. After all, God has no physical dimension yet everything happens, according to the mystical mind, at his command. How, the kabbalists wanted to know, did this work? Isaac wasn't the first to solve the problem; the *Bahir* had already suggested that the answer lay in the mystical pillar than ran from heaven to earth. But Isaac was the first to explain the answer by using symbols that people could relate to. Like many before him he adopted the scheme set out in the *Sefer Yetsirah*.

The *Sefer Yetsirah* had hinted that the numbers from one to ten, together with the 22 letters of the Hebrew alphabet, were the tools through which the world was created. The numbers were more than just digits: they represented ten interconnected entities which progressively descend from heaven to earth, pouring pure divine thought from one to another, gradually transforming it into earthly cause and effect. The upper entities of this hierarchy reflect the profundities of divine wisdom, understanding and knowledge, the lower stages embrace the more earthly qualities of spirituality and physicality. The ten stages are known as *sefirot*. The *Sefer Yetsirah* mentioned them but didn't explain them; *Bahir* discussed them but only as very fluid and undefined concepts. Isaac was the first person to define them and to begin to outline their symbolism.

Isaac associated the lower *sefirot* with the qualities that King David attributed to God in the biblical book of Chronicles: greatness, power, beauty, eternity, splendour and kingship. These ideas continued to develop and evolve over the centuries, but by explaining the *sefirot* symbolically, and by giving them names, Isaac the Blind, abundant in light, laid the foundation for generations of Kabbalistic thought.

Isaac's writings are not easy to understand. Like all mysticism, Kabbalah is opaque at the best of times and, given that he lived at its very dawn, it is not surprising that his theories and ideas are foggy. He is difficult to read and much of what he says is unintelligible, even to those well versed in Kabbalistic matters. The pioneer of the scholarly study of Jewish mysticism, Gershom Scholem, whose familiarity with Kabbalistic sources was second to none and who is considered the giant in his field, wrote, 'I myself cannot pretend to understand more than half the material transmitted in his name.'[19]

Despite his efforts to confine the knowledge of Kabbalah to a small, closed circle of associates, Isaac was unsuccessful. Provence, where he lived, was politically connected to the kingdom of Aragon on the western side of the Pyrenees. The Jewish communities in the two regions were in close contact. Students regularly travelled from Aragonese towns to study in the larger and more prestigious Talmudic colleges in Provence. A good number of these students came into contact with Isaac's Kabbalistic teachings, which they picked up from his disciples or from people whom they had met. When they went home the students took their newly acquired Kabbalistic knowledge back with them.

As a result, from around the year 1220 the town of Gerona, home to the largest of Aragon's Jewish communities, grew into an active centre of Kabbalistic thought. Its leading lights were Rabbis Ezra and Azriel, two men whose similar names have led to centuries of confusion. Ezra and Azriel were serious, committed theoreticians of the early Kabbalah. But they were not able to instil the same sense of discipline into their circle as Isaac the Blind had demanded from his followers in Provence, and it earned them a sharp rebuke.

Living at a safe distance from Provence and less inhibited about publicly discussing mystical doctrine, some of the more enthusiastic members among Ezra and Azriel's associates decided to launch an initiative to publicise Kabbalah among the population at large. They taught mystical ideas freely to audiences who were not part of the closed elite and who in turn were happy to discuss what they had learned publicly. It was the first time that Kabbalah had broken out from the protective embrace of its austere, solemn guardians. It would not be the last. The unwanted attention distressed Isaac and his Provençal associates greatly.

Isaac had no hesitation in making his displeasure known. 'I was filled with great concern,' he wrote, 'when I saw scholars, men of understanding and pious, engaging in long discourses and presuming in their books and letters to write about great and sublime matters … I have also heard concerning the men of Burgos that they openly hold forth on these matters in the marketplaces and in the streets.'[20]

Too old to travel himself, Isaac sent his nephew Asher to Gerona, to rein in the overenthusiastic promoters of Kabbalah. How successful he was is hard to know. For when he arrived he found himself embroiled in a completely different sort of controversy; one in which he was pitted against those who rejected the very teachings and ideas of Kabbalah itself. Rejectionists who regarded Kabbalah not as a mystical science but as out-and-out heresy.

THE BEGINNING OF OPPOSITION

Like any new doctrine, Kabbalah was susceptible to criticism and opposition. Unlike many new doctrines, however, the opposition to Kabbalah was fiercer and more sustained than its exponents could have expected. Kabbalah did not fit into the traditional scheme of things. And, therefore, the traditionalists rejected it.

The traditionalists maintained that Judaism was constructed upon an interwoven system of biblical and rabbinic sources that provided the rationale for its customs, laws and beliefs. There were no authoritative traditional sources, not even hints, which supported the idea of *sephirot*, none which demonstrated the validity of combining words and letters for mystical effect, and none which justified the various complex system of meditations in which kabbalists engaged when directing their prayers.

The only authority for these practices – and it was a very weak one – was the *Sefer Yetsirah*, a relatively late document in the long chain of Jewish writings and very much on the fringes of mainstream Judaism. In the eyes of traditionalists the *Sefer Yetsirah* didn't count for much at all.

Without biblical or rabbinic sanction, without a recognised tradition rooted in antiquity and developed through interpretation and analysis, Kabbalah was supremely vulnerable to the charge of heresy. It was a charge hurled at Isaac the Blind's nephew Asher when he arrived in Gerona. And despite his education and learned argumentation, Asher found himself unable to deflect the criticism hurled at the upstart mysticism by outraged dedicated opponents such as Meir of Narbonne.

Meir devoted much of his life battling against increasingly strident attempts, mainly by Dominicans, to convert Jews to Christianity. He had no time for the distractions and fantasies of Kabbalah. Anticipating criticisms which would rarely be repeated until the nineteenth century, Meir regarded mysticism as little more than mythology and superstition. In 1888 the pioneer of modern Jewish history, Heinrich Graetz, described Kabbalah as obscurantism, which deluded sound sense and led the weak astray.[21] Graetz was writing seven centuries after Kabbalah's birth. Meir of Narbonne, who lived at the very place and time in which Kabbalah was putting down roots, felt even more strongly. He regarded the *Bahir* as a forgery, mocking it for meaning 'light' even though no 'light shines through it'.[22] He described the teachings of the kabbalists as 'empty words, chaff before the wind, devoid of sense'. Asher tried as best he could to defend Kabbalah against these charges, writing a polemical response, but he failed to dent Meir's onslaught. Asher knew that his side had been let down by the very people whom Isaac had sent him to Gerona to deal with: men who taught Kabbalah in public and opened it up to the criticism and mockery of its enemies.

For all its popularity, Kabbalah has never been far from criticism. Throughout history its defenders have sometimes swayed opinion in their favour, at other times they have been overcome. The fundamental disadvantage that Isaac the Blind and his nephew Asher were under was that they were kabbalists pure and simple; they had no reputation in other fields of Jewish learning. Unlike Isaac's father, *Rabad*, they were not acknowledged as masters of Talmud or Jewish law, disciplines which would have strengthened their reputation and given them greater credibility. In early thirteenth-century Spain, when the birth pangs of Kabbalah were causing its devotees so much pain, the doctrine was crying out for a champion whose learning in all fields was so deep that he was worthy of respect from every quarter.

Fortunately, there was such a man. His name was Moses ben Naḥman. He is known to the Jews as *Ramban* and to the wider world as Naḥmanides. He was a Talmudist, a mystic, a communal leader and something of a genius.

THE ENLIGHTENED WILL UNDERSTAND

Moses son of Naḥman was born in Gerona in 1192, shortly before Kabbalah made its first appearance in that city. It is believed that he trained and practised as a physician, although nothing is known about his medical career. His formidable reputation rests on his religious scholarship, his prolific writings and his commentaries on the Torah and Talmud. A charismatic leader, he was appointed as the chief rabbi of Catalonia. In due course he would become the acknowledged spokesman and rabbinic authority for Spain's extensive Jewish population.

In his old age Moses was summoned by royal command to defend his faith in a formal debate, or disputation, in Barcelona, in the presence of King James and much of his court. His opponent, Pablo Christiani, a Dominican friar who had converted from Judaism, had requested the disputation in order to teach the Jews the error of their ways and to impress upon them the truth of Christianity. The King agreed and summoned the son of Naḥman to speak for his religion. For four days Moses and Christiani hurled biblical quotes and theological speculations at each other. Eventually, with the atmosphere becoming ever more heated and the spectators ever more aggressive, Naḥmanides begged the King to bring the disputation to an end. King James agreed, presented Naḥmanides with 300 *dineros* and declared that he had never heard anyone who was so wrong present his case so well.

It was a pyrrhic victory. Shortly afterwards Naḥmanides was charged with blasphemy by the Bishop of Gerona. By now over 70, he left the country and boarded a ship to the Holy Land.[23] It was then that he wrote his famous commentary on the Torah, a remarkable fusion of textual analysis, theological investigation, caustic academic criticism and Talmudic argumentation, concluding as often as not with tantalising Kabbalistic hints, intelligible only to those steeped in mystical lore.

But that all took place when his years were waning. Long before then he involved himself in a controversy that was tearing apart the intellectual landscape of the rabbinic world.

In 1191 Moses Maimonides, the greatest of all post-Talmudic Jewish thinkers (and the father of Abraham who practised Jewish Sufism), created turmoil in the rabbinic world. He wrote a book for the growing number of acculturated Spanish Jews who had been raised within the Jewish tradition but who struggled to reconcile their faith with the cultural outlook of the society in which they lived. Confused and perplexed, these people were torn between two apparently incompatible and competing systems: the traditional teachings of their rabbis on one hand and fashionable Islamic philosophy on the other. Based on Aristotelian principles, this philosophy seemed to teach a wholly different outlook on life. Maimonides composed his book to help them synthesise both world views, to help them remain true to their faith and yet adopt an intellectual position compatible with the twelfth-century understanding of modernity.

Maimonides's *Guide for the Perplexed* was a difficult and enigmatic book, which concealed more than it explained. Its publication caused convulsions in Jewish communities across Europe and North Africa. This was the time when the Inquisition was pursuing the last adherents of the Cathar faith, and, although Jews were not directly involved, the rabbis of southern France could not help but be touched by the repressive intellectual atmosphere. They issued a local ban on Maimonides's writings, which they sought to extend across the Jewish world. Fierce rows broke out between Maimonides's supporters, mainly based in Spain, and the French rabbinic authorities. It was as much a clash of cultures as a question of law: a conflict of outlook, between the scholastic legalism of Jews in Christian Europe, and the more philosophical, quasi-mystical views of their co-religionists in the Islamic world.

Like many communal leaders, Nahmanides found himself drawn into the controversy. Unlike others, he refused to take sides, although it is not hard to discern where his sympathies lay. In a letter sent to one of the principal belligerents he made an impassioned plea for understanding. Maimonides's philosophy, he argued, had led to a revival of Judaism among those who had previously abandoned their faith. Instead of attempting to impose prohibitions upon his writings, he continued, it would be more beneficial to recognise that differences existed between communities. The glue of Scripture and Talmud held them all together but beyond that each community had a different outlook, which could not be legislated away by any single religious authority. Not just that, but the Jews of Yemen attributed almost saintly status to Maimonides, due to the wise counsel he had afforded them when they were threatened with forcible conversion to Islam.

Despite his tolerant appeal, Nahmanides was unable to effect reconciliation between the two camps. In the spirit of the Inquisition, the French rabbis even persuaded the Dominicans to burn Maimonides's books. It was a sobering moment, the irony of which was only fully appreciated eight years later, when the

Church built a pyre in Paris and burned every copy of the Talmud that could be found in France.

Naḥmanides nevertheless remained true to his breadth of vision. His scholarship was extensive and his literary output diverse. He wrote biblical commentaries, poetry, ethical works, Talmudic elucidations and a small number of Kabbalistic works, including an explanation of the first chapter of *Sefer Yetsirah*. And although he wrote few texts devoted exclusively to Kabbalah, Kabbalistic concepts permeate his other writings, particularly his poetry and his commentary to the Torah.

Despite his wide range of intellectual interests, when it came to spreading mystical teachings Naḥmanides was very much on the side of the conservatives. He may have been the communal leader, but as far as his Kabbalistic works were concerned he showed no interest at all in the outside world. He was the acknowledged leader of the Gerona kabbalists, but shared none of the proselytising enthusiasm of his older colleagues in the city, who had aroused the ire of Isaac the Blind for teaching Kabbalah in public.

For Naḥmanides, the only permissible way to transmit Kabbalah was direct oral instruction from teacher to student. Kabbalah was not a rational science; it could not be conveyed through writing. In his Commentary to the Torah he warned his readers not to enquire or try to apply reason to any of his mystical allusions, 'for my words will not be understood, or known at all, through reasoning or comprehension, other than from the mouth of a wise Kabbalist into the ear of an understanding recipient'.[24]

We can get a flavour of his obscurity in his interpretation of the phrase 'and this is the blessing', with which the penultimate chapter of the Torah begins: 'According to the way of Truth [the very words] "and this" *is* the blessing ... the enlightened will understand.'[25]

It wouldn't be accurate to describe Naḥmanides as just a Kabbalist; he was far more than that. He was the first mainstream rabbinic figure to include Kabbalah in his repertoire, and for the best part of a century he was regarded by other kabbalists as their leading authority. He may not have approved of discussing

Kabbalah in writing, but his followers had no hesitation in writing books that deciphered and explained his Kabbalistic method.[26]

Naḥmanides's conservatism did not appeal to all. After his death those who believed that Kabbalah should be taught openly gained the upper hand. They propelled Kabbalah away from whispered conversations in secret enclaves and cast it into the glare of daylight. In doing so they overcame Kabbalah's fundamental shortcoming, that it lacked the sanctity and gravitas of tradition.

Most religious systems develop from a set of beliefs grounded in myth, revelation or prophecy, sometimes all three. But although Kabbalah owed allegiance to the Bible and the Talmud, there was very little in ancient Jewish doctrine that gave credence to its basic principles. The idea of the ten *sefirot*, the divine emanations, had been creatively linked to verses in the Bible, but we can be pretty sure, even if the early kabbalists weren't, that biblical authors knew nothing of the *sefirot*. The biblical prophets may have ascribed powers to God, but it was the kabbalists who yoked those powers together into a system of *sefirot*.

The inability to appeal to tradition was a weakness that left Kabbalah vulnerable to criticism from its opponents. But the generation of kabbalists after Naḥmanides turned this weakness into a strength. They took advantage of Kabbalah's flexibility. Kabbalah, like all philosophies, was the product of human reason and ingenuity. Human, novel and rootless, early Kabbalah was far more flexible than any long-established religious tradition.

As Peter Burke has pointed out,[27] ideas may change when they spread from one place to another. Kabbalah had migrated, first from Provence to Gerona, and it was now being taken up by a new group of enthusiasts in the kingdom of Castile. As it journeyed it changed. These developments were enough to create a divide between those who held to the old ways and those who believed they stood on the threshold of something new.

On one side of this divide were the students of the now dead Naḥmanides, led by his most important disciple, Shlomo ben

Adret. On the other side were a group of men, the best-known of whom has given us one of Kabbalah's most intractable historical problems. His name was Moses de León. He was either the most important literary figure in the entire history of the Kabbalah, or he was a man who has been lauded far beyond his actual deeds. It all depends on how you look at it.

Radiance

A PRECIOUS JEWEL

The Zohar is the most important, the best-known and in many ways the definitive book of the Kabbalah. Profound and obscure, lightly narrated yet mystifying in meaning, the Zohar is regarded by some as second only to the Bible in holiness. In certain circles it has even supplanted the Talmud, normally regarded as the authoritative interpretation of the biblical tradition. Yet nobody had heard of the Zohar until the thirteenth century, when reports of its existence began to emerge from a town in Castile.

Today, its influence is felt across the whole spectrum of Jewish religious life; passages from it have entered the mainstream Jewish liturgy while some of its customs, such as studying all night on the traditional anniversary of the giving of the Torah, have become an accepted feature of the yearly calendar.

Those who elevate the book to the same level as, or even beyond, the Talmud maintain that it was written by Shimon bar Yohai. Living in the second century, bar Yohai was a pupil of Rabbi Akiva who emerged unscathed from the *Pardes* and was later extolled as a hero of the Palace literature. With a teacher like Akiva, it is not beyond the bounds of possibility that Shimon bar Yohai could have composed a book that is so central to the mystical tradition. But the evidence is against it.

The most immediate difficulty is that, if it was composed in the second century, the Zohar must have lain concealed and unknown for eleven centuries. We can be sure that mystical luminaries like Abu Aharon, Isaac the Blind and Naḥmanides had never heard of it; they would have said so if they had. But in the latter half of the thirteenth century, in a small Castilian town among a circle of up to that moment minor kabbalists, it suddenly emerged radiant and splendid into the light. It was an unbelievable moment. If you believe it.

The argument in favour of Shimon bar Yoḥai's authorship relies on a story in the Talmud, in which Shimon was a fugitive from the Roman government. He had made the mistake of publicly denigrating the achievements of the Empire. It seemed innocent enough at the time; hearing his colleague Yehuda praising Rome for building markets, bathhouses and bridges in occupied Israel, Shimon retorted that the occupiers had only done all this for their own benefit. 'They built markets to accommodate prostitutes, bathhouses to pamper themselves, bridges to collect tolls.' Unfortunately Shimon's complaint was overheard, a report was sent to the authorities and he was sentenced to death. He fled with his son Eleazar to a cave in the desert, where they remained for 12 years, sustained by a miraculous spring of water and a carob tree, buried up to their necks in sand for most of the day so as not to wear out their clothes. When they finally emerged from their isolation, they were so spiritually charged that their gaze set fire to everything they looked at. So intense were they that a voice issued from heaven ordering them back to the cave for another year, to calm down and prepare for their return to human society.[1]

Elsewhere, the Talmud hints at Shimon bar Yoḥai's mystical credentials, by comparing him to Moses. Unlike all other prophets, who experienced dim and obscure heavenly visions, rather like peering through a frosted window, Moses's revelations were sharp and detailed. The window through which he gazed upon heaven was crystal-clear. The Talmud implies that Shimon was granted the same level of insight.[2] But while the Talmud only suggests this obliquely, the Zohar categorically asserts Shimon bar Yoḥai's mystical pre-eminence.

The Zohar gives details of its own authorship, explaining that Shimon bar Yoḥai wrote the book during his 12 years hiding in the cave:

> Rabbi Pinḥas used to visit Rabbi Reḥumai by the shore of Lake Kinneret. He was a venerable man, full of days and his eyes could no longer see. He said to Rabbi Pinḥas: I have had a trustworthy report that our companion bar Yoḥai has a jewel, a precious gem and I have looked upon the light emitted by this jewel and it is like the light of the sun emerging from its sheath, illuminating the entire world. This light extends from the heavens to the earth, and will continue to illumine the whole world until the Ancient of Days comes and sits upon the throne ... Go my son, go and follow this jewel which illumines the world, for the hour is now ripe for you. He left him and prepared to go on board a ship with two other men. He saw two birds, darting low over the lake. He called to them and said 'Birds, birds, darting low over the lake, have you seen where bar Yoḥai is?' He waited a little. 'Birds, birds,' he said, 'go and come back to me.' And they flew away. They embarked and set off across the lake. Before they had disembarked the birds returned and in the mouth of one of them was a message that said that bar Yoḥai had left the cave, together with Rabbi Eliezer, his son.
>
> He went to him and found him transformed, for his body was covered with mould. He wept and said 'Alas, that I should see you so!' He replied: 'Blessed is your portion in that you have seen me so, for had you not seen me in this state, I would not be in this state.'[3]

The precious jewel in this anecdote is, of course, the Zohar, whose light illuminates the whole world. Zohar means radiance or splendour. Like the book *Bahir*, which means bright, the name *Zohar* alludes to the book's spiritual luminescence.

The Zohar is able to tell us that it was written by Shimon bar Yoḥai during the 12 years that he and his son were in the cave. What it cannot tell us is what happened to it during the thousand years or so prior to its arrival in Spain. That is a mystery.

Mystery should not surprise us. Mysticism is, by definition, mysterious. Things do not happen in the world of concealment in the same way that they happen in the revealed world. Why shouldn't an unknown book written in a cave in the Israeli desert over a millennium earlier, suddenly and without fanfare land in a small town in Spain?

Some people were surprised. In 1500 the Portuguese Jewish astronomer Abraham Zacuto published his history of the world. In it he recorded a testimony by Isaac of Acre, who is thought to have been a former pupil of Naḥmanides. Living in the Holy Land, Isaac had heard of the discovery of the Zohar. He was puzzled; if the book was what it was claimed to be, why had it emerged in Spain, rather than in Israel? And what of the conflicting stories that Isaac had heard about its origins? Some people said that Shimon bar Yoḥai had written it and that Naḥmanides had sent it from Israel to his son in Catalonia, that the wind had then blown it to Aragon, or perhaps Alicante, and that it had fallen into the hands of a man known as Moses de León. But others said that Shimon bar Yoḥai had not written it at all, that this same Moses de León had composed it himself using the power of the Holy Name. Apparently, so people said, Moses de León was a spendthrift; he always needed money and had attributed the book he was writing to the ancient sage Shimon bar Yoḥai, in order to sell extracts for the highest possible price.

In 1305, Isaac travelled to Spain to investigate the Zohar for himself. He met Moses de León, who categorically denied that he had written the book. He even offered to show Isaac the original, which he had at home, in order to prove that it had been written by bar Yoḥai. As so often happens in these stories, however, other powers intervened. Moses died before he could produce the book. Meanwhile, Moses's wife insisted that no such original copy of the book ever existed, that whatever de León wrote had come straight from his own head.[4]

Isaac of Acre was the first person, as far as we can tell, to throw doubt on Shimon bar Yoḥai's authorship of the Zohar. Instead, he raised the possibility that the book had been written in the thirteenth century by Moses de León. That, of course, would explain why nobody had heard of it until that time.

In the nineteenth century, when the historical investigation of religion started to become a formal academic discipline, scholars of the Kabbalah began to enquire more deeply into the Zohar's origins and authorship. It wasn't just that its lengthy concealment and unexplained sudden appearance seemed unlikely; there were also questions to be resolved about the content of the book itself.

WHO WROTE THE ZOHAR?

The Zohar varies so much in style and substance from one part of the book to another, that it is obvious to modern critics that it is composed of several different documents knitted together. Some of the documents have even preserved their original names.[5] The language, too, is problematic. Most of it is written in a stylised Aramaic. Yet in second-century Israel, when the Zohar is supposed to have been written, scholarly and religious literature was written in Hebrew. Aramaic was the vernacular, spoken in the markets and the streets. As Eitan P. Fishbane has pointed out, a text like the Zohar, which aims to draw a veil of secrecy over itself, is not likely to have been written in the language understood by ordinary people when the authors had the opportunity to compose it in a more cryptic tongue.[6]

The chronology and family relationships are confused, Shimon bar Yoḥai 's son-in-law is presented as his father-in-law and some characters turn up in the second century even though it is clear from other, more reliable sources that they will not be born for several generations.[7] Nor is the geography right. The descriptions of the various locations in Galilee where the narratives are set do not correspond with the topography and geography of that region. And the plant and animal life described is more like that found in Spain than in Israel. All this points to an authorship later than the second century, most probably in Spain.

Gershom Scholem was in no doubt about its authorship. The clincher for him was the apparent similarity between the style of the Zohar and some of the other, verifiable Kabbalistic writings of Moses de León. Isaac of Acre's testimony had first directed critical attention towards de León; 600 years later Gershom Scholem came up with even more persuasive, literary evidence in favour of the Spaniard's authorship. For the best part of 50 years, Scholem's scholarly authority and outstanding reputation led nearly every academic investigator to accept that he was right: that the Zohar, this voluminous, complex, deeply insightful book, was all written in Spain in the course of one lifetime in Aramaic, by a man who otherwise only wrote Hebrew and whose other writings, despite similarities noticed by Scholem, do not even begin to approach the Zohar in terms of style, complexity or insight.

Scholem's theory that Moses de León wrote the Zohar has not been rejected by everyone; many reputable Kabbalah scholars still hold to it. But increasingly a new generation of scholars is uncovering evidence that suggests the book's authorship was more complex than Scholem had imagined: indeed, that the Zohar is not a book at all. Rather, it is a compilation of different manuscripts by different authors, which for a couple of hundred years circulated independently, or were packaged together two or three at a time, in small collections. Despite being described as a book, as Isaac of Acre's testimony confirms, it was not a single, unitary work. It wasn't until the first printers bound together all the manuscripts they could find into a single volume that the Zohar received its final form. And that was not until the end of the sixteenth century, long after the manuscripts had first surfaced in Castile.[8]

The most likely view today is that the Zohar should properly be described as a body of literature, created by a group of Castilian kabbalists, but which includes some earlier material that may go back even as far as the eleventh century, long before Moses de León.[9] And this theory has led to another, which, if valid, gives us a remarkable insight into the politics of early Kabbalah, and the battle for authenticity between different schools of Kabbalistic thought. It is a struggle between the Castilian kabbalists, who included Moses de León, and the older school who held to the mysticism of the now dead Naḥmanides, which had been carried forward by his disciple, Shlomo ben Adret.

As we saw earlier,[10] when it came to the transmission of Kabbalah, Naḥmanides was firmly in the conservative camp. Like Isaac the Blind, he believed that mystical insights should only be communicated by word of mouth, to students who had sufficient understanding not to be misled. Furthermore, the scope of permissible mystical investigation was limited. Kabbalah for Naḥmanides and his successors in Gerona was a closed, esoteric system. There was only so far one could go, particularly when it came to investigating the nature of the *sefirot*.

In contrast, in Castile, Moses de León's generation of kabbalists took a more adventurous approach. Not only were they prepared to spread mystical doctrine through their writings, they were also far more creative in their manner of doing so. They expressed their creativity through imagery, and storytelling.

Ever since the book *Bahir*, the ten *sefirot* had symbolised aspects of divinity which could never be reduced to mere words. Giving the *sefirot* names like Wisdom, Understanding, Love and Might, the early kabbalists, first in Provence and then in Naḥmanides's Gerona, had sought to define the divine forces which governed the world. They knew that those forces were far more than their mere names, but words and names were all they had. But the kabbalists of the Zohar in Castile elevated the discussion to a new, higher level. They constructed metaphors, to explain not just the names but the functions of the *sefirot*. They linked these metaphors to passages in the Bible. The words and phrases of the Bible became the gateway to graphic, poetic descriptions of the cosmic drama, and to the connections between the forces that govern the revealed and concealed worlds.

Above the *sefirot* was *En-Sof*, the unknowable, unapproachable, Source of Sources, the concealed God, so remote that he cannot even be contemplated, let alone discussed. Literally meaning 'without end', *En-Sof* is the utterly transcendent, infinite divinity, who in a manner incomprehensible to created matter, made manifest the *sefirot*. They, by transmitting divine bounty from one to another, like sap through the Tree of Life, blood through Cosmic Man, collectively turn nothingness into substance.

Even the plants of the field were recruited to help explain how the spiritual forces operate. Each plant, and every herb, symbolises a different spiritual mystery. Trees have varying properties, depending on the particular spiritual channels which flow into and through them. The Bible is the key to it all:

> Rabbi Judah said: What is the meaning of the verse 'God made each one corresponding with the other' (Ecclesiastes 7.14)? The Holy One, blessed be he, made the earth like the pattern of the heavens, and everything alludes to what is above. … For Rabbi Jose said: The trees through which wisdom is revealed, for example, the carob, the pistachio and so on have all been constructed according to a single propagation. All those that bear fruit, apart from apples, are a single mystery, but the paths are separate. All those that do not bear fruit, that is the large ones, apart from the willows of the brook, which have a mystery of their own, derive their nourishment from the one source. And each of the smaller ones, apart from the hyssop, had the same mother.
>
> All the herbs in the earth, to which powerful princes have been assigned in heaven, have each a mystery of their own based on the heavenly pattern. Therefore it is written 'You shall not sow your field with two different kinds of seed' (Leviticus 19.19), for each one enters on its own and leaves on its own. This is the meaning of 'Do you know the ordinances of heaven? Can you recognise its dominion in the earth?' (Job 38.33), … Everything in the world is a mystery of its own and the Holy One, blessed be he did not wish to reveal or confuse them, and so he gave them all names.[11]

Significantly, the Zohar rarely refers to any of the *sefirot* by name. It assumes that its readers are sufficiently skilled in Kabbalistic interpretation to understand what it is talking about. In the above passage the various plants symbolise different *sefirot*. The apple which bears edible fruit, the willow which does not, and the hyssop, a shrub, each stand alone. Each is a plant which receives special attention in the Bible; their *sefirotic* nature is distinct from other vegetation.[12]

The symbolism of the Zohar is fanciful, complex and obscure. And so, even as the various Zohar texts were themselves being written, so, too, were commentaries, explaining what its symbols mean. Yosef Gikatilla, one of the leading kabbalists in Castile and a contemporary of Moses de León, composed *Gates of Light*, a sort of mystical encyclopaedia designed to explain the Zohar's symbolism to the uninitiated. In his introduction he pointed out that a person's name is not the person themselves, but merely puts us in mind of them, their personality and traits. Similarly, each of God's names in the Bible puts us in mind of distinct spiritual qualities, such as wisdom, mercy or might. Each of these qualities is uniquely associated with a particular *sefira*.

Gikatilla describes how the *sefirot* are arranged in the branched hierarchy known as the Tree of Life. The entire body of the tree is the elemental, four-letter name of God, the true pronunciation of which is believed to have been lost. The trunk of the tree is the name that God used when he first disclosed himself to Moses at the Burning Bush.[13] All the other divine names are either branches and twigs that hang from the tree, or roots spreading out beneath.

He explains how the divine names are sometimes hidden within the words and letters of biblical verses. Such verses are ciphers to be decoded by rearranging their letters to disclose the divine name they conceal. Finally, he lists dozens of synonyms used in Kabbalistic texts as coded references to the different divine names.

Through their writings and discussions, the Castilian kabbalists deliberately and enthusiastically discarded the reticent, subdued approach of Naḥmanides and his students to the teaching of Kabbalah. They did this by drawing upon the ancient rabbinic technique of *midrash*, a form of Bible commentary which uses narrative as one of its principal devices. The Zohar is written as just such a narrative: it purports to be a chronicle of Shimon bar Yoḥai's wanderings with a group of friends through Galilee. Most of the group are historical characters, known from Talmudic and other rabbinic sources. As they travel from place to place they see wondrous things, have deep and profound discussions and recount miraculous events of which they have heard. From time to time they encounter strangers who deliver mystical insights, inspire new ideas and reveal extraordinary new truths. Although the material is presented as a series of stories, much of it is arranged in the form of a running commentary on the Torah, each biblical phrase or verse inspiring a digression into a new narrative or insight. Indeed, the kabbalists believe it is these insights which are the true essence of the Torah, the Bible's words and sentences themselves being nothing more than gateways to the profound truth which lies behind them:

> Rabbi Shimon said: Woe to the man who says that the Torah intended simply to relate stories and the words of commoners, for if this were the case, we ourselves at the present time could make a Torah from the words of commoners and do even better. If the intention was to deal with the affairs of this world then the secular books in the world contain better things … But all the words of the Torah are exalted and are supernal mysteries … The narratives of the Torah are the garments of the Torah. The value of a garment resides in the body and the value of the body resides in the soul. The fools in the world look only upon the clothes, which are the narratives of the Torah; they know no more, they do not see what is beneath the clothes … The wise … look only upon the soul, which is the foundation of all, the real Torah. And in the time to come they are destined to look upon the soul of the soul of the Torah.[14]

Just as the Torah conceals deep mysteries, so are the Zohar's stories designed to teach mystical lessons. But one contemporary theory claims that the whole structure frames a powerful polemic, a vast complex allegory, which is more political than mystical. It is a polemic which seems deliberately to extol the Zohar authors' new approach to the promotion of Kabbalah, and to distinguish it from the now obsolete methods preferred by Naḥmanides.

The polemic relies on the Zohar's occasional description of Shimon bar Yoḥai as spiritually superior to Moses. It is a bold claim; in Jewish tradition Moses had always been recognised as the greatest of all prophets, the miracle worker who humbled the mighty Pharaoh, who led the Israelites from slavery to freedom, who ascended Mount Sinai to receive the Torah and who, uniquely in human history, engaged in direct, crystal-clear dialogue with God. 'Mouth to mouth I speak with him,' says God of Moses, 'manifestly, and not in riddles, for he sees the likeness of God.'[15]

As we saw above, the Talmud implies that Shimon bar Yoḥai experienced the same quality of divine revelation as Moses. But this is as far as the Talmud goes; it doesn't elaborate on the type of revelations that Shimon receives, nor does it seem particularly bothered that Shimon and Moses have this particular quality in common. The Zohar, however, does go further. Boaz Huss, who has developed the theory that the Zohar contains a polemic against Naḥmanides, draws his readers' attention to a passage in which Shimon tells his companions that he has seen what no other person has seen since Moses's second ascent to Mount Sinai, and that whereas the Bible says that Moses was unaware his face shone, he, Shimon, was fully conscious of his own radiant visage.[16] Furthermore, the image of Moses which the Zohar projects in several passages is of a humble, uncertain, hesitant leader. Shimon bar Yoḥai, on the other hand, is presented as clear, decisive and confident.

Huss argues that, in describing Moses as modest and cautious, the Zohar is referring not to the biblical prophet but to another Moses – Moses Naḥmanides. The argument is not fully persuasive, but it is compelling; the uncertain Moses in the Zohar represents the cautious, conservative Naḥmanides; the unafraid, self-aware Shimon bar Yoḥai symbolises the new school of Castilian kabbalists, confident in their knowledge and free to reveal it openly. 'Happy is the generation among which Shimon bar Yoḥai dwells,' says the Zohar, 'for its king is a free man. Free to lift his head to reveal and to explain matters without fear. And to say what he wishes without trepidation.'[17]

Of course, it is hard to know what impact, if any, this apparent polemic against Naḥmanides and his school had. It did take time for the Zohar to become popular; it wasn't really until it emerged from the printers' presses in the early sixteenth century that it achieved the sort of canonical status it enjoys today. But serious kabbalists knew it and drew from it from the days of its first appearance in Castile. Some, like the fourteenth-century Italian Kabbalist Menaḥem Recanati, made use both of the Zohar and of the mystical hints in Naḥmanides's Bible commentary.

Recanati was almost the first Jewish mystic to work in Italy since the days of Abu Aharon. Only one major figure preceded him. He owed very little to either Naḥmanides or the Zohar. His name was Abraham Abulafia. He was a very strange character indeed.

THE DISSIDENT KABBALIST

Much of the Zohar's popular appeal is due to its simple, storytelling format. But, like all good mysticism, it is what lies beneath the surface which really matters. The Zohar's compelling, often cute stories of Shimon bar Yoḥai 's wanderings through Galilee with his friends are only a device to capture the reader's attention and assist their memory. Concealed behind the narrative is a dense symbolic description of how God acts on the world, explained through the system of forces known as *sefirot* that flow from heaven. The mystical enquiry into how God does things is called theosophy, from the Greek *theos* meaning god, and *sophia*, wisdom.

But knowledge of God is not the only sort of mysticism. Those early mystics who descended to the Chariot were seeking a more intimate connection, an experience of God rather than an understanding. In that regard Abraham Abulafia had more in common with the early mystics than his own contemporaries. He also aimed for ecstatic, mystical experiences, which he accomplished by contemplating the divine names and meditating on the complex permutations of their letters.[18] Abulafia was by no means unique in concentrating on the divine names; his own pupil, Yosef Gikatilla, had, as we saw earlier, written his *Gates of Light* to explain their mystical properties. But Gikatilla was first and foremost a Castilian Kabbalist, focusing on understanding rather than experiencing God. Abraham Abulafia, on the other hand, saw himself as a prophet; perhaps even as the Messiah.

Abraham Abulafia was born in Saragossa in Spain in the year 1240. At the age of 20 he left home in search of the mythical river Sambatyon. A figment of the early rabbinic imagination, Sambatyon was said to be an impenetrable watercourse, on the other side of which lived the ten lost tribes of Israel. Impenetrable because it hurled rocks and boulders all week long; the river only rested on the Sabbath. But as it is forbidden to cross water on the holy day, nobody had ever managed to cross. Apart from one man, and it was a mystery how he had done it. His name was Eldad the Danite; he had lived 400 years earlier. Abraham Abulafia set out to replicate his feat, to cross the Sambatyon. He failed. He was forced to turn back after stumbling into a war zone, his path blocked by battles between the Mamluk Sultanate and an army of invading Mongols.[19].

For much of the next 20 years, Abulafia travelled between Israel, Spain, Greece and Italy. Pausing for a while in Capua, a little way north of the modern city of Naples in southern Italy, he immersed himself in the study of the *Guide to the Perplexed*, Maimonides's controversial philosophical work. The book's critics were still vigorously attacking it; Abulafia's philosophy teacher, Hillel of Verona, was one of those agitating in its defence.

Some time in the 1260s Abulafia left Capua and travelled to Barcelona, where the disputation between Naḥmanides and Pablo Christiani had recently taken place. Naḥmanides had probably left the city before Abulafia arrived; he had set sail for the Holy Land a couple of years after the disputation, having been accused by the Bishop of Gerona of blasphemy. But he was still venerated by the city's Jews and his teachings were almost certainly one of the factors that attracted Abulafia towards mysticism. The other factor was his unexpected exposure to Sufi writings.

Barcelona was a vibrant port that acted as a hub for ships from across the Mediterranean. Like many medieval trading and transport centres, it was a place where ideas, stories and patterns of thought from different cultures came into contact and cross-fertilised. One of the city's lesser-known industries was the copying of Sufi texts from Arabic to Hebrew. We do not know for certain whether Abulafia came across these texts, or whether he came into contact with Sufi ideas in any other way. But it is likely. For something profound happened to Abulafia in Barcelona. When he arrived he was a student of Maimonides's rationalist philosophy. By the time he left he had been transformed into one of the most influential kabbalists in history. Almost certainly the oddest.

Abulafia continued to travel, teaching small groups of students most of whom, he complained, abandoned him. He expressed disappointment with them, though it is hard to discern the reasons. For although he wrote prolifically and provided his readers with far more biographical detail than any other Kabbalistic writer, he rarely explained directly what he meant. As Harvey Hames has put it, 'Once one gets used to the way Abulafia thinks, then deciphering the meaning of the text becomes an interesting challenge and there is a feeling of achievement when what looks like utter gibberish suddenly takes on meaning.'[20]

Abulafia's mysticism is based on an interweaving of Maimonidean philosophy and the power of the Hebrew language. Based on techniques developed by the Pietists of Germany he devised methods for permutating the letters of the divine names with other letters of the alphabet. The Hebrew alphabet is made up exclusively of consonants, each of which can carry one of seven vowels. In Abulafia's system, the seeker after mystical ecstasy meditates upon each consonant, combining each vowel with it in turn. The permutations are written down, so that the mystic visualises as well as inwardly articulates the sounds. The use of special breathing techniques and adopting particular body positions adds a physical dimension to his introspection.

Intense concentration is required, and a conscious act of will. 'When you feel that your heart is already warm and when you see

that by combinations of letters you can grasp new things which by
human tradition or by yourself you would not be able to know and
when you are thus prepared to receive the influx of divine power
which flows into you, then turn all your true thoughts to imagine
the Name and His exalted angels in your heart as if they were
human beings standing or sitting about you.'[21]

Teaching these techniques to his students was as essential to
Abraham Abulafia as practising them himself. It was his firm belief
that he would only be able to fulfil his destiny through his role as a
teacher of mystical secrets. It was a destiny of which he had always
been aware, signified by the propitious year of his birth, 5000 in
the Hebrew calendar – the very beginning of the sixth and final
earthly millennium. It was Abulafia's lot to become nothing other
than the Messiah of the redemption. Of this, everything suggests,
he was certain.

In the year 1279 Abulafia set out to achieve his destiny. He had
been living in Sicily, where he had come across the teachings of
the twelfth-century abbot Joachim of Fiore. He discovered that the
Joachimites shared his belief that the world was on the threshold
of a new era, and that the final apocalypse was at hand. Abulafia
regarded this as a sign that he was obliged to prepare both the Jews
and the Christians for the approaching end. He was to do this using
the full extent of his mystical and philosophical powers. And there
was something extremely important he had to do at the outset.

Since his mission was to prepare the Christians as well as the Jews,
there was one man who was essential to his task. Pope Nicholas III
would be his conduit into the Christian world. It was imperative
that Abulafia meet him, to teach him of the divine names and
to induct him into the changes which would come about in the
redemptive age. Abraham Abulafia set off for Rome.

Abulafia himself tells us what happened next. He had intended
to meet the Pope in Rome, in St Peter's, the heart of the Church,
on the eve of the Jewish New Year, a most propitious time for him.
When he arrived in Rome he found to his dismay that the Pope
had decamped to his summer home in Soriano. Unfazed, Abulafia
followed him there. The Pope must have had forewarning of his

arrival, for according to Abulafia he instructed his guards to arrest him, take him to the city gate and burn him alive. Somehow Abulafia was told of all this before he arrived, because he tells us that he paid no attention to his informers. Instead he sat and practised meditation, saw visions and wrote a book of testimony about his impending rescue. He then continued with his journey to Soriano.

It turned out that he had been right to be complacent. On arrival at the palace in Soriano he discovered that the Pope had died the previous night, smitten by a plague. This was not a figment of his imagination; corroborating Latin sources confirm that Pope Nicholas III died suddenly, stricken by an apoplexy, before a confessor could be brought.[22] Abulafia was arrested, kept in a dungeon for a fortnight and then released without charge or ceremony.

Whether or not Abulafia was really on his way to see Pope Nicholas when he died or whether the whole episode was a product of his imagination, based on his subsequent knowledge of the Pontiff's sudden death, is a question we can't answer. In any event the Pope did not announce that Christianity had been subsumed into Abulafia's notion of Judaism and Abulafia was not proclaimed Messiah. His messianic destiny, not to mention his tremulous anticipation in meeting the most powerful man in Christendom, had fizzled out into a non-event.

Abulafia returned to Sicily. Things turned out little better for him there. In 1282 the leaders of the Palermo Jewish community wrote to Rabbi Shlomo bin Adret, Nahmanides's former pupil, who had succeeded him as leader of the Jewish community in Barcelona. They wanted to know what to do about Abulafia. Political conditions were unstable in Sicily; the island had recently rebelled against the French king Charles I and the atmosphere was tense. The last thing Palermo's Jews wanted was one of their own people predicting the end of Christianity and claiming to be the Messiah.

Adret, acknowledged as a leading authority in Jewish law, responded with a fierce letter attacking Abulafia's mysticism and his claims. He placed Abulafia and all his writings under a ban.

Abulafia wrote back fiercely, attacking the doctrine of the *sefirot*, the very essence of Spanish Kabbalah. The row brought into sharp focus the tension between Kabbalah's two very distinctive, apparently irreconcilable approaches. On the one hand Spanish Kabbalah focused on the *sefirot* and the mystical nature of the commandments; on the other Abulafia's Kabbalah was driven by a desire for mystical, ecstatic communion, gained through contemplation and manipulation of the divine names.[23]

Abulafia's quest for ecstasy had deeper roots; it stretched all the way back to those early mystics who had descended to the Chariot. But the Spanish system had greater staying power. Abulafia was an intense personality, difficult to understand and by his own word impossible to get on with. This may explain why, despite his prolific writings, his legacy did not have the impact he desired upon future generations.

Indeed, the next major figure in Italian mysticism drew not upon Abulafia's work, but upon that of the Spanish kabbalists. He was a man named Menaḥem Recanati. He was more of a synthesiser than an innovator; he brought a degree of coherence to the tangle of ideas that had proliferated in Spain over the past half-century. Coherence and systemisation were exactly what Kabbalah needed at this stage in its development.

A DIVINE KISS

The second half of the thirteenth century was far and away the most creative period in Kabbalah's early history. The texts that would eventually be collated into the work we know as the Zohar sat, as yet hardly acknowledged, at the centre of the Castilian fellowship's literary endeavour. At this early stage they jostled for attention with greater and lesser works, many of which did not survive the devastation to be visited upon Spain's Jews in the decades to come, the traumas of forced conversion and the upheavals of expulsion. It is an unfortunate consequence of European history that only a small proportion of what was written by Spain's community of kabbalists has survived to the present day.

In 1240, shortly after the French rabbis had persuaded the leadership of the Dominican order to burn Maimonides's books, cartloads of Talmud manuscripts were publicly burned in Paris. It turned out to be the first of many such immolations which carried on until 1559. Ostensibly it was only the Talmud that was to be burned, condemned due to the misapprehension that it was because of this book that the Jews did not convert to Christianity. But although their brief was to seize copies of the Talmud, many of the inspectors who raided Jewish study houses and synagogues could not read Hebrew. They had no idea if they were seizing copies of the Talmud or anything else. If it was written in Hebrew, it went onto the pyre.[24] Nobody has any idea of what other works were lost during the conflagrations, and there is little doubt that the many Kabbalistic treatises that have survived from this time are only a small remnant of those which once circulated. Often we only know of a work's existence because it is mentioned by someone else. Someone like the Italian Kabbalist Menaḥem Recanati.

Although he lived in Italy, Menaḥem Recanati had a voluminous library of works composed by the generation of Spanish kabbalists who produced the Zohar. The extent of his library is evident from the many citations from Castilian works that he includes in his own books. He was not unique in drawing on this earlier literature; in fact what distinguished the kabbalists of his age from the Zohar generation is their dependence on those who went before them. There is a lack of innovation in Recanati's work; his preference is to enlarge upon and explain the teachings of those who preceded him, unsystematic and incoherent as they often were. The Kabbalah of the Zohar generation was characterised by a profusion of ideas and theories that frequently had little relation to each other. Recanati's genius was to begin to unravel the tangled threads of Castilian Kabbalistic doctrine, to begin to impose some order and coherence upon the discipline.

Although living in Italy, Recanti's Kabbalah was rooted firmly in Spain, the land in which Abraham Abulafia's writings remained under a ban. In none of his writings does Recanati pay any attention to his Italian predecessor. His affinity to the Spanish Kabbalah of the *sefirot*, rather than Abulafia's routes to ecstasy through the power of the alphabet, comes across most clearly in the work for which he is best known, his Commentary on the Torah. Time and again he quotes from the Zohar, often in quite lengthy passages. It was the first time that the Zohar had been brought to the attention of an audience outside Spain.

Perhaps Recanati's most important contribution to the future of the Kabbalah was through his interpretation of one particular biblical passage. He could not have foreseen the impact his interpretation would ultimately have, and probably would not have believed it had he been told.

When Moses's brother Aaron died in the wilderness, the book of Numbers says that his death was 'by the word of God', or, if translated literally, 'by the mouth of God'. The same is said of Moses. These brief statements were explained by the Talmud[25] as meaning that their death came about through a divine kiss. Since we all have to die, this must be the best way of all. The idea of death by a divine kiss was, unsurprisingly, one which appealed to the mystical imagination of kabbalists of every stripe and shade, from the romantic to the ecstatic.

For Abraham Abulafia, death by a kiss meant a person who dies absorbed in a state of ecstasy while uttering the divine name. Recanati's view was different. Based on the Zohar, he maintained that death by a kiss is a temporary state experienced by someone who is so absorbed in their prayer or study that, just as ripe fruit falls from the tree it no longer needs, so the fully actualised soul abandons its body and cleaves instead to the divine presence.[26]

The importance of Recanati's view has less to do with the concept of death by a kiss, upon which many books can and have been written, than on the impact his explanation had on a student of Kabbalah who lived two centuries later, one who also lived in Italy, and was not a Jew but an Italian nobleman.

His name was Count Pico della Mirandola; he was possibly the most erudite and distinctive scholar of the entire Renaissance. We shall hear more about him soon. His distinctiveness was not only that he approached Kabbalah from a Christian perspective. It was also that he saw Kabbalah as one of the world's great wisdoms, particularly efficacious when blended with the knowledge of how nature operates. In the early Renaissance this knowledge was more a matter of belief than science. They called it magic, by which they meant something far more profound and consequential than the word implies today. Magic had never been far from the world of Kabbalah and now, due to the work of Pico della Mirandola and his Kabbalist teacher Yohanan Alemanno, it was about to get a lot closer still.

YOHANAN ALEMANNO'S KABBALISTIC MAGIC

As his name implies, Yohanan Alemanno's family were originally of German parentage. His grandfather had moved first to France and then to Spain, from where the king of Aragon had sent him on a mission to the Vatican. Yohanan lived in Florence during the latter decades of the fifteenth century, and the intellectual climate of that city at the dawn of the Renaissance pervades his writings.

Alemanno's study of Kabbalah convinced him that events on earth could be influenced by drawing down the supernatural powers that flowed through the *sefirot*. This drawing down could be done by reciting the divine names, such as those which are found in a Torah scroll. Mystical minds, used to seeing what lies behind the immediately obvious, recognised that divine names are encoded within the Torah's narrative, so that even though what appears on the surface may be profound and sacred, beneath it lies an even deeper, concealed wisdom, the very blueprint of the cosmos itself. As long ago as the third century, Rabbi Oshaya Rabba had declared that God consulted the Torah when creating the world.[27]

Alemanno believed that the Torah could also be used as an instrument of magic. When the Kabbalist-magician recites the words of the Torah, with the proper concentration and having performed the correct preparations, the divine spirit will descend upon him 'to such a degree that the scroll will give him power to work signs and wonders in the world'.[28] But this can't be achieved by any old Kabbalist. The essential first stage is for the aspiring

Kabbalist-magician to become fully acclimatised to receiving the divine forces, long before he dares endeavour to harness them for practical purposes. Only after repeated exercises will he be sufficiently immersed in the art of what has become known as 'practical Kabbalah' to receive the divine spirit with sufficient intensity to achieve his desired ends.

In Alemanno's scheme there is nothing heretical about using the Torah for magical purposes. Even Moses used it in this way according to Alemanno, drawing down divine emanations to part the Red Sea.[29]

Alemanno insisted there was no possibility of Kabbalistic magic being used for any purpose other than the good. Practitioners of black magic, he said, would have to look elsewhere for their art. They might profitably try using the magic of the astrologers, an inferior magic, which, because it is based on the stars rather than the *sefirot*, is rooted in the physical universe. It can never be as pure or efficacious as the spiritual magic of the practical Kabbalist.

Alemanno's magic came in for severe criticism from a contemporary, Elijah del Medigo. It was impossible, del Medigo asserted, to bring spiritual forces into the world as magicians claim to do. Using the Torah in an attempt to do so is akin to idolatry. He didn't mention Alemanno by name in his broadside, but both men lived in Florence, both were teachers of Pico della Mirandola, and his reticence about identifying the target of his criticism may simply have been for reasons of diplomacy. As we shall see, Pico's circle included some of the most powerful people in Florence. It may not have been judicious for either man to be seen publicly quarrelling with the other.

Outside of Italy, the life of the Kabbalah, if one can use such a term, was fairly quiet for most of the fourteenth and fifteenth centuries. In Spain, kabbalists came and went. There were no spectacular innovations and little external influence. Until 1492, when the Jews were expelled from the Iberian Peninsula, an event which, traumatic as it was, heralded a whole new flowering in the Kabbalistic world.

But we stay in Renaissance Florence, where the next great development in the history of Kabbalah was about to take place. Yohanan Alemanno's pupil, Pico della Mirandola, was about to introduce Kabbalah to a Christian world that had never known it, and that was unprepared for its appearance.

Christian Cabala

THE IMPETUOUS GENIUS

In 1274 the Catalan philosopher Ramon Llull experienced a life-transforming revelation on the Puig de Randa, a mountain on the island of Majorca. It inspired him to compose his *Ars Magna*, a Great Art, based on scientific, philosophical and mystical principles which he believed connected Islam, Christianity and Judaism, the three religions of the thirteenth-century Iberian Peninsula.

Llull's Art was similar in at least two respects to Spanish Kabbalah. He described a hierarchical system of divine attributes, resembling the *sefirot* of the Kabbalah. And he devised a technique for meditating upon combinations of words and letters, not too different from that being developed at the same time by Abraham Abulafia. The only significant point of difference was that Lull meditated upon the Latin alphabet, whereas Abulafia immersed himself in Hebrew.

The Zohar, Llull's *Ars Magna* and the letter-based meditations of the Spanish-born and trained Abraham Abulafia were all products of a remarkable moment in European history: the almost-peaceful cohabitation and intellectual cross-fertilisation of Islam, Christianity and Judaism. It was a uniquely Iberian phenomenon which flourished but briefly. Contact between philosophers, theologians, poets, doctors, artists, grammarians and dreamers in each culture led to a blossoming of knowledge and ideas that eventually resonated across Europe and North Africa. In such a rich, shared, intellectual climate it is little surprise that Llull's Art evoked aspects of Kabbalah, or indeed that influences flowed the other way.

But there were differences, too, between Kabbalah and *Ars Magna*, and not just in the disparity between the languages on which they were each based. Llull's Art was constructed upon scientific principles, utilising the four universal elements, fire, air, earth and water, and their corresponding qualities, heat, cold, dry and damp. Llull's was a natural science, something Kabbalah never claimed to be.[1]

Llull's missionary aim was to hasten the conversion of Jews and Muslims to Christianity by uniting their faiths. Two hundred years later a young Italian nobleman attempted the same synthesis. He regarded Kabbalah as a unifying principle between the faiths, and he laid the foundations for the Christian interpretation of Kabbalistic principles. The mantle of first Christian Cabalist sits atop the shoulders of Count Giovanni Pico della Mirandola. His story begins a few years before he was born.

Round about the year 1460, a monk from Macedonia brought a bundle of Greek manuscripts to Cosimo de' Medici in Florence. Cosimo, founder of the Medici dynasty, head of the powerful family's bank, supreme patron of the arts and ruler of Florence in all but name, impatiently seized the documents. Arguably, this was the moment that heralded the birth of the Renaissance.

Unarguably, the manuscripts' arrival in Florence turned out to be the most significant event in the Kabbalah's history since the appearance of the Zohar in Castile 200 years earlier. And yet the documents contained not one word of Kabbalah. Nor did they have anything to do with Judaism, or even the Jews.

The manuscripts were known as the *Corpus Hermeticum*, the Hermetic Writings. Composed, so everyone believed, in the deepest reaches of antiquity, the writings had a venerable pedigree. The third-century Church father Lactantius had relied on them to prove the beliefs of Christianity. A century later, however, Augustine had condemned them for their praise of Egyptian magic, and for the false prophecies of their author.[2] Their author was thought to have been an Egyptian priest-magician, a supposed contemporary of Moses named Hermes Trismegistus, or 'Hermes Thrice-Great'.

The manuscripts brought by the monk had been hidden away, forgotten and disintegrating, in a Byzantine store room for many centuries. But Constantinople, capital of the once powerful Eastern Roman empire of Byzantium, had fallen to the Ottomans in 1453. Collectors in the know, powerful men like Cosimo who had a network of agents scavenging for just such things, gradually began to hear about Byzantine booty: documents long thought lost, treasures and relics whose existence had been forgotten or never known, that were now finding their way onto the market. Chief among these desiderata were the Hermetic manuscripts. As soon as he heard about them Cosimo snapped them up.

Once the manuscripts were in his possession, Cosimo summoned Florence's leading Greek scholar, Marsilio Ficino. Just a few months earlier Cosimo had commissioned Ficino to translate the works of Plato for him. Now, Cosimo ordered, Ficino was to put Plato aside and translate Hermes instead. Hermes, after all, was a contemporary of Moses whereas Plato, as everybody thought they knew, was a pupil of the prophet Jeremiah.[3] Cosimo believed, and Ficino concurred, that the more ancient sage should be translated first.

It wasn't until much later, in 1614 in fact, that Isaac Casaubon demonstrated that the *Corpus Hermeticum* was not an ancient Egyptian work. Rather, it had been written in the Christian era. Its alleged author, Hermes Trismegistus, had almost certainly never existed. Like the Sibylline Oracles, another literary classic of antiquity, its authors had managed to give the impression that it was far older even than its true venerable pedigree. But at the beginning of the Renaissance this wasn't known. Instead the humanist spirit of the times, which asserted that the literature of the ancients was wisdom to be studied, had led Cosimo de' Medici to commission Marsilio Ficino to translate an ancient Greek manuscript into Latin. The *Corpus Hermeticum*, imagined to be a trove of ancient wisdom and magic, was now freely available in Florence, to those with the skills and education to understand it. Its presence would lead Kabbalah into pastures new and quite unexpected.

It was Giovanni Pico della Mirandola who first wove a connection between the Hermetic Writings and Kabbalah. He did so in the belief that he could bind them, together with other ancient wisdoms, into a single universal philosophy that would prove, from first principles, the beliefs of Christianity. Little did he imagine that this ambitious project would lead him to be known one day as the founder of Christian Cabala. Always Cabala with a 'c' and not a 'k', because that is how it was spelled in Florence.

Pico lived a short, but action-packed life. Without doubt one of the greatest intellects of the Renaissance, his personal life veered from one crisis to another. A gentleman scholar, with wealth and privileges appropriate to his status, Count Pico was a welcome guest at many of the great houses of Italy. In 1486, at the age of 23, he was returning to his university in Perugia, having just spent some time studying philosophy at the Paris Sorbonne. He decided to break his journey in the Tuscan city of Arezzo. It isn't known why he chose to stop there, or indeed how long he stayed. What is known is that while in Arezzo he fell madly in love. The intensity of his fervent, all-consuming passion was marred only by the fact that the young woman, Margherita, was already married – to Giuliano Mariotto de' Medici.

As his name indicates, Giuliano was a member of the wealthy Medici family of bankers. Although his personal star had never risen as high as that of his eminent cousin Lorenzo, who had now succeeded his grandfather Cosimo as de facto ruler of Florence, Giuliano was still able to call upon powerful and fearsome allies to help him avenge himself upon the young scholarly upstart. On 10 May 1486 Pico made a run for it, taking with him only his retinue of servants, 20 horses, crossbowmen and, of course, Margherita. Opinion is divided even today over whether it was an elopement or an abduction.

Wealthy, charismatic, highly intelligent and good-looking, the only qualities Pico seems to have lacked were those of how to be a successful fugitive. The townspeople, outraged by his behaviour, were single-minded in their duty to Giuliano. The Podestà, the chief magistrate, rang the bells, assembled his men and ordered them to track Pico down. Two hundred volunteers joined in. Pico was overtaken at Marciano, close to the Sienese border. Heavily outnumbered, it was only due to the skill of his horse that Pico escaped with his life. Eighteen others were not so lucky.[4]

Pico and his secretary were brought back to Arezzo, where they were thrown into gaol. But the young count had one trump up his sleeve: Giuliano had secured the loyalty of the townspeople both due to local pride and because of his status as a member of Lorenzo de' Medici's family. But Pico himself was one of Lorenzo's treasured and intimate friends. Like his grandfather Cosimo, Lorenzo the Magnificent was an ardent patron of culture and knowledge; his inner circle comprised the elite of Renaissance Florence. Leonardo da Vinci, Michelangelo, Botticelli and Machiavelli were just the cream of the luminaries who graced his court. Pico was in there, too. Outmanoeuvred by an opponent with such connections, Giuliano Mariotto de' Medici could only fume as behind the scenes his eminent cousin Lorenzo negotiated the impetuous count's release.

The episode in Arezzo might have been nothing more than a tale of courtly love and betrayal were it not for the project that Pico had been working on when Cupid smote him. A project he seems to have continued even as he was being treated with chivalrous favour in an Arretine dungeon. Between Pico's capture in May 1486 and the following October, the Sicilian Flavius Mithridates translated upwards of 3000 folios of Kabbalistic texts into Latin on his behalf. Although the folios are undated, we know they were translated at this time because of the occasional notes that Mithridates scribbled in the margins, alluding to Pico's troubles in Arezzo.[5]

Born Samuel ben Nissim Bulfarag, Mithridates had converted from Judaism to Christianity some 20 years earlier. Since then, he had acquired a reputation for preaching polemics against the Jews and, it appears, a penchant for young boys.[6] But whatever the calumnies he levelled at the Jews in public, the translations he carried out for Pico show that he retained a profound understanding of Judaism, deep enough to comprehend even the obscurities and complexities of Kabbalah. Without Mithridates it is unlikely that Pico would ever have mastered the theology of the *sefirot*, which demanded a deeper immersion in rabbinic and Kabbalistic traditions than he had so far attained. Nor would he have become conversant with the manipulation of divine names. Pico had started to learn Hebrew, his early teachers including Mithridates himself, the philosopher Elia del Medigo and the Italian Kabbalist Yohanan Alemanno. But Kabbalistic wordplay demands a knowledge of the language far beyond anything that even the young prodigy Pico could yet muster. As for a knowledge of rabbinic tradition, it was Pico's misunderstanding of its nuances which enabled him to trace the origins of Cabala further back into history than could possibly have been the case.

So Pico was obliged to lean heavily on Mithridates for his Kabbalistic knowledge. And although Mithridates translated many Kabbalistic texts into Latin for Pico, a rigorous analysis by Chaim Wirzsubski[7] of the young count's Cabalistic knowledge shows that he ultimately depended upon Mithridates's translations of just two masters, both formerly residing in Italy: Abraham Abulafia and Menaḥem Recanati. These two thirteenth-century Jewish kabbalists unwittingly became the twin pillars of Christian Cabala. Equally unwittingly, they were responsible for finally rupturing the bond between Pico and Margherita. When she indicated a few months later that she was willing to return to him, he displayed no interest.[8] He was now in Rome, with his mind on greater things. Poor Margherita found herself discarded.

By early November 1486 Pico had finished the work that would lead to the next great crisis of his life. It was a project of unbounded ambition. Its goal no less than the ultimate summation of Truth; its tools every known ancient body of knowledge. With a particular emphasis on the entirety of the world's philosophic, esoteric and magical literature.

Drawing on sources as varied as Thomas Aquinas, Albertus Magnus, natural magic, Orphic hymns, Chaldean oracles, the *Corpus Hermeticum* and, of course, Kabbalah, Pico constructed

900 philosophic principles, or theses, which he argued were all reconcilable with each other and which, when assessed as a coherent whole, would prove, beyond any scientific or philosophical doubt, that Christianity was the one true faith. Among his 900 principles were 72 that he had derived from Kabbalah. Seventy-two was not a random number; the book *Bahir* refers to 72 names of God, and in Kabbalistic lore the longest and most intricate of God's names comprises 72 letters.

Pico was not content with simply compiling and publishing his theses. He was a young man of far-reaching ambition, and he was certain he had just constructed the greatest philosophical synthesis ever attempted. So important did Pico consider this work, his *Conclusiones*, that he published his book in every Italian university and offered to pay the travel expenses of any independent scholar who wished to travel to Rome to debate with him. With typical hubris, he proposed to Pope Innocent VIII that a public, scholarly debate be held, in January 1487, to discuss his findings.

Pico was still three months short of his twenty-fourth birthday. He was impetuous. The Pope was not. Indicating that he might be willing to sponsor a debate, he first submitted Pico's conclusions for inspection to the College of Cardinals. It was not the idea of a debate that concerned him; such events were frequent in medieval scholarship. It was the sheer scale of Pico's work, the novelty of the themes he covered, his age and somewhat tarnished reputation that made his proposal a matter that Innocent did not feel impelled to rush into.

The College of Cardinals were not as outraged by Pico's *Conclusiones* as they might have been. It wouldn't have been surprising if they had regarded the whole project as a pagan heresy, drawn as it was from the wells of occult and esoteric literature. But they did not reject it. In fact, of the 900 theses in Pico's *Conclusiones*, the Cardinals found fault with only 13. Of these, only one had anything to do with Cabala, and it didn't even occur in the section containing the 72 Cabalistic statements. But there could have been little doubt, even in Pico's mind, that it was the most astonishing and controversial of all his propositions.

In the section of his *Conclusiones* where he lists the principles that he derived from natural magic, item number seven states that 'there is no greater knowledge capable of proving the divinity of Christ than magic and Cabala'.[9] Pico said no more than that, he did not expand on what he meant, but there was no doubt in the minds of the Cardinals. The statement implied that that magic and Cabala were more fundamental to Christian faith than the Gospels. They rejected it as false, erroneous, superstitious and heretical. The Cardinals demanded that the proposition be deleted, together with the 12 other contentious items that they found.

Pico agreed to the deletions but could not hold back from defending himself. Along with the revised version of his *Conclusiones*, he submitted an Apology. But in reality it was not so much an apology as a defence. It did not go down at all well in the papal court. Rather than accepting his revised submission and agreeing to a debate based on the remaining 887 theses, on 4 August 1487 the Pope condemned the whole of Pico's *Conclusiones* and charged him with heresy. Pico fled to France, where he was arrested and, once again, imprisoned. For the second time in Pico's short life Lorenzo de' Medici sent envoys to negotiate his release. He returned to Florence in 1488.

Shortly before his condemnation by the Pope, Pico published his Apology, together with a document which he had intended to read as his introduction to the scholarly debate. Despite the controversy which surrounded his *Conclusiones*, it is this introductory essay which history has come to judge as Pico's finest work. Known today as the *Oration on the Dignity of Man*, it has been described as the 'most succinct expression of the mind of the Renaissance'.[10]

In his *Oration*, Pico argues that humanity, the pinnacle of creation, is responsible for its own spiritual elevation or decline. God has made humanity 'a creature neither of heaven nor of earth … in order that you may, as the free and proud shaper of your own being, fashion yourself in the form you may prefer. It will be in your power to descend to the lower, brutish forms of life; you will be able, through your own decision, to rise again to the superior orders whose life is divine.'[11]

The human power to shape its own destiny is achieved, according to Pico, by comparing and contrasting the collective wisdom of all philosophical systems. 'For these reasons, I have not been content to repeat well-worn doctrines, but have proposed for disputation many points of the early theology of Hermes Trismegistus, many theses drawn from the teachings of the Chaldeans and the Pythagoreans, from the occult mysteries of the Hebrews and, finally, a considerable number of propositions concerning both nature and God which we ourselves have discovered and worked out.'[12]

Cabala, for Pico, was an extremely ancient component of this collective wisdom. It was, of course, nowhere near as old as he imagined; his conviction that Cabala was ancient was the result of relying too heavily on Abraham Abulafia and misunderstanding him. He had read in Abulafia that Kabbalah was revealed to Moses when he received the Ten Commandments on Mount Sinai. Abulafia was using the word Kabbalah in its literal sense, as a tradition that had been received. He meant that on Mount Sinai God had taught Moses a set of principles, a key to interpreting the Torah. Pico, however, seems to have understood Abulafia to mean that the Kabbalah as he knew it was revealed to Moses, almost as an off-the-shelf package. It is far from likely that this was Abulafia's intention. But Abulafia's writings were always obscure and dense; one can hardly blame Pico for misinterpreting him.

Nevertheless, Pico's belief that the Cabala had been handed down to Moses on Mount Sinai and transmitted through the generations opened up radical new possibilities for Christianity. Cabala's apparent biblical roots gave it an unchallengeable level of authority. If Pico was right that Cabala proved the existence of the Trinity and confirmed the supernatural nature of Jesus's name, then Christian belief would be unassailable. More than that, Pico would be justified in his claim that Cabala was essentially a Christian doctrine, and not Jewish. 'I discovered in [books of the Kabbalah] not so much the Mosaic as the Christian religion. There was to be found the mystery of the Trinity, the Incarnation of the Word, the divinity of the Messiah; there one might also read of original sin, of its expiation by Christ, of the heavenly Jerusalem, of the fall of the demons, of the orders of the angels, of the pains of purgatory and of hell.'[13]

Pico argued that the superiority of Kabbalistic doctrine made it the supreme defence against the dark side of magic. In the 15th of his magical conclusions Pico wrote that it could only be possible for magic to be successful if it was explicitly and implicitly allied with Cabala.

The goal of Cabala, for Pico, was to achieve an intellectual ecstasy in which the soul would ascend beyond the body, absorbed into a mystical unity with God. This was the true meaning of the perfect death by a divine kiss granted to Aaron and Moses, the Kabbalistic interpretation of which he had encountered in Recanati's writings. Pico identified this kiss with the verse in the Song of Songs, 'let him kiss me with the kisses of his mouth'.[14] The Song's lovelorn narrator yearns, he maintained, for *Mors Osculi*, death by a kiss, a temporary mystical state in which the soul is so overwhelmed by ecstasy that it abandons the body altogether. Pico's elaboration of this theme has been described as representing 'the most poetic, perhaps the only truly poetic, motif that the Italian Renaissance borrowed from Talmudic legend'.[15]

Death by a kiss was not to be Pico's destiny; his passing was far more prosaic. His career never really recovered from the disastrous reception given to his *Conclusiones*. Pico remained under papal condemnation until Innocent VIII's death in 1492, but received a pardon the following year from his successor, Pope Alexander VI. By this time, however, he had fallen under the austere influence of the controversial Florentine friar Savonarola, who persuaded him to rid himself of all his possessions and give away his income to his nephew.

Pico died in 1494 at the age of 31, on the day that the city of Florence fell to the Emperor Charles VIII. The cause of his death is unknown; some say he was poisoned by his secretary.[16] He is buried in San Marco in Florence; Savonarola preached at his funeral. Upon his death the mantle of Christian Cabala was passed to his associate, Johannes Reuchlin.

THE ART OF THE CABALA

Johannes Reuchlin met Pico in 1490. Aged 35, he was eight years older than the prodigal count. A prominent lawyer in the German territory of Württemberg, Reuchlin had already studied Greek in Basel, published a Latin lexicon and begun to study Hebrew. Now he was spending a year in Rome, supervising the education of the Duke of Württemberg's son Ludwig and soaking up the cultural ambience of Renaissance Italy.[17]

No details have survived about the meeting between the two men, but it is evident that Reuchlin came away inspired. He threw himself deeply into his Hebrew studies and for the first time took an interest in Cabala. So much so that within four years he published his first Cabalistic book. Entitled *De Verbo Mirifico*, On the Miraculous Word, it isn't a classic; his opus magnus of Cabalistic scholarship was still to come. But the book did establish one important principle, from which to a great degree the whole of subsequent Christian Cabala derives.

De Verbo Mirifico takes the form of a discussion between a Jewish Kabbalist, a Greek and a Christian. The Christian is called Capnion, which is a Greek translation of the name Reuchlin; like many Renaissance scholars, Reuchlin chose to refer to himself using a Hellenised nickname. The discussion between the three fictional disputants ranges widely, across science, religion, the occult and philosophy. But the main aim of the trialogue is to explore the mystical properties of names and words, and in so doing to identify the one name, the wonder-working word, that trumps all in its miraculous powers. This name is revealed in the third part of the book as a variant spelling of Jesus, formed in Hebrew characters by the insertion of a single letter to the unutterable four-letter divine name known as the Tetragrammaton. The construction of this new name was not his idea – Pico had already alluded to it – but Reuchlin developed it and spelled out the wonder-working properties of what was now the five-lettered Pentagrammaton. When used in conjunction with the Cross, the miraculous name can, among other things, repulse pirates, tame camels, overpower demons and even revive the dead.[18]

Reuchlin's book marked a turning point in the early history of Christian Cabala. It introduced Cabala into northern Europe and laid the foundations for Reuchlin's much more important next book. It was 23 years before he was ready to publish it, but when he did his reputation as the first systematic exponent of Christian Cabala was cemented. Before then, however, a row broke out, not of his making, which saw him tried for heresy and very nearly destroyed him altogether.

The Reuchlin Affair, as it is now known, took place in the wake of the expulsion of the Jews from Spain in 1492, when much of Europe was closed to them. In 1509 Johannes Pfefferkorn, a Jewish convert to Christianity, managed to persuade the Holy Roman Emperor Maximilian I to seize and burn all Jewish books throughout his territories. Pfefferkorn was working to a plan that would complete the eradication of Judaism from the continent and ease the conversion of Europe's Jews to Christianity.

The backlash against Judaism was in part a reaction against the scholarship of people like Ficino, Pico and Reuchlin, Renaissance humanists who concentrated their scholarly energies on the literature of ancient times and who, in the case of Hebrew, saw it as a tool to advance their understanding of Christianity. Reuchlin already had a reputation as Christian Europe's outstanding Hebrew scholar, a status he had acquired in 1506, when he published his *Rudiments of Hebrew*, the first Hebrew grammar and dictionary written for Christians. When Emperor Maximilian decided to establish a commission to evaluate Pfefferkorn's confiscation policy, he invited Reuchlin to join. The Emperor could not have been too surprised when Reuchlin turned out to be the sole commissioner to speak out against the policy, and to recommend its abolition.

Reuchlin's stand aroused the ire of the ecclesiastical authorities. The Inquisitor General brought charges against him for heresy and called upon the theological faculties in Paris, Cologne and Louvain to condemn him. The matter trundled through the courts until

1520, when Pope Leo X finally ruled against him. Reuchlin was financially and emotionally ruined; he died two years later.[19]

It is striking that the Reuchlin Affair took place at the same time as the Protestant Reformation was gaining traction. Reuchlin was no Protestant; he believed that his work on Hebrew and Judaism was fully at one with Catholicism. But Luther's reforms, with their emphasis on *sola scriptura*, the literal understanding of the Bible, are unlikely to have succeeded had it not been for Reuchlin's defence of Hebrew, the language of the Old Testament. Pfefferkorn certainly blamed Reuchlin for the Reformation. After Pope Leo delivered his verdict, Pfefferkorn wrote, 'Yes, Reuchlin, if the Pope had done this to you eight years ago, Martin Luther and your disciples ... would not have dared to wish or contemplate what they are now publicly pursuing to the detriment of the Christian faith. Of all this, you alone are the spark and the enabler, to drive the holy church into error and superstition.'[20]

And yet in 1517, despite the heresy trials and the attacks on his reputation, Reuchlin managed to publish his seminal work, *De Arte Cabalistica*, On the Art of the Cabala. He dedicated it to Pope Leo X, Lorenzo de' Medici's son, in the hope that this would encourage Rome to support him in his battle against his opponents. He praised Leo for his father's support of the 'Italian philosophy of the Christian religion' in the face of attacks by 'sophists'; it was a none too subtle hint that the Pope should join the fight against obscurantism, just as his father had done through his support for the Renaissance.[21] Three years later, when Leo announced his verdict condemning Reuchlin, it was clear his flattery had got him nowhere.

Reuchlin was Pico's successor in the development of Christian Cabala. He had two great advantages over his younger Florentine teacher. The 1492 expulsion of Jews from Spain, two years before Pico's death, had resulted in a proliferation of previously unknown Kabbalistic texts. Carried by refugees for whom books were the most treasured of their meagre possessions, and augmented by the revolutionary new technology of printing, the amount of Kabbalistic material at Reuchlin's disposal far exceeded that which had been available to Pico. Whereas the Italian count had relied primarily on Latin translations of the works of Abraham Abulafia and Menaḥem Recanati, the German lawyer was able to read a far more representative range of Kabbalistic works, including the Zohar and several books by Abulafia's former pupil Yosef Gikatilla.[22]

As a result, On the Art of the Cabala was far more structured in its exposition than anything attempted by Pico. It was the first systematic Cabalistic work directed at a Christian audience. It would become the 'bible of the Christian Cabalists'.[23]

As with De Verbo Mirifico, the book was presented in the form of a discussion between three people: a Pythagorean philosopher, a Muslim and a Cabalist. The choice of a Pythagorean reflected Reuchlin's interest in the mathematical philosophy of the ancient Greek magus Pythagoras, a system which he believed had originally derived from Cabala and could be rediscovered within it.[24] Since each letter of the Hebrew alphabet has a numerical value, and as Hebrew was the language with which the world was created, Reuchlin concluded that the whole of creation can be reduced to mathematical symbolism. Not only were 'letters and names signs for things, but such things are themselves signs for other things'.[25]

The art of Cabala, the reason why the book is so called, lies in understanding how to magically manipulate these signs and symbols, in order to approach and commune with the angels. Cabala was a gift from God, essential for salvation. A contemplative art, it was the pinnacle of human desire. Cabala was not an obscure Jewish mysticism that had been adapted for Christian interest. It had always been intended for Christians; its primary purpose was to teach the messiahship of Jesus.

Reuchlin's Christian Cabala differs in important ways from that of the Jewish kabbalists. Unlike the Jews, most Christian Cabalists were not ecstatic mystics; with the exception of Pico's death by a kiss they rarely referred to revelations or mystical experiences. Instead, they saw Cabala as an ancient philosophy which strengthened the understanding of Christianity.[26]

Reuchlin's pioneering work on Christian Cabala never achieved the prominence within the Church that he must have hoped for. It was overtaken by events: the Reformation, Counter-Reformation and Europe's religious wars left little space for the development of an esoteric theology, particularly one rooted in Judaism. Although scholarship in Christian Cabala did carry on for another couple of centuries, it blended into the broader occult, used in conjunction with magic, numerology, astrology and the wisdoms of the ancient world.

The Jews took little interest in Christian Cabala; they had their own concerns. The exile from Spain, a catastrophe of unimaginable proportions, had shaken their world, forcing them to reappraise their beliefs and priorities. One consequence was that Kabbalah was thrust into a new direction, fundamentally altering the way it would now be conceived. To understand this we need to travel to the hills of northern Galilee, to a village which was as yet wholly unaware of what was about to happen to it. The village's name means a lookout or panorama and is written in English as Safed. Locals pronounced it as Tz'phat.

The City of Mystics

In 1492, as the final act in over a century of anti-Jewish legislation, pogroms and persecution, the Jews were expelled from Spain. Many had already converted to Christianity, some out of genuine belief, others because it was just so much easier to live as a Christian than as a Jew in a hostile religious environment.

There were precedents for such an expulsion. In 1290 the Jews had been thrown out of England and in 1306 the same had occurred in France. But Spain was different. Jews had lived there since the third century, coexisting with Christians and Muslims in an environment that has come to be known as *convivencia*.

The three religious communities lived side by side, traded together, worked for each other and, although maintaining distinct religious and cultural practices, for the most part got on reasonably well. It was a tolerably successful, pluralist community. Nobody had raised an eyebrow in 1315 when the mystic Ramon Llull had composed a fictional dialogue in 1315 between a Christian, Muslim and Jew. None thought it odd that the Christian nobleman Rodrigo, better known as El Cid, led military campaigns for both Christian and Muslim rulers. And no protest had been raised when the Talmudist Shmuel ibn Naghrilla served as vizier of Muslim Granada for over 30 years, even though the ancient Pact of Umar technically forbade Jews from holding public office in Muslim lands.

But that had all changed. The first upheaval had been in 1212, when a Christian force defeated the Muslim Almohad dynasty. Subsequent battles drove the Muslims out of almost the whole of Spain, with the exception of Granada. The new militancy turned Christian hearts against the Jews and the Jews turned their hearts against the *conversos*, their former co-religionists who had converted to Christianity. Then the Inquisition weighed in. From 1390 endeavours to convert the Jews to Christianity increased substantially. Jewish communities were torn apart by riots and pogroms. The *conversos* got it from both sides: from the Jews for their abandonment of their ancient heritage, and from the Christians, resentful at sharing the privileges of emancipation with people who, although baptised, looked, spoke and in many cases clandestinely behaved as Jews.

When Granada, the last Muslim province in the peninsula, fell in January 1492, King Ferdinand and Queen Isabella were confirmed in the view that they had been blessed with divine favour. On 31 March 1492 they decreed that the Jews who had not yet converted were either to receive baptism or leave the country. The Crown probably expected that most would convert, thereby eliminating the Jewish religion from Spain while allowing them to retain the tax revenues of the new *conversos*. They were wrong. An estimated 80,000 souls left. Maybe not a lot when we consider the upheavals and slaughters of the twentieth and twenty-first centuries, but a large number for those days, when world populations were far lower.

Contemporary accounts tell of the chaos as the Jews tried to flee. The few ships whose crews were willing to carry them were overcrowded. Storms overturned the boats or drove them back to Spain. Pirates from North Africa saw them as easy prey. Hunger and disease took their toll. Those who did eventually make it to safety ended up scattered in ports across the shores of the Mediterranean. Slowly, new communities of Spanish exiles began to take root and grow. And where Spanish Jews could be found, so, too, could the Kabbalah, that they carried in their books and in their minds.

The expulsion of the Jews from Spain was a tragedy for the families, and for the Jewish nation. But it led to the blossoming of the Kabbalah, which was now spreading far and wide. The Zohar was printed for the first time, in Salonica, Cremona and Mantua. Its printing did not pass without controversy, critics fearing that it would foster heretical thought. The editor of the Mantua edition recognised the danger, but absolved himself, noting that 'even if we admit that some individuals might be misled by it, and their hearts be affected by impurity, this has no bearing in the matter, for we are not concerned with fools or the wicked'.[1] His printing press was turning out books for the upright of heart; he could not take responsibility for those in whom corruption was already implanted.

A further gateway was thrown open for the Kabbalah in 1517, when the Ottoman Emperor captured the Holy Land. Spanish exiles who 20 years earlier had found their way to Istanbul packed their bags again, setting off for their ancestral home. Some went to Jerusalem, others to a village in the hills of Galilee. A small village, where a remarkable transformation in the nature and fortunes of the Kabbalah would take place. Its name was Safed. It did not remain small, or a village, for long.

It has been estimated that when the Ottomans conquered the Land of Israel the population of Safed comprised 200 to 300 households. Thirty years later this number had grown to 1175; over the course of the following 20 years it almost doubled again. The town's growth was fuelled by low taxation, a booming textile industry and the particular skills in weaving and dyeing that the exiles had brought with them from Spain. The climate was good, too; summer temperatures in hilly Safed were closer to those in Spain than to lower-lying locations in the Holy Land.[2]

Safed held a particular attraction for serious students of the Kabbalah. Galilee was where, according to the Zohar, Shimon bar Yoḥai and his mystical fellowship had lived and learned. Never mind that the narrative is believed today to be imaginary and the scenic descriptions inaccurate. As far as the Zohar's readers were concerned these were the very hills among which Shimon and his companions had wandered, the fields in which they'd held their mystical communions, the tracks and pathways they had traversed, the land in which they had learned the secrets of the cosmos.

It was in Galilee that the *Idra Rabba*, or Great Assembly, is said to have taken place. The most ecstatic of all the experiences that Shimon bar Yoḥai and his companions shared, its account is arguably the most important narrative of the Zohar. The Great Assembly was where the deepest, most powerful and secret mysteries were revealed, mysteries that had not been disclosed since Moses stood on Mount Sinai, secrets so powerful that three of the companions did not return to this life; they died, as had Moses and Aaron before them, through a divine kiss. Only seven from the original fellowship of ten remained. Three, seven and ten, the configuration of the *sefirot*; three above who do not show themselves in the cosmos, seven below that shape and build the material universe, ten altogether.

> It is taught that ten entered and seven emerged. Rabbi Shimon [bar Yoḥai] was happy and Rabbi Abba was sad. Rabbi Shimon said something and they saw those three. The angels of heaven were taking them and showing them the hidden storerooms on high, because of the honour due to them. They brought them to the mountains of pure balsam. Rabbi Abba was consoled. It is taught that from that day forward the companions did not leave Rabbi Shimon's house and that when Rabbi Shimon was revealing secrets, only they were present with him. And Rabbi Shimon used to say of them: We seven are the eyes of the Lord, as it is written, 'these seven, the eyes of the Lord (Zechariah 4.10)'. Of us is this is said.
>
> Rabbi Abba said: We are six lamps that derive their light from the seventh. You [i.e. Shimon bar Yoḥai] are the seventh over all, for the six cannot survive without the seventh. Everything depends on the seventh.[3]

There were many reasons for a Kabbalist to live in Safed, the most important being its proximity to the village of Meron, the traditional site of Shimon bar Yoḥai 's tomb. In the sixteenth century the tomb became a magnet for the mystically inclined. Its appeal has never diminished, it is still a site of pilgrimage today; hundreds of thousands flock there each year on the anniversary of the date upon which Shimon, the supposed author of the Zohar, is believed to have died.

When the first kabbalists arrived in Safed during the 1520s and 1530s the exile was still weighing heavily on their minds. Their forebears, the Spanish kabbalists, had invested their creative energies in studying the mysteries of the *sefirot* and seeking to draw closer to God. The Safed mystics were too concerned with the challenges of life to indulge in such speculative activity. Instead they embarked on a mystical quest to comprehend the significance of their exile, to understand its purpose and the manner in which it foreshadowed the ultimate redemption.

They were not the first kabbalists to take an interest in the idea of redemption. As Gershom Scholem pointed out, the earlier kabbalists had also recognised that the end of days was approaching and the age of the Messiah dawning, but these subjects rarely played a part in their speculations. For the early kabbalists the key to cosmic redemption was the mystical elevation of their own souls. But the disaster of 1492 injected a new urgency into the messianic quest. It was made all the more pressing by a long-standing mystical calculation which predicted that 1492 itself would be the very year in which redemption would begin.[4] The fact that catastrophe arose in the place of redemption threw into sharp focus the knife edge upon which the cosmos was balanced. Apocalypse and salvation were two sides of the same coin.

The coin seemed to turn in 1502, when the Kabbalist Asher Lemmlein turned up in Istria, across the bay from Venice, to announce the coming of the Messiah. His followers began preparing for the redeemer's arrival, adopting ascetic practices and donating their possessions to charity. But it was a false alarm. Lemmlein died, his followers dissipated and the redemption drew no nearer.[5]

Thirty years later the *converso* Solomon Molcho took matters into his own hands. He returned to the Jewish faith, circumcised himself, recruited an enthusiastic following and proclaimed himself

Messiah. Sadly, he fared no better than Lemmlein. He made the fatal mistake of trying to enter into a treaty with the Holy Roman Emperor. The Emperor handed him over to the Inquisition, who burned him at the stake for heresy.

Solomon Alkabetz, the leading light among Safed's earliest kabbalists, took a more measured view. He moved from Salonika to Safed because of a remarkable experience he'd shared with a fellow Kabbalist, Joseph Karo. He wrote to his former brotherhood in Salonika to tell them about it.

Joseph Karo is best known today as the author of two great compendia of Jewish law, in which he very occasionally forsakes traditional legal reasoning in favour of a ruling from the Zohar.[6] He claimed to receive regular instruction from a heavenly voice that spoke personally to him. In his letter to the Salonika brotherhood, Alkabetz recounts how he, too, had heard this heavenly voice.

He explained how he and Karo had spent the whole night of the *Shavuot* festival studying, in accordance with a custom first mentioned in the Zohar. While they learned, Karo's mystical heavenly mentor spoke to them both. 'Go up to the Land of Israel,' proclaimed the voice, 'for not all times are opportune. There is no hindrance to salvation, be it much or little. Let your eyes not have pity on your worldly goods, for you eat of the goodness of the higher land … Make haste, therefore, to go up to the land, for I sustain you here and will sustain you there …'[7]

TRANSFORMING THE EXILE

The kabbalists of Safed perceived a mystical link between the exile from Spain and Adam and Eve's expulsion from the Garden of Eden. Before the first couple ate the forbidden fruit the cosmos had existed in perfect harmony. When they were expelled from the Garden and thrust into the physical world a rupture opened up in the cosmos, destroying its harmony. The tenth *sefira*, known as the *Shechina*, which represents the divine presence on earth, was torn away from her partner *Tiferet*. It was as if she, just like Adam and Eve, had gone into exile.

Because Adam and Eve had caused disorder in the cosmos it became the task of their descendants to restore the primordial harmony. The human soul is the link between heaven and earth, and it is an axiom of Kabbalah that what people do down here affects what goes on up there. Cosmic harmony could only be restored when the *Shechina*'s exile was ended, and that could only be orchestrated from earth by mystical activity in the human soul.

The early kabbalists in Safed saw it as their responsibility to engage in this mystical activity, to end the exile of the divine presence and bring the universe back to perfection. One way to accomplish this was to experience exile mystically within their own souls, identifying themselves with the sufferings of the *Shechina*.

In order to replicate the humiliation and exile of the *Shechina*, Solomon Alkabetz and his brother-in-law Moses Cordovero would walk barefoot through the hills and villages of Galilee, bruising and tearing their feet on rocks and thorns, in acts of self-imposed mortification. On their wanderings they would visit the graves of ancient rabbis, where they would discuss Kabbalah, 'in the belief that proximity to the last resting-place of the ancient teachers powerfully assists the spontaneous generation of mystical ideas'.[8] Moses Cordovero reported that as they wandered their mouths would, of their own accord, proclaim words of Torah. In Kabbalistic theory this type of involuntary speech, a sort of speaking in tongues, has its origins in the *Shechina*, indicating that their self-imposed exile had indeed established a link between their souls and the displaced divine presence.[9]

Although Alkabetz was older than Moses Cordovero, and his mystical master, it was the younger man who was regarded as the leading Kabbalist in Safed. He gathered the town's mystical elite into a close-knit fellowship; studying together and living an austere, pious life, hedged about with precise restrictions. Among other things they were to banish all profane thoughts from their hearts and falsehoods from their lips, never to become angry or speak evil of any person or even of an animal, only to converse with each other in Hebrew, give charity every day, confess their sins before each meal and sit on the ground each night to mourn the destruction of the Jerusalem Temple.[10]

Still, it wasn't all doom and gloom. The ascetism of Cordovero's kabbalists was tempered by their religious duty to be joyful on Sabbaths and festivals. On these days their sparse meals became celebrations: they would drink, sing and elevate their hearts in blissful anticipation of the messianic age.

Cordovero wrote prolifically. About 30 of his works are known, of which ten have been printed. Among them is his *Explanation of the Precious Light*, the first ever comprehensive commentary on the Zohar.[11] Part of his commentary was incorporated into his most famous work, *The Pomegranate Garden*. In his introduction he describes how he had led a dissolute life until a revelation at the age of 20 snapped him out of his complacency and propelled him into a quest for enlightenment. It was then that he met Solomon Alkabetz, who led him to the portals of wisdom and understanding 'sweeter than honey that exudes from the comb', awakened him in the study of the Zohar and showed him 'the keys to its gates'. The complexity of the subject he studied left him so perplexed and confused, his heart 'drowning in the sea', that he decided to take a pen and ink and arrange the material in a systematic order.[12] The result was a book of 32 'gates', each containing several chapters. It was the first structured presentation of the Kabbalah and, although written in the flowery language that only a medieval mystic could conjure up, it remains a classic of Kabbalistic scholarship.

Kabbalah's popularity had snowballed in the wake of the expulsion from Spain and the consequent dispersion of Iberian Jews across the Mediterranean. Its mystical obscurity helped deaden the pain of being a refugee; immersion in its mysteries offered an escape from harsh realities. But as an intellectual system, Kabbalah itself had hardly progressed for three centuries. Moses Cordovero, the greatest Kabbalist since the days of the Zohar's authors and of Abulafia, did not come up with any important new insights. Instead, his genius lay in the manner in which he gave structure to Kabbalah, setting out its ideas and principles in a clear, systematic fashion.

In doing this, Cordovero merely continued the same process that the Zohar authors had followed. For the Kabbalah of the Zohar was essentially a thirteenth-century way of expressing ideas that had been around for a very long time. As Yehuda Liebes has shown,[13] many Kabbalistic ideas had their origins in ancient sources. The influence of medieval Jewish philosophy, particularly that of Maimonides, was to systematise ideas and beliefs, packaging them up into concepts that appealed to the rational mind. The authors of the Zohar did something similar, taking references in the Bible to God's attributes and attaching them to specific *sefirot*, creating a system of concepts that merged scattered biblical and mythical ideas into a semi-coherent whole.

But the world had moved on since the thirteenth century. The concepts that the Zohar had developed and the questions it addressed did not necessarily satisfy the curiosity of sixteenth-century minds. Kabbalistic thought had fossilised and despite his achievements Moses Cordovero had effectively systematised a fossilised system.

Moses Cordovero died in 1570 at the age of 48. Joseph Karo delivered the funeral address. As his coffin was being carried to the grave, Isaac Luria, a recent arrival in the town, observed two pillars of fire proceeding before it.

Cordovero was dead and it was clear to all that the expected redemption of the Jews from exile had still not materialised. Nor did the restoration of cosmic harmony appear any closer. But one thing had changed. The baton had been passed to Isaac Luria. He knew exactly what to do with it.

Luria had only been Cordovero's student for six months when the older man died. It may well have been the most important six months in the entire history of Kabbalah. Inspired by Cordovero, Luria set off on a path that would change the nature and understanding of Kabbalah for ever. His great genius was to weave all the various ideas, concepts and doctrines of Kabbalah into one integrated, internally consistent mythical system. In doing so, Isaac Luria had a more profound impact on the Kabbalah than had the combined intellects of all kabbalists during the preceding three centuries.

THE LION OF SAFED

Isaac Luria's life story is so hedged with legends and tales of fantasy that uncovering the historical details of his life is not easy. Lawrence Fine, in an outstanding biography, concludes that he was probably born in Jerusalem but that his family moved to Egypt when he was a child.[14] He remained in Egypt until his mid-30s, earning his living as a merchant dealing mainly in pepper, cucumber, wine, wheat and leather.

Trade was not Luria's thing, however. His passion was learning. As a young man he joined a rabbinic circle where he contributed to various works of legal scholarship. He studied with David ibn Zimra, the author of several Kabbalistic works, and it may have been with him that he first started to develop his ideas. But it was his discovery of the Zohar that took him away from both his rabbinic and business colleagues.

According to one account of Luria's life,[15] more legendary than biographical, he saw a man in a synagogue holding an unfamiliar book, which he clearly could not read. Intrigued, Luria asked what it was. The man confessed that he didn't know, explaining that he was a *converso*, a Jew who had converted to Christianity in the years leading up to the expulsion from Spain, who now wanted to reconnect with Judaism. He had brought this book to the synagogue with him, not knowing what it was but so as not to feel out of place among people who each had their own prayer book. Luria took a look and realised that the book was the Zohar, of which he had heard but which he had never seen. He persuaded the stranger to sell him the book and for the next six years he secluded himself on Jazirat al-Rawda, his uncle's island in the Nile, wholly immersed in the Zohar.

In 1570 Luria arrived in Safed, where he joined Moses Cordovero's mystical fellowship. Given Cordovero's status as the city's pre-eminent Kabbalist, it is likely either that Luria had already established a reputation for himself before arriving or that Cordovero perceived some extreme mystical quality in the newcomer that made him want to draw him in. But within six months Cordovero was dead, and two years later so was Luria. The tremendous reputation and huge saintly regard in which Isaac Luria is held are the product of no more than 30 months in Safed. One can only wonder what he might have achieved had he lived beyond the age of 38.

Many years ago Gershom Scholem stated that any attempt to concisely survey Luria's Kabbalah is to 'risk error and court misunderstanding. Nevertheless the risk must be taken if we want to clear the way to a satisfactory understanding.'[16] The short description which follows can only be the dimmest reflection of a system so complex and uncertain in nature that Luria's original conception may never be fully comprehended, let alone expressed in words. The difficulties of comprehension are made all the harder since Luria's ideas seem to have evolved and changed as he taught them, and then were only transmitted second hand, through the writings of his students.

Luria, often referred to as the Ari, an acronym of his name which in Hebrew means 'lion', was blessed with an unusual combination of profound psychological insight and extraordinary creative energy. The mystics of Safed claimed that the Ari, among very many other things, could read signs and letters on one's forehead, knew the language of the burning candle and the flaming coal, and spoke directly with Elijah and the angels.[17] His chroniclers, of whom his principal student, Hayyim Vital, was the most prolific, devote pages to enumerating his qualities and recounting his deeds. It is little wonder that they believed, as did he, that he bore the soul of the second-century rabbi, hero and putative author of the Zohar, Shimon bar Yohai. Who in turn bore the soul of Moses.

One of the themes which the Ari integrated into his all-embracing Kabbalistic scheme is that of transmigration, the idea that after death souls travel from one body to another. The concept had been around for some time in Jewish mystical circles, originating in the eighth or ninth century in Iraq. By the tenth century the rationalist philosopher Saadia Gaon, who wrote the first scientific commentary on the *Sefer Yetsirah*, was denouncing it as 'madness and confusion'.[18] But belief in transmigration continued to gain currency. The book *Bahir* mentions it[19] and Naḥmanides accepted its existence while insisting that it was not to be discussed or publicised. The Zohar has no such qualms, seeing transmigration as the method by which a bad or inadequate soul can live again in order to redeem itself.

Gradually the idea arose that souls might reincarnate more than once, cartwheeling in great chains from one body to another. And these souls might also divide. Just as one candle transfers its light to many, so one soul may illuminate many bodies. Conversely, a single body may contain sparks from different souls, and some sparks from a single soul might be incarnated into human bodies, while other sparks from the same soul remained in heaven.

It was this complicated, fragmentary system that Isaac Luria systematised. He did not make it any less complicated. Far from it: the Lurianic doctrine of transmigration is highly complex. But he took a holistic view of the cosmos and regarded reincarnation as just one element in a complex, organic system.

In this system all souls derived from that of Adam. The ultimate goal of transmigration was that souls would become perfected as they travelled from one body to another, being subsumed back into Adam's primordial soul when they had reached ultimate perfection. Once all souls were restored and Adam's soul whole again, the world would be redeemed. The world needed redemption, not because of Adam and Eve's error with the forbidden fruit, but because the cosmos was flawed due to a different, even greater catastrophe which had taken place at the moment of creation.

Lurianic Kabbalah contains many complex and impenetrable elements. Almost certainly, the most striking and dramatic is the account of how this catastrophe happened, and what could be done about it.

Everyone agreed that, before the world was created, God was all that existed. This led to an intractable problem; if God was all there was, yet wanted to create a world that was remote from him, where could he put it? If there was nothing beyond God, how could creation happen? There seemed to be no space for the world.

Luria's answer, which he developed from earlier Kabbalistic theories, was that God withdrew into himself. It is as if he concentrated his essence so as to leave a void in the centre within which creation could take place.

The process of withdrawal is known as *tzimtzum*. Bizarre as it may sound, *tzimtzum* anticipates, from the opposite perspective, the science of cosmology. In the theory of the Big Bang, the visible universe started out as an imperceptible cluster of highly dense matter that expanded into the cosmos that we inhabit. In Luria's theory of Kabbalah, God concentrated his light into himself, leaving a void that expanded and filled with creation.

The void was not entirely empty. It contained negative forces, left behind by the retreating light. While these forces had been contained within the divine light, and diluted by its infinite size, they had been negligible. Now that they were all that existed within the void, they coalesced into a dense mass. Out of this mass, four worlds emanated, each from the other. The lowest of these four worlds is the material world that we inhabit.

A ray of divine light was sent back into the void. This ray is known in Kabbalistic terminology as Primordial Man. Additional rays burst forth from the eyes of Primordial Man. These rays would become the light of the *sefirot*. They were collected in ten vessels, specially created for the purpose.

But then the unthinkable happened. As the light of the *sefirot* flowed into the vessels they became progressively unstable. The receptacles for the light of the three upper *sefirot* remained resilient but the seven lower ones shattered. Some of the light they contained fell as sparks to earth, where they lay, trapped, beneath the broken shards of the vessels.

The broken husks of the vessels encapsulate the severe, negative force of Judgement; the divine sparks trapped beneath them are the positive, divine potencies of Compassion and Mercy. With the negative forces trapping the positive, evil was given a free rein in the world. Evil can only be defeated by liberating the trapped, positive sparks.

The sparks are freed and elevated to their rightful heavenly place when righteous people carry out the divine commandments with the right intention. The practical consequence of the drama of the trapped sparks is to regulate the lifestyle and daily actions of the individual. Cleansing the soul through penitence, performing good deeds, keeping the commandments with joyful enthusiasm and praying with the right intention are all necessary behaviours which will assist with the repair of the cosmos, and bring perfection to the created world in which we live.

As part of his programme for an intensively focused religious life, Luria adapted Moses Cordovero's practice of visiting the graves of departed rabbis, communing with their souls to add impetus to the task of cosmic healing. Unfortunately, integrating one's soul with the departed is no easy matter. It is not just a question of visiting a graveside. Great preparation is necessary. One's spirit needs to be purified through the constant pursuit of righteousness, humility and joy. Acts of mortification and penance need to be performed before the planned communion takes place. And it all has to be carried out according to a strictly prescribed regime.

It wasn't just the preparation that mattered. What to do at the graveside itself was just as important. Upon arrival at a saintly soul's grave, the mystic went through a series of mental exercises to achieve an appropriate level of trepidation and concentration. Then, when he was ready, he would stretch himself out upon the grave and form an image in his mind of the deceased doing the same. Once he was certain that the two were stretched out together in parallel he would meditate on the binding of his soul to that of the departed. Finally, by concentrating on the soul of Adam, from which all souls derive, he would seek to elevate both souls together to the upper realm. Effective communion with the dead was something only the most skilled and saintly adepts could perform successfully. But the reward, in terms of cosmic healing, was well worth the effort.

Needless to say, the system of Kabbalah which Isaac Luria constructed is far more complicated than this brief outline. It has been subjected to a wide range of interpretations and it contains many elements that we have not touched on. The bottom line, though, is that the cosmos is in need of repair. It is this process of repair which the Kabbalist is mandated to bring about, by removing the shards of the vessels, the shells as they are known in Kabbalistic terminology, thereby elevating the divine sparks trapped beneath and restoring them to their rightful place.

Luria wrote very little. His only surviving written legacy is a few comments on passages in the Zohar and three mystical table hymns to be sung on the Sabbath. Nearly everything that we know about him comes from books and documents written by his students. His students don't always agree with each other, and sometimes the same student contradicts himself in different books. We can see this most clearly in the work of Hayyim Vital (pronounced Vee-tal), Luria's most talented student and the one who devoted more effort and time than anyone else to recording his teachings.

Over the course of 20 years Vital produced several versions of Luria's Kabbalah. There are contradictions between his different versions. Sometimes this is because his understanding of a particular teaching evolved. At other times, however, the contradictions reflect the difficulty of conveying Luria's system coherently, or the fact that the way in which Luria himself had expressed a particular idea had changed.

Hayyim Vital had an unfortunately high opinion of his own self-importance, which can make it difficult to read his work objectively. Lawrence Fine quotes a passage from Vital's diary in which he claims that Luria only came to Safed for his benefit, for the purpose of perfecting Hayyim Vital's own soul. Once Vital had learned as much as his master could teach him there would be no further reason for Luria to remain in this world.[20]

This was not simply the bragging of an inflated ego. Vital had no qualms about speaking his mind; he was just as forthcoming about his shortcomings. He tells his readers that before arriving in Safed he had wasted two years practising alchemy, had cursed his parents, drunk forbidden wine and displayed anger towards his wife. He recorded the penances that Luria prescribed for him to neutralise all these offences.

Vital jealously guarded his extensive expositions of Luria's work, refusing to allow them to be published. He was worried that Luria's teachings might be misunderstood by those who had not learned directly from the master's mouth. But he offended Luria's other students by his refusal to share his recollections of the master with them. An accommodation was reached in 1575, three years after Luria's death, when his former students acquiesced to his demands. They signed a document in which they undertook to study the Kabbalah with Vital but never to reveal any of the mysteries he taught them without his express permission.[21]

Vital's ban on the publication of his own writings did not hold. In 1587, while he was dangerously ill in Safed, his brother sold them. Copies circulated clandestinely in Safed and Jerusalem until 1620, when Vital died. Then they appeared openly.

Safed's fame as Kabbalah's centre of innovation barely outlived Luria's students. The economic boom which had fuelled the town's growth faded almost as rapidly; by the end of the sixteenth century the population was dwindling and no new teachers of stature were emerging. But Luria's teachings had spread far.

The opportunity to spread the Ari's Kabbalah to communities in distant lands was eagerly taken up by Israel Sarug, a man who does not figure among the lists of Luria's known disciples, but who claimed to have been one of his first students. While Safed drifted back towards its former status as a small, unremarkable hill town, Sarug travelled to Italy, teaching Lurianic Kabbalah wherever he could find a ready audience. He was given the most fulsome reception in Venice. Home to a large community of Spanish Jews, descendants of those who had been exiled a century earlier, Venice was a thriving centre of Kabbalistic activity, the undisputed home of Kabbalah in Italy.

Israel Sarug may not have had much of a relationship with Luria; indeed, if he really was not a student then he may never even have met him. Nevertheless, Sarug more than anyone else is responsible for the transmission of Luria's innovative Kabbalistic system from the backwater of Safed to the canals of Venice and from there into the great centres of Renaissance Europe. It was in such places that the next phase in the history of Kabbalah, both Jewish and Christian, was about to begin.

Cabala and the Occult Sciences

COSMIC HARMONY

The expulsion of the Jews from Spain brought unexpected benefits to Italy's Christian Cabalists. Up to now, the only works of Kabbalah they'd had access to were the writings of Abraham Abulafia and Menaḥem Recanati, both of whom had lived and worked in Italy. Now Spanish exiles were arriving, bringing new books and traditions with them.[1] Reuchlin had been able to access Kabbalistic material that Pico had never seen. His contemporaries in Italy had an even greater opportunity. They could lay their hands on books and manuscripts that Reuchlin, who lived too far away, never had an opportunity to peruse.

Cardinal Egidio da Viterbo, who had met Pico in his youth, took full advantage of this new opportunity. One of the Church's leading intellectuals, Egidio took the refugee Hebrew grammarian Elia Levita into his home, supporting him and his family for ten years. In return Levita taught him Hebrew and Aramaic, giving him the tools to study the newly arrived Kabbalistic books in their original language. Egidio's library, renowned as one of the great collections of his time, was a repository of Kabbalistic works. He even had a rare, complete manuscript of the Zohar, which he had obtained at great trouble and expense from Damascus.

To Egidio's mind, the opportunity presented by Christian Cabala was far greater than simply proving the truths of

Christianity. In his books he argued that the opportunity offered by Cabala to Christians marked a transformation in human history, one which would lead to the spiritual unity of mankind. This transformation would be expressed through the reform of the Catholic Church, a cause for which he was a passionate advocate.[2]

Egidio's optimism was misplaced. Christian Cabala is not remembered for its contribution to Church reform. Instead, its revival took it off in a wholly different direction, one which Jewish kabbalists knew nothing of or, if they did, showed very little interest in.

From its earliest origins, the Kabbalah of the Jews had remained firmly within its own cultural boundaries. Its very name implies as much: Kabbalah means the 'received' tradition, a tradition which was handed down, promulgated no further than its designated recipients, strictly contained within the scope of its sources. Kabbalah's sacred text is the Jewish Bible, its philosophy purports to derive from the second-century rabbi Shimon bar Yoḥai and its mythology was crystallised into the Zohar. It is a self-contained system, and was always so, even before the Zohar first emerged. The Chariot descents were based on the visions of the biblical prophet Ezekiel; the *Sefer Yetsirah* is rooted in the first chapter of Genesis. Any external philosophies which may have influenced it, Neoplatonism, Sufism or Gnosticism, are only of interest to outsiders. kabbalists themselves have never given them a second thought. Kabbalah's extremities are the Jewish nation's literary, spiritual and cultural traditions.

Christian Cabala is not similarly constrained. When compiling his *Conclusiones*, Pico della Mirandola consulted every arcane and spiritual discipline known to him, believing that they could all be integrated into a single, universal truth. Even though he singled out Kabbalah, along with magic, as the most efficacious proof of Christianity, he regarded each discipline that he drew upon as a valid component of a universal Whole. Each and every one was capable of being combined with any other to illuminate a particular truth or proposition.

This distinction enabled Christian Cabala to do something denied its Jewish ancestor. Christian Cabala could be integrated with any other ancient philosophical system, provided only that the other system was valid, at least to a sixteenth-century mind.

And so, at the same time as Cardinal Egidio da Viterbo was building a library of Kabbalistic texts and writing his treatises, in Venice the Franciscan friar Francesco Giorgi was driving Cabala into new territory, blending it together with Pythagorean numerology and the theories of proportion developed by the first-century Roman architect Vitruvius. Integrating language, numbers and geometry, Francesco Giorgi (also referred to as Zorzi) transformed a philosophy that seeks to prove the truth of Christianity into a blueprint of the universe.

Giorgi's mystical philosophy is that the whole of creation exists in a state of perfect harmony; Cabala is its symbolic representation. His great book, *De Harmonia Mundi*, describes the celestial accord in which the heavens, the stars and the earth all dwell, perfectly proportioned and linked together by number: a sort of mystical geography, as Giulio Busi puts it.[3] The angelic hierarchies, the planets and the lower worlds are all connected, all immaculately synchronised. For Giorgi, the music of the spheres is melodious indeed; the Architect of the cosmos has constructed an edifice of elegant symmetry, united by number and navigated through Cabala.

Giorgi, whose writings cover thousands of pages, was the leading Christian Cabalist of his time, following directly in the footsteps of Pico della Mirandola and Johannes Reuchlin. He echoed their endeavours but in none of the works that he had printed during his lifetime did he refer to them by name. His reluctance to name them may have been a matter of self-protection. Giorgi was a respected churchman, well known within Venetian diplomatic circles. He would naturally be reluctant to associate publicly with men of whom the Church was suspicious.

Born into an aristocratic family, Francesco Giorgi was recognised as Venice's most skilful preacher. Well versed in Hebrew literature, he had good connections with the city's Jews. As a young man he had travelled through the Holy Land, frequently referring to this experience in his writings, as if it had a formative impact on his life. In 1530, when England's Henry VIII hoped that Jewish Bible interpretation might provide him with a legal justification for divorcing Catherine of Aragon, Giorgi was the obvious man for the King to turn to.

Before she married Henry, Catherine of Aragon had been married to his brother Arthur. Although biblical law forbade a man from marrying his brother's wife, the Pope had allowed the wedding on the grounds that the marriage between Catherine and Arthur had not been consummated. Now that he wanted to get out of the marriage, Henry's advisers argued that the Pope had been wrong; he had had no right to overturn a biblical prohibition. Catherine's supporters, however, were pointing to a different biblical injunction, one which instructed a man to marry his childless brother's widow, in order that children could be raised in the deceased brother's name. Faced with one biblical text which invalidated his marriage to Catherine and another which made their union obligatory, the only way out that Henry could see was to seek an opinion from a Jewish legal authority. He had to know whether this biblical obligation to marry his brother's widow applied to him, or only to Jews.

Henry sent his envoy Richard Croke to Francesco Giorgi in Venice. Giorgi introduced Croke to Elijah Halfon, a rabbi who specialised in Jewish law. He confirmed that the obligation only applied to Jews. Henry was not compelled to marry his brother's widow.

On the face of it Giorgi seems to have played only a minor, introductory role, but in practice his intervention was far more strategic than it seemed. Not every rabbi agreed with Halfon's ruling; indeed, Henry's opponents in the Vatican had recently engaged a Talmudist who argued the opposite, that the law applied to everyone, not just Jews. Giorgi knew enough about Halfon to know that he considered the laws of the Torah to be binding only upon Jews, which was exactly the answer Richard Croke was looking for.[4] Giorgi chose Halfon carefully; he knew him not only as a Kabbalist, but as one who was sympathetic to the Christian study of Cabala, believing that it was evidence of the imminent approach of the messianic age.

Taking his cue from Pico, Giorgi heard the wisdoms of the ancient world as instruments performing in a divine orchestra. Cabala was the concertmaster, uniting them all in a great cosmic symphony. Pico and Giorgi sought Truth. Other inspired thinkers believed they could harness the harmony of the universe to practical effect. Most of the time their motives were for the good of humanity; the number of esoterics who used their arts for nefarious ends were probably very few. Nevertheless, even right-thinking occultists were easily misunderstood. None more so than the Cabalist, philosopher and sorcerer Heinrich Cornelius Agrippa.

KABBALAH MEETS MAGIC

Giorgi wasn't the only Christian Cabalist drawn into Henry VIII's great matter. In 1531 Heinrich Cornelius Agrippa wrote to Eustace Chapuys, telling him that he had 'invincible arguments' for the legality of Catherine of Aragon's marriage to Henry VIII.[5] Chapuys, who was the Holy Roman Emperor's ambassador to England, sent a dispatch to the Emperor, asking him to instruct Agrippa to intervene on the Queen's behalf. However, Agrippa backtracked, declining to become involved.

History has not been kind to Agrippa. The latter part of the sixteenth century saw an outcry against witches and witchcraft. A witch-hunting craze raged across Europe, powered by mass hysteria as much as anything else. Innumerable innocents met terrifying deaths at the hands of enraged, superstitious mobs. The villain traduced at the heart of this craze, portrayed as a sorcerer whose black dog was a demon in disguise, was the pious Christian Cabalist and philosopher of magic Heinrich Cornelius Agrippa. As we shall see, he was severely misjudged.

Agrippa's first entry onto the public stage was in 1509, when he delivered a lecture at the University of Dôle in Burgundy. His topic was Johannes Reuchlin's Kabbalistic book On the Miraculous Word. Agrippa explained to his audience how Reuchlin's book had dealt with the role of magic in the service of religion. It was a topic which would define much of his future career.

That winter Agrippa visited Abbot Johannes Trithemius, a known expert on demonology. Both men agreed that the reputation of magic had been tarnished and needed to be restored.[6] By magic they meant harnessing those invisible forces in which everyone believed: angels, planets, spirits, rays and even mere potencies. The two men were acute to the danger that magic could be used for bad purposes as well as good. But they were confident that dark forces would not harm them, as long as they followed Pico's advice to only use magic in conjunction with Cabala.

Agrippa's visit to Trithemius resulted in him composing the first draft of his most famous book, *De Occulta Philosophia*. It wasn't until 1533 that he was ready to publish, 20 years after he had completed the first draft.

In his book, Agrippa discusses three types of magic – natural, celestial and religious. Natural magic applies to this world, celestial magic to the world of the stars, while the highest of the three, religious magic, operates upon the heavens. The practice of religious magic requires the correct use of Cabala, expressed through the permutation and re-combination of the letters of the Hebrew alphabet and their mathematical equivalents. Those sufficiently skilled in this Cabalistic magic have the power to reach the angels and divine spirits, drawing down beneficial forces for the greater good of the world.[7]

Unlike Solomon Alkabetz and Moses Cordovero, who were studying Kabbalah in Safed at exactly the same time in order to purify their souls, Agrippa's Cabala was eminently practical. By harnessing the angelic hierarchies in his service, he aimed to bring about positive material change and beneficence in the world. Both Agrippa and the Safed kabbalists believed in the importance of a penitent, pious life. Where they disagreed fundamentally was on the purpose of their mystical endeavours. For Agrippa the purpose of Cabala is to restore the human soul to its original divine status, through the wonder-working name of Jesus. For the Jewish mystics the goal of Kabbalah is to approach as closely as is humanly possible to the final mystery, the knowledge of that which may not even be contemplated, the unknowable essence of God.

Quite why Agrippa, out of all the Christian Cabalists, was so vilified may never be fully understood. As Klaus Reichert points out, Agrippa was no wizard. Everybody in the sixteenth century, even the early pioneers of science, believed that they were surrounded by demons and witches. Agrippa's Cabalistic attempt to harness supernatural powers in the service of the material world was part of the early scientific revolution, even though it wasn't understood in those terms in his day.[8]

His reputation was not helped by the black dog that went everywhere with him. A legend circulated that when Agrippa died the hound leapt to its own death in a river, thereby proving that it had been his familiar spirit all along. But this legend alone does not explain the full extent of his demonic characterisation. During the latter part of the sixteenth century, Europe was in religious turmoil. Luther's Reformation had spawned the Counter-Reformation, the Catholic Church was censoring and controlling the publication of books and the continent was riven by religious warfare. It was a time of turmoil and fear, a time in which the conditions were ideal for the persecution of outsiders. And in a superstitious world, nobody was more of an outsider than a sorcerer, wizard or witch. The origins of the witch-hunting craze of which Agrippa was a victim lie in the political and social unrest of the times. But the *coup de grâce* to Agrippa's reputation was delivered, not by a crazed witch hunter, but by the French political theorist Jean Bodin.

Although best known for his work in support of the sovereignty of the monarch, Bodin also wrote fiercely against demonology and witchcraft, in whose existence he unquestioningly believed. He fulminated against Pico's blending of magic with Cabala and attacked Agrippa for following in the Italian count's footsteps.

It was Bodin's closely argued assault on Agrippa which did most to construct his image as the demonic sorcerer of black magic. As the late Dame Frances Yates shows, it was this picture of Agrippa as the black magician that created the stereotype on which Christopher Marlowe's play *Doctor Faustus* is based. When Faustus, the man who will shortly sell his soul to the devil, is urged by a good angel to lay aside his book of magic, he replies that he intends to be as cunning as was Agrippa. Torn between two angels, Faustus rejects the advice of the good one, and follows the malevolent influence instead. He draws Cabalistic and magical symbols, again an allusion to Agrippa, and conjures up the devil. From that moment his fate is sealed. It is more than likely that Marlowe's Faustus was inspired, at least in part, by Bodin's diabolical portrayal of Agrippa.

FORSAKEN BY ANGELS

Not all of Christian Cabala was about angels, spirits and magic. The French Cabalist Guillaume Postel was captivated by the feminine element in Kabbalah which seeks reunification with the male principle. The Zohar had developed this dichotomy into a highly charged sexual metaphor which illustrated the divine forces underlying animal and human reproduction on earth.

The metaphor relies on visualising the arrangement of the *sefirot* as the outline of a cosmic man. The ninth of the ten *sefirot* occupies the position of the phallus. The tenth, the female, lies beneath it. The created world is sustained by divine forces which flow from the highest *sefirot* to the lowest in a continuous process of emission. When the ninth *sefira* emits its efflux into the tenth, the metaphor is decidedly sexual. The ninth *sefira*, the masculine principle, is usually called *yesod*. The tenth, the feminine principle, is *Shechina*.

In 1547 Guillaume Postel met Joanna, an Italian woman whom he came to regard as his spiritual mother. He considered her the personification of *Shechina*, regarded her as a messianic figure and believed she would issue in a new era of world harmony. He believed that Joanna was Christ reappeared on earth. It goes without saying that the idea of a female Christ was heretical in the eyes of the Church.

The sixteenth century was a time when male attitudes to women were going through significant change. A literary debate, the *querelle des femmes* or 'the woman question', was provoking strong opinions both for and against female superiority over the male.

Within the terms of this debate, Postel was no liberal. He equated Joanna with the *Shechina*, precisely because he maintained that women were inferior to men. Paradoxically, their inferiority made them morally superior. They could not be held responsible for sin in the same way as men could, and their different souls meant they had spiritual insights denied to men. Saintly women were 'vessels for the divine presence'.[9] Their inferiority allowed the power of the divine to work more strongly through them. For Postel, Joanna was the ideal representation of such a woman.

Postel was condemned by the Inquisition for his views, but unlike many others he escaped a death sentence. His books (including any he hadn't yet written) were banned, but when he appeared before the Inquisition in Venice it was decided that rather than being a heretic he was simply insane. He spent the rest of his life in prison or under house arrest, but with far more freedom than was normal. Yvonne Petry suggests that the verdict of insanity was a deliberate tactic to protect him from being declared a heretic. For, whatever his views about Joanna and the feminine aspect of Cabala, Postel, like many Christian Cabalists of his day, had a phenomenal intellect. 'His scholarship was reluctantly admitted by all who knew him, even by those who called him a heretic or lunatic. The consensus of his peers was that Postel was extremely learned and intelligent but that his attention had been diverted into frivolous and dangerous areas, primarily due to his dabbling in Jewish mysticism.'[10]

In July 1550 Postel met the English mathematician John Dee. Dee, a member of the nobility and highly influential within Queen Elizabeth's court, counted every significant work of Christian Cabala among the thousands of books in his library. His interests spanned the entire spectrum of mathematical enquiry, from practical computation to Cabalistic numerology. His prowess with numbers led him to compile navigational charts, invent mechanical gadgets, of which one was a flying crab, and write the preface to an English translation of Euclid's *Principles of Geometry*.

Dee used mathematics to conjure up angels. He described a seance in which he and his associate Edward Kelley had one of Agrippa's books open before them. On the page were mathematical and alphabetical tables, to be used for summoning angels. He didn't see the angels that he summoned, but Kelley did, or at least he claimed to have done so. The angels Michael, Gabriel and Raphael all spoke to Dee, through Kelley's mouth.

Sadly, Kelley seems to have been deceiving Dee, but that is not the main point. Dee was confident that the spirits he summoned were angels and not demons, because he was using Cabalistic techniques to call them, and ever since Pico's day it had been known that Cabala was a guaranteed defence against demons and black magic.[11]

In 1583 Dee left England for Europe. He believed himself to be on a messianic mission: before he left London he declared that the angels had assured him he would be the Prophet of the Last Days.[12] A green angel appeared to him when he was with Kelley in the Polish city of Kraków. It advised him to seek an audience with the Bohemian Emperor Rudolf II, in Prague, a mission he did not hesitate to perform.

Rudolf's Prague was a magical place, the epitome of a sixteenth-century Renaissance city, a place of art and science, astronomy, magic, alchemy and, of course, Cabala. Fashioned into a site of culture and learning by its eccentric, frequently reclusive, mystically enthralled emperor, the city became a lodestone for the wise, the weird and the wonderful. The astronomers Tycho Brahe and Johannes Kepler worked there, as did Rabbi Judah Loew, the mystical, activist Kabbalist, of whom we shall hear more shortly. The Emperor's personal physician was the occultist Johann Pistorius and according to legend the famed Polish alchemist Sendivogius successfully transmuted lead into gold in the Emperor's chamber.

Unfortunately, Dee did not flourish in Prague. The Emperor gave him an audience but turned against him when it became clear that all Dee wanted was to deliver a message from the angels urging Rudolf to repent his sins. Dee's sojourn went from bad to worse and six years after his departure from England he returned, leaving Edward Kelley behind.

In his heyday Dee had espoused a political philosophy based on a mystical conception of Elizabeth's benevolent reign. He advocated the creation of a renewed English empire in Europe and the New World, views which catapulted him to the highest echelons of the royal court. His favour won him the Queen's personal favour, at least for as long she looked kindly upon his allies within her circle. She even stepped in to protect him when he found himself accused of being a conjuror. John Dee's star had shone brightly in the Elizabethan court.

But that had been before he travelled to Europe. In his absence, things changed. His circle in the royal court fell from favour. When he came back to England Dee found that he no longer had Elizabeth's patronage.

Now the accusations that he was a conjuror began to be heard more loudly. Dee became a target for witch hunters. He reached rock bottom when James I, himself an expert on witches and demons, succeeded Elizabeth on the throne. James's book *Daemonologie*, which had been published in Scotland shortly before he ascended the English throne, was a proof of the existence of magic and witchcraft, and a handbook for the punishments to be meted out to practitioners of the black arts. Much of what James describes, the witches' gruesome potions, their power over the elements, and vindictive chants, is familiar to us from Shakespeare's contemporaneous portrayal of the three 'weird sisters' in *Macbeth*.

As his life neared its end Dee found himself abandoned, living in penury and ostracised by those whom he had formerly called friends. He appealed to James to bring to trial the foreign enemies and traitors who had accused him of being a sorcerer, but James was the wrong man to look kindly on a suspected conjurer. Dee's appeal was in vain. Forsaken by his angels he died alone and in poverty, a victim of the decline of the Renaissance and the ascent of superstition.[13]

BLURRING THE BOUNDARIES

Christian Cabala was rarely studied in isolation. In its earliest days Pico had regarded it as one ancient truth among many, albeit the most important in proving the beliefs of Christianity. Even

Reuchlin, a more systematic Cabalist than Pico, had discussed 'practical Kabbalah', which is magic performed using Kabbalistic techniques and therefore free of dangerous or demonic influences. Like Pico, Reuchlin also believed that Cabala had some things in common with the ancient Greek philosophy of Pythagoras.

By the beginning of the seventeenth century Cabala was allied to many popular esoterica, of which magic, alchemy, astrology, Hermeticism and Pythagoreanism were just the most prominent in a complex occult landscape. Occultists who spoke of Kabbalah intended neither the mystical theology of the sages of Safed nor Cabala as Pico and Reuchlin understood it. Indeed, much of what was claimed to be Kabbalah bore very little relation to the real thing in either of its doctrinal manifestations. As Gershom Scholem put it, Kabbalah 'became a kind of banner under which the public could be offered just about anything … the word Kabbalah stirred up reverential shudders and enveloped all.[14]'

The first man known to incorporate elements of Kabbalah into alchemy was the sixteenth-century Italian priest Giovanni Agostino Pantheo. In his alchemical recipes he applied the Kabbalistic technique of treating letters as numbers to show that words in different languages can be connected by their numerical values. He showed that the value, using the Latin alphabet, of the alchemical code word for 'matter' is 72, the same as the reckoning in Hebrew of God's supreme name. He associated each of the Hebrew characters in God's four-letter name with one of the cardinal elements: air, water, fire and earth. The numerical values of each of the four letters represented the respective proportions of these elements in different stages of the alchemical process. Pantheo was not practising Kabbalah as such, but he was using it as a tool to advance his alchemical speculations.[15]

The Swiss medical pioneer and alchemist Paracelsus used Cabala as an adjunct to magic. Blending the two together can speed up organic processes to accomplish in a month that which takes nature a year. A dictionary of Paracelsus's terminology explained Cabala as a 'divine science, that reveals to us God's teaching concerning the Messiah, brings about friendship with the angels for its practitioners, bestows knowledge of all natural things and, shadows having been driven away, illustrates the mind with divine light'.[16]

With the boundaries between different occult arts so blurred, it is easy to overlook those Cabalistic elements that found their way into sixteenth-century literature. In her fascinating study *The Occult Philosophy in the Elizabethan Age*, Frances Yates highlighted the occurrence of Cabalistic motifs in the classic literature of the time. We have already seen how Christopher Marlowe's Doctor Faustus practised magic tinged with Cabala. Yates shows that Spenser's *Faerie Queene*, Shakespeare's *Merchant of Venice* and *The Tempest*, and Milton's *Paradise Lost* among other works all owe a debt to Pico, Reuchlin, Giorgi and the long line of kabbalists who sit behind them.[17]

Of all the ancient esoterica and pseudo-sciences that became yoked together with Cabala, its only one true bedfellow was magic. Not just among Christian Cabalists. Magic had always been a subject of interest to the Jewish kabbalists. Magic after all is a creative process; an echo of the first creation, a human attempt to emulate in some small way the unknowable mysteries hinted at in the ancient *Sefer Yetsirah*, the Book of Formation. There is no creative act greater than that performed by the Creator of the Universe when he brought the human race into being. It became an aspiration for the magically minded Kabbalist to replicate this act through the creation of a living humanoid. Not a human being, but an animated replica. It was called a golem. The word translates as lump.

Golem

THE MAN WHO DIDN'T MAKE A GOLEM

The most famous golem of all didn't exist. Of course, it is most likely that no living golem has ever existed, but even so there is no doubt in the mind of most historians and scholars that the humanoid allegedly made by Rabbi Judah ben Bezalel Loew, best known as the *Maharal* of Prague, was never anything more than a legend. Some say it was the inspiration for Mary Shelley's *Frankenstein*.

The Hebrew word *golem* means a lump or shape. A golem is an artificial person made out of a lump of earth or clay. Moulded into the shape of a human, and animated by signs and spells, a well-made golem is able to move and has enough understanding to obey the instructions of its creator. However, according to most authorities, it cannot speak and it certainly has no soul. It is a sort of medieval, clay robot made by magical, Kabbalistic means.

The person who makes a golem must be a skilled Kabbalist, learned and righteous. They have to be versed in the arts of golem-making, to know how to control their creation, and how to destroy it should it turn dangerous. Judah, the *Maharal* of Prague, had all these qualities and, although he almost certainly never made a golem, the legend of his humanoid became popular because everybody knew he could have made one had he wanted to.

Judah Loew was born some time between 1512 and 1526. He wrote prolifically, but in none of his books does he mention his birthplace, the date of his birth or any information at all about his early years and youth. The earliest known fact is that by 1553 he was the Chief Rabbi of Moravia, living in the town of Nikolsburg in the south of what is now the Czech Republic. Twenty years later, for reasons which are as uncertain as the events of his youth, he left his job and travelled to Prague. There, he devoted himself to a school he founded, and commenced his extensive literary activity.

Loew's writings are dense and complex, but at first sight they do not appear to be particularly Kabbalistic. Until one realises that his ideas are rooted in Kabbalah. Unlike every major Kabbalist who preceded him he deliberately used non-technical language. Although he mentioned the *sefirot* often, and themed each of his major books around one of them, the whole thrust of his writing is directed, whether consciously or not, at people who are unfamiliar with the complexities of mystical jargon. He approaches the issues he writes about from the perspective of a Kabbalist, but while his head may be in the heavens, he keeps his feet firmly on the ground. So much so that, despite his Kabbalistic world view, his name and thought rarely figure in later Kabbalistic literature. Isaiah Horowitz, whose compendium of Jewish scholarship surveys the full spectrum of Kabbalistic literature, mentions neither his name nor his books.[1]

Yet Horowitz was a young scholar in Prague when Loew was its leading rabbinic intellectual. He must have been familiar with his writings; he may even have been educated in Loew's school. It is probable that Horowitz did not mention Loew in his book because it did not occur to him that Loew was, at the core, a Kabbalist. For Loew was particularly scathing about those seeking knowledge of God, which he saw as a distortion of faith. One cannot say what God is, he argued, because he is essentially unknowable. The *sefirot* cannot tell us anything at all about God, all they can do is to reflect our way of understanding him.[2]

An independent thinker, Judah Loew was militant about the need to address social inequity, improve education and oppose religious coercion. In his books he frequently digresses from a mystical or theological exposition into a discussion about education, community or the law: the sort of subjects that would have preoccupied a campaigning religious activist for social justice in the middle of the sixteenth century.

In 1592, Loew met Emperor Rudolf II, the man John Dee had unsuccessfully urged to repent. There is no record of what the Emperor and Loew discussed, but legend, both Jewish and Bohemian, has more than made up for the deficiency. In one Czech legend, the first meeting between the Emperor and the Kabbalist took place because of a royal decree expelling the Jews from Prague. Loew made it his business to confront the Emperor and plead for the decree to be revoked. When Rudolf refused to see him, Loew stationed himself on a bridge that the Emperor had to cross to reach his castle. As his coach drew near, the royal escort demanded that Loew step aside. When they saw that the rabbi had no intention of moving, they threw stones at him. As the stones flew through the air they turned to roses. The Emperor, astonished at what he was witnessing, stepped out of the coach and invited Loew into his castle. The decree of expulsion was rescinded and from that moment on Emperor Rudolf II and Rabbi Judah Loew became the best of friends, sharing Kabbalistic and occult secrets as only two mystically inclined enthusiasts can do.

The only inconsistency in this legend is that Loew left Prague only a few months after meeting the Emperor. Another version, perhaps more accurate, is that he left because, rather than becoming friends with the Emperor, he had somehow provoked his ire and was forced to leave.

Judah Loew is perhaps the only rabbi who has become a cultural icon in a European city. He could justifiably be regarded as the patron rabbi of Prague. His tomb is in the city's overcrowded, topsy-turvy Jewish cemetery, so crowded that graves have been built upon each other, vertiginously toppling in every direction. It is a place of pilgrimage for Czechs as well as Jews: a site to pray for a miracle, or to wait to see one occur.

His statue stands outside Prague's New City Hall. To his left a young girl is offering him a rose. She is his granddaughter and, so they say, the unwitting cause of his death. Judah had been ill for days; he knew that his death was approaching. But he also knew that the angel of death has no power over someone while they are engaged in the study of Torah. For three whole days he immersed himself in his books, keeping the destructive angel at bay. Then his granddaughter arrived, bearing a rose. 'Smell this,' she innocently declared. The rabbi, distracted, lifted his head to smell the rose. The angel of death saw his opportunity and pounced; a fleeting moment was all he needed.

There are many legends about Judah Loew. He was that sort of man and Prague is that sort of place, a city that lends itself to magic and fairy tale. One legend more than any other has come to define his memory; it is the reason why so many people have heard of him, even though the legend was originally told about someone else altogether and in any event there is no truth to it all. It is, of course, the legend of the Golem of Prague.

The golem that Rabbi Loew is said to have created is credited with many exploits. Some stem from a book of short stories about Loew and his golem, which was published in 1909 by Yudl Rosenberg of Warsaw.[3] The legend begins with the Jews of Prague living in a state of fear, constantly attacked by their enemies and receiving no assistance from the authorities. Rabbi Loew decided that the only solution was to create a monster of a man who would strike terror into the hearts of the foe and wreak vengeance upon them if they persisted.

Taking water and clay, the *Maharal* kneaded a man-shaped figure. He uttered Kabbalistic formulae over it and wrote *emet*, the Hebrew word for 'truth', upon its forehead. The creature stirred into life, huge and fearsome in appearance. Loew sent it out to patrol the streets and instructed it to return to the attic room in the city's synagogue every night.

At first, everything went well. The golem did its job, the enemies were suitably terrified and a sense of security returned to the Jewish ghetto. But, little by little, the golem began to play up. It started to playfully damage objects in the markets and streets. Then it began vandalising the town. Finally, it started to attack people. (Different versions of the legend add varying levels of detail and colour to these offences.) Things got to a point where the *Maharal* realised that the golem had to be destroyed. He ordered it up to its attic room and instructed it to lie down. He took some water and erased the first letter of the word *emet* from its forehead. The word now read *met*, Hebrew for 'dead'. The golem reverted to being a man-shaped lump of clay.

THE GOLEM OF CHELM

From the middle of the nineteenth century, until they were wiped out during the Shoah, the inhabitants of the Polish town of Chelm had the misfortune to be the butt of Jewish humour.

Known ironically as the 'sages of Chelm', the Jews of the town were ridiculed for their foolishness. It was said that the beadle of the synagogue would walk through the town every morning to wake his congregants. When they saw that his footprints were spoiling the look of the freshly fallen snow, they picked him up and carried him. Another time, when they were all tired of worrying, they decided to pay the same beadle two roubles a week to worry for them. Until they realised that now he was earning two roubles a week, he had nothing to worry about.

Nobody knows for certain why Chelm acquired a reputation as the Jewish city of fools. It may have been because it was where the first golem legend originated. A seventeenth-century manuscript describes how Eliyahu of Chelm, a noted Talmudic scholar of the previous century, had used *Sefer Yetsirah*, the Book of Formation, to create a golem. He hung a tablet around its neck bearing the Hebrew word for 'truth', and set the creature to work, performing menial tasks for him. Then something went wrong (the manuscript does not say what) and the rabbi had to destroy the golem. As Judah Loew would do, he rubbed out the first letter of the word for truth, changing it to the Hebrew for dead, and the golem returned to dust.

This legend is almost certainly the blueprint for the tales about Rabbi Judah of Prague's golem. The Prague legends are more numerous and relate far greater detail, but the similarities between the two narratives are too great to overlook. Eliyahu and Judah were contemporaries, and it is likely that in the legend's telling and retelling its relatively unknown protagonist was replaced by one who evoked a greater sense of mystery. The tale about a little-known rabbi in Chelm was transmuted into one concerning the far more famous *Maharal* of Prague, a charismatic, inspirational leader about whom other tales of wonder and fantasy were already circulating.

HOW TO MAKE A GOLEM

The earliest report of golem-making appears in the Babylonian Talmud.[4] It is a very short report and somewhat enigmatic.

> Rava created a man. He sent him to Rabbi Zeira. He [Rabbi Zeira] would speak to him, but he wouldn't answer. He said to him, 'You are from the Fellowship, return to your dust.'

The passage is odd, as is the manner of its construction. In the original text the sentence 'Rava created a man' is made up of three Hebrew words, two containing three letters and one with four: ten letters altogether. The three words are all anagrams of each other and the additional letter in the third word is equivalent in the Hebrew alphabet to the number three. To complicate things further, the three letters can also be rearranged into the Hebrew word for a limb. A Kabbalist, believing that God created the world through the utterance of words, would undoubtedly find this significant.[5]

The passage in the Talmud continues:

> Rav Ḥanina and Rav Oshaya would sit every Sabbath evening and study *Sefer Yetsira*, and a three-year-old calf was created through it, and they would eat it.[6]

Why they would choose to eat a magically created calf is not explained in the Talmud. One suggestion is that they could not afford to buy food, and the calf was created through the medium of the Book of Formation, *Sefer Yetsirah*, to provide them with their Sabbath meal. Most kabbalists, however, are less likely to be interested in this than in the fact that artificial life can be created by studying *Sefer Yetsirah*.

The creation of animated figures is one of the most ancient forms of magic. In ancient Egypt, miniature clay figures known as *ushabti* were placed into a coffin, to speak on behalf of the dead. The Colossus of Memnon, a giant statue in the Theban Necropolis of Egypt, was believed to sing at dawn. Simon Magus, the magician who is mentioned in Acts of the Apostles, is said to have boasted that he could animate statues so that they appeared to be men. And King Solomon's legendary throne was furnished with metal images of men and animals invested with the power of speech. The expectation that a humanly created being should have the ability to speak might explain why Rabbi Zeira was unimpressed by the mute man that Rava sent him.[7]

Judah Loew had a different explanation for Rava's mute golem. Rava just didn't have the spiritual power to create something that was the same as him. Man cannot create man, any more than God can create God.[8]

There is a mystical logic to the aspiration to create a golem. The Bible says that God created humanity in his own image; therefore his creative powers must also be present in the human soul. It follows that creating a living being is not simply a way of demonstrating one's prowess in the magical arts; it is a sacred act, emulating the divine in order to draw closer to God.

The earliest detailed instructions on how to make a golem appear in the writings of Eleazar of Worms. The process begins with the study of *Sefer Yetsirah*, for which one has to put on white clothes. Eleazar does not say which sections one has to study in *Sefer Yetsirah*, but presumably if you can't work that out for yourself then you have no business trying to make a golem in the first place.

To form the golem, one has to take virgin soil from a place in the mountains which has never been ploughed. The soil is to be mixed with 'living' water, generally understood as coming from a running stream or river, and the dough shaped into the form of a human. Having created the inanimate form of the golem, the next stage is to pronounce the correct formula over it. This is done by constructing 221 permutations of the letters of the Hebrew alphabet, all of which is to be done by referring to the instructions and tables that Eleazar provides in his *Commentary to the Sefer Yetsirah*. In another of his books Eleazar describes a second stage, in which the alphabet is combined with each of the letters in God's four-lettered name.

Elsewhere in his many writings Eleazar offers additional instructions, or amends his original ones slightly. But nowhere does he state that he actually made a golem. Eleazar's instructions seem to be theoretical, to educate his readers, rather than to report on a process he himself undertook. Unlike another, unknown author, who claimed to have witnessed an attempt to create a golem, one which nearly went horribly wrong.

In his book, probably written in the thirteenth century, the anonymous author describes a version of the golem-making ritual in which the creators walk around the lifeless creature, reciting the alphabet 462 times. It is the process of circumambulation which gives the creature the power to move, but the golem's craftsman has to walk in a forward direction. This particular golem was being created by a group of students, and they mistakenly walked backwards instead of forwards. They began sinking into the earth until they were buried up to their navels, unable to extricate themselves. Fortunately their teacher heard their screams. He told them to repeat the permutations of the letters while thrusting themselves forward. Gradually they gained traction and corkscrewed themselves out of the earth. We are not told what happened to the golem.

Some of those adept in other occult disciplines also took an interest in golem-making. The alchemist and physician Paracelsus devised a recipe for making a miniature person which was neither magical not Kabbalistic, but might have been based on a theory put forward by the Kabbalist-magician Yohanan Alemanno. In his commentary on the Song of Songs, Alemanno argued that the power of language alone, even when applied using the tools of Kabbalah, could never be enough to animate a lump of clay. To make a working golem one needed to be skilled in medicine and natural science. The golem's body had to be made from the same elements as that of a human, and in the correct proportions. Whether Paracelsus, who is considered a forerunner of modern medicine, was really influenced by the magically minded Kabbalist Alemanno is a matter of debate. But it is certain that in early modernity the idea of creating a living humanoid fired many imaginations, not just those of the mystically minded kabbalists.[9]

Making a golem was a dramatic act of Kabbalistic theatre, but it was not a skill that a Kabbalist was required to develop. Unless one held Abraham Abulafia's view that the whole purpose of making a golem was an internal one that conferred spiritual benefit on the person creating it. Weighing out the correct ingredients (Abulafia requires dust, flour and water, not clay) and reciting the complex, golem-making letter combinations generate an influx of wisdom, drawing the golem's maker closer to God. From this point of view, the golem is nothing more than a by-product of a much more intimate spiritual process. This process is facilitated by first making a model of a human, but the key intention is to concentrate the mind, not to bring the human-shaped lump of dough to life.

Indeed, for Abulafia there is a creative act that is far more important than the making of a golem. He quotes the statement in Genesis that Abraham and Sarah 'made souls in Haran'. The greatest of all deeds, says Abulafia, is to make souls. 'And this deed is, according to our opinion, the culmination of all the good deeds. Therefore, every wise person ought to make souls much more than he ought to make bodies, since the duty of making bodies is [solely] intended to make souls. Thereby man will imitate his maker ...'[10]

Abulafia does not explain how one performs this greatest of all deeds, the making of souls. It is not the sort of instruction one commits to writing. But one does not need to know how to make a soul to be aware of the threats and dangers that await it in the world of creation. Taking care of souls, one's own as well as those of others, guarding them from the entrapments of evil, is a primary duty of the Kabbalist. And of all the dangers confronting the soul in this world the most immediate threat is its possession by a negative force, a demonic spirit. Known in Kabbalistic terminology as a *dybbuk*.

Good, Evil and the Life of the Soul

HOW TO DEAL WITH A DYBBUK

Behind all the theories, symbols and complexities of Kabbalah there is one simple, fundamental idea. Everything in the created world corresponds to its source in the divine realms. The cosmos is a fully integrated, self-reflecting whole.

The human body is a reflection of the Primordial Man, who was formed when God withdrew into himself to create the cosmos. Primordial Man's limbs are the *sefirot*, to which the structure and placement of our limbs correspond. Our actions have an effect on the domains above, and what happens above influences life below. The Jerusalem Temple was constructed under divine inspiration as an earthly microcosm of the heavenly throne, its architecture a model of the celestial chariot. When the inhabitants of Jerusalem were exiled, so too was the *Shechina*, the tenth of the *sefirot*. Feminine in nature, *Shechina* denotes God's earthly presence. When her exile ends she will be reunited with her masculine counterpart *Tiferet*, cleaving together just as male and female do on earth. Kabbalah is not shy about sexual imagery. The union of human bodies is far more than a natural urge. It is the earthly representation of the unity of the cosmos.

There is symmetry in the cosmos. Everything has an opposite: positive and negative, sacred and profane, hidden and revealed, left and right, light and dark, good and evil. The negative forces are the product of the cosmic catastrophe at the moment of creation, when vessels designed to contain the divine light shattered. Sparks of light fell to earth, where they lay trapped beneath the broken shards of the vessels. The broken shards represent the negative forces of evil; beneath them lies the positive, divine light. Humanity's task is to remove the husks, elevate the sparks and thus repair the flaws in the cosmos, restoring it to pristine unity. But our task is hampered, for we ourselves are riven by competing, opposing forces. Humanity is as flawed as the cosmos it is charged with repairing.

The human soul, too, is a microcosm, a pale reflection of the divine will. When Isaac Luria prescribed penitences for a soul, his intention was greater than just improving the fate of the person affected. Repairing a soul has a positive, cosmic significance. Conversely, when a person sins and then fails to heal their soul, a corresponding breach appears somewhere within the cosmic fabric.

The domain of evil is called in Kabbalistic terminology the *Sitra Aḥra*, the 'Other Side'. An inversion of the divine world, it is the abode of dark forces. Angels oversee the world we live in, demons dwell on the Other Side. Satan doesn't play a big part in Kabbalistic mythology although he does appear occasionally, as himself, or in the guise of the bad angel Sama'el. It is not Satan who should worry us most. The things we should most fear are demons.

The greatest danger is when a demon clings to our soul. A clinging demon is called a *dybbuk*. The Hebrew verb from which the word *dybbuk* is derived is also used to describe the cleaving of a pious soul to God. The two states are mirror images of each other.

Kabbalistic folklore is full of stories about demonic beings. Demons themselves frequently took the shape of cats or black dogs. Sometimes they attached themselves to lost, dead souls who for one reason or another had not been able to transmigrate successfully. The demon would then guide the renegade soul into the body of a living person. This gave the soul a refuge, and the demon an opportunity to take control of the possessed person's body.

Most frequently, the unfortunate person whom the *dybbuk* possessed was a woman. The image of a *dybbuk*, usually male, penetrating her body is both sexual and an illustration of the doctrine of opposites. Male and female, living and dead, pure and impure, all fused together in one human body. Exorcising a *dybbuk*, removing the destructive forces from a pure soul, is not just an imperative to save a person who has been possessed. It is a battle in a cosmic war.

Of course today we talk about mental health, not possession by *dybbuks*. But in times gone by, possession by spirits was a common way of explaining behaviours that could not otherwise be understood. So common that even those who were not mentally ill but who simply deviated from social norms were frequently considered to be possessed. Jewish women believed to be possessed by *dybbuks* would have fared no better in Christian society, where they would have been condemned as witches. It is no coincidence that between the sixteenth and eighteenth centuries, when fear of *dybbuks* was at its peak, the Church burned to death between 300,000 and one million men and women condemned for witchcraft. Superstition was most pervasive in those years between the Renaissance and the Enlightenment, the very years we call the beginning of modernity.[1]

Exorcising a *dybbuk* involved removing it from the body in which it had taken up residence, and returning it to the world of the dead. In this way a small piece of the cosmic order would be restored. The *dybbuk*, of course, did not want to go. A dramatic, terrifying ritual was required to force the reluctant spirit out of the body in which it was squatting. The ceremony was conducted in the synagogue, in the presence of ten men who had purified themselves through fasting and ritual immersion. They would all dress in the white shrouds in which a corpse is buried, wreathed in prayer shawls, their heads and arms bound with the sacred parchments worn in daily prayer.

The exorcist would address the *dybbuk* directly. Listing the offences that the soul had committed during its human life, which might include apostasy, talebearing, suicide, murder or ritually deviant conduct, the exorcist would both cajole and threaten the *dybbuk*.

With the *dybbuk* fully cognisant of the trouble it was in, and the appeal to its better nature concluded, the ark in the synagogue containing the scrolls of the Torah was opened. Seven scrolls were removed, seven blasts were blown on seven rams' horns and seven black candles lit. Curses were proclaimed, incantations recited, and seven different combinations of the 42-letter name of God pronounced.

Hayyim Vital recorded instructions received from his teacher Isaac Luria for expelling a *dybbuk*. It was imperative that the exorcist remained strong-hearted, displaying no fear. The spirit was to leave the body only between the big toe and its nail; any other exit route might cause permanent damage to the possessed person. Crucially the spirit was to be warned, with threats and imprecations, against entering anybody else. There is no place for the world of the dead in the abode of the living.[2]

THE TEMPTRESS OF THE NIGHT

If women were in danger of penetration by dead souls, men faced an equally menacing, even more explicitly sexual, opponent. The story of Joseph della Reina shows just how dangerous this opponent could be, and how fragile are the boundaries between this world and the Other Side.

The earliest version of the story was recorded in 1521 by Abraham ben Eliezer Halevi. Exiled from Spain, Abraham was one of the first kabbalists to study in Safed. The story appears in his commentary on the Zohar entitled *A Letter on the Secret of Redemption*.[3]

The hero of the legend, the selfsame Joseph della Reina, was almost certainly not a fictional character. He is thought to have lived in the century before the tale was first recorded. The story itself, however, is clearly fictional, though there may be a grain of truth behind the tale.

Rabbi Joseph della Reina was, if the legend is to be believed, a man of profound mystical insight, one of very few people in the whole course of history whose home the immortal prophet Elijah would visit to engage in mystical conversation. But despite this undoubted honour, Joseph bore a great sadness. It overwhelmed him every time he stepped into the street from the small courtyard he shared with his neighbours. He only had to glance at his fellow mortals to be subsumed in sorrow and grief. He just could not bear to see the suffering and violence of the world; it distressed him far beyond any reasonable measure. He knew, of course, as every true believer does, that the promised Redeemer was making haste, but he wasn't coming fast enough for Joseph. He prayed each day that this would be the one on which redemption will come.

Eventually Joseph could stand it no more. He knew he wasn't allowed to do this, but he conjured up Elijah. It was a great offence; it was one thing for Elijah to choose to visit him, quite another for Joseph to summon the prophet. Elijah, when he arrived, was furious. He grew even angrier when he discovered that he had been summoned to teach Joseph the forbidden secrets that would restore the *Shechina* to her rightful place amongst the *sefirot*, thus bringing about instant redemption. But Elijah found it impossible to resist Joseph's urgent sincerity, for the yearning for redemption is infectious. He agreed to teach Joseph the secret of how to initiate redemption, but warned him that it was a highly dangerous undertaking. To restore the *Shechina* and bring about salvation Joseph had to do nothing less than eliminate utterly all the destructive powers of evil, a feat he could only accomplish by crossing to the Other Side and capturing its rulers, the demon Asmodeus and his bride, the temptress Lilith.

Asmodeus, king of the demons, made his literary debut in the book of Tobit. Written probably in the second or third century BCE and included in the Apocrypha, Tobit is a window onto the magical and superstitious beliefs of its time. One of the characters in the book, the unfortunate Sara, was married on seven separate occasions, only to suffer the death of each of her husbands on their wedding night, slain each time by Asmodeus before the marriage could even be consummated. This diabolical feat provided Asmodeus with the credentials to become the villain of many subsequent Jewish folk tales. Ultimately, however, he was proved vulnerable. A tale in the Talmud relates how he was taken prisoner by an envoy of King Solomon and forced to assist in the building of the Temple.[4] Joseph della Reina would have known this story, and it may well have given him the confidence to believe that he, too, could prevail over Asmodeus.

Defeating Lilith was a different matter. She was far more pernicious. Lilith is portrayed in her many legends as the archetypal temptress, arousing desire in men as they sleep at night and subordinating them to her powers. She is mentioned in the Talmud as a long-haired, winged demon who seduces men who sleep alone.[5] Her full biography was finally disclosed in the eleventh century, when she was revealed in a satirical polemic as Adam's first wife. She took umbrage when Adam insisted that she lie beneath him. When he refused to reverse positions and allow her to lie on top, she stormed out of the Garden of Eden.[6] The Lilith legends, all written by men, disclose more about the fantasies of their authors than they do about the sex life of demons.

Apprised of the true characters of Asmodeus and Lilith, Joseph della Reina fasted and prayed with his students, exactly as Elijah had instructed him. At the appropriate moment, he pronounced the unknowable, secret, mystical name of God. At once the skies opened, heavenly trumpets sounded and bolts of lightning hurtled from the sky. Joseph and his students swooned into a deep trance. When they awoke they found themselves on Mount Seir, once home to the biblical Esau, now the abode of Lilith and Asmodeus. Two massive black dogs, foaming at the mouth, eyes ablaze and snarling, were hurling themselves down the slope towards them.

Before setting off on this dangerous mission, Metatron, Prince of the Divine Presence, had given Joseph two sacred chains, inscribed with the secret name of God. Now, Joseph hurled the chains over the charging dogs. As if they had a mind of their own, the chains wrapped themselves around the frenzied hounds. The dogs shuddered to a halt. Their canine bodies dissolved before his eyes, gradually revealing the prone forms of the rulers of the demons, Asmodeus and Lilith, in all their vile repulsiveness, bound fast by Joseph's chains.

The first part of his mission was complete. Joseph della Reina had captured the king and queen of the demons. Now all he had to do to bring about redemption was to lead them off the mountain and deposit them, enchained, at the feet of Elijah.

A terrible choking sound came from the demons as the rabbi dragged them down the mountain. They begged him for water. But Joseph had been warned not to give them anything at all. If he did, they would escape from his clutches. Still, the demons would not take no for an answer. Telling him that they were parched to the point of expiry, they implored him, if he wouldn't give them water, to at least revive their spirits with a sweet scent. Joseph thought about it. There could surely be nothing wrong with that; it didn't fall into the category of giving. He lit some incense. It was his eternal error.

As the first wisps of smoke entered Asmodeus's nostril, his shape began to change once again. Before Joseph's eyes, there now stood the body of the Devil. In front of whom the hapless rabbi was still burning his incense. Looking to all the world as if he were engaged in devil worship, the greatest of all idolatries, Joseph della Reina had fallen headlong into the demons' trap.

Worse was to come. Lilith, transformed now into a beautiful succubus, embraced him. A crowd of ululating wraiths drew close. A wedding canopy sprang up around them. The chanting grew louder, and he heard the sound of a glass breaking. Before Joseph della Reina knew what was happening, he had been wed to Lilith, queen of the demons. He was well and truly trapped. There was no escape.

As the story of the pious rabbi shows, the boundaries between this world and the Other Side are thin and porous. Everything is connected, and, when joined in the wrong way, even the best intentions are no protection against the pollution of the soul. Joseph's ambition to bring about redemption was an arrogance. Instead of freeing the holy sparks he had entrapped them even more deeply. The correct path leading to the end he desired would have been to concentrate on the repair of his own soul. The moral of the story is that nobody, not even Elijah's intimate friend, can force the coming of the redemption.

THE DESCENT OF THE SOUL

The soul is exposed to multiple dangers in this world. Yet perfidious demons, envious succubi and parasitic *dybbuks*, terrifying as they may be, are the least probable of all the perils a soul is likely to face. Far more insidious are the self-inflicted dangers to which the soul is likely to fall victim. Dangers brought about by drawing too close to the Other Side, by paying attention to the Evil Inclination, the human tendency to sin. 'For the inclination of a person's heart,' says Genesis, 'is evil from their youth.'[7]

Human souls, vulnerable to blemishes caused by sin, can always be repaired through penance and even reincarnation. Even so, the outlook is bleak for new souls, which are always born pure and have yet to be exposed to the realities of this world.

In its early life, the new soul knows nothing of this bleakness. Indeed, its first experiences are sublime. Formed in the highest of the seven heavenly palaces by the union of two *sefirot*, a newly created soul descends, palace by palace, on its journey to earth. It pauses in the fifth palace, known as the upper Garden of Eden, where it joins all the other created souls who are waiting to be allocated a body. The body is a garment for the soul, providing it with a physical form. Because nothing spiritual can exist in the earthly realms unless it is attired in physicality.

Originally new souls flowed daily, in their thousands, into the fifth palace. But when the Temple in Jerusalem was destroyed, the creation of new souls ceased. The chamber is less crowded now. One day the last soul will leave its sanctuary.

Before descending to earth the soul is taken to the earthly Garden of Eden, to help it acclimatise. From there it ascends once more, to the heavenly throne, where it is wreathed with seven crowns, shown the splendours reserved for those who live a virtuous life, and, lest it become too proud, given a vision of the sufferings of the wicked. Now aware of the gravity of life on earth, the soul is met by the angel Gabriel, who will introduce it into its body. Two guardian angels fly down with them. They will accompany the soul for the whole of its life, one watching over it from the left and one from the right.

The guardian angels don't have an easy time of it. All souls are born with free will, which the angels are powerless to override. If a soul wishes to go off the true path and expose itself to danger from the Other Side, the angel's job becomes so much harder. And at those moments in history when the evil in the world outweighs the good, some unfortunate souls are doomed to be sinful from the start. For when a soul is born into the world, it passes a pair of scales. If the pan of the scales that is filled with sinfulness sits lower than the pan of righteousness, then the soul is vulnerable to the influence of the Other Side. This doesn't mean that the soul is impure or sinful, but it does make the job of the guardian angel harder, protecting its charge from the temptations and perils that will be placed in its way. If on the other hand righteousness weighs more, then the soul is assured a more blissful life, and its guardian angel a more tranquil existence.[8]

Of course the soul was not created simply to experience earthly life. There are different interpretations of the ultimate purpose of the soul but the common thread between them all is the idealised Kabbalistic goal of cleaving to the *Shechina*, the *sefira* in closest contact with the physical world.[9]

The desire to cling to God is a theme that runs like a thread through the history of Kabbalah. The Kabbalistic term for this cleaving is *devekut*. It comes from the same Hebrew root as *dybbuk*. Both are examples of cleaving, the one positive, the other negative. The journeys to the heavenly Chariot attempted by the early mystics were an expression of *devekut*. So, too, was the state of ecstasy alluded to by Abulafia and Recanati in their discussions of death by a kiss.

Devekut need not involve out-of-body experiences and withdrawal from the world. Naḥmanides places it on an almost mundane level. For the twelfth-century mystic from Gerona, cleaving to God meant thinking constantly about him.

Remembering and loving him 'to the point that one speaks to people with one's mouth and tongue, while one's heart is not with them, but before God'.[10]

There is, of course, a danger of drowning in such assimilation. The anonymous author of a twelfth-century Kabbalistic work, *Gates of Righteousness*, begged his teacher to impart to him some power that would allow him to safely assimilate into the great ocean of the divine. 'For it much resembles a spring filling a great basin with water. If a man should open the dam, he would be drowned in it and his soul would desert him.'[11]

Whether a soul turns out to be righteous, sinful or, like most of us, something in between, its journey to and through the world is little short of remarkable. So remarkable that some people just did not believe it; they thought it too fanciful to be true. They felt much the same about Kabbalah in general. Just as there were those who saw truth in Kabbalah, there were others who didn't believe a word of it. As well as its advocates, Kabbalah had its opponents. Those opponents were not few in number. It is time for us to hear their voices.

Critics and Crisis

A LION ROARS

Kabbalah's popularity was never greater than among the Jews of late Renaissance Italy. The old ways of understanding the world were giving way to the first stirrings of science; curiosity was in the air. But science arrived in a world used to magic and superstition, in which demons, spirits and angels continued to roam, a world which, while experimenting with the congruity of the natural, still believed in the supernatural. In its early days, science walked hand in hand with the occult, with alchemy, astrology and, of course, Kabbalah. For some early scientists, Kabbalah, with its interest in how the supernatural worked, was an obvious companion.

Judah Ḥamitz, of whom we shall hear more shortly, studied medicine in Padua before immersing himself in Kabbalah. The physician, naturalist and Kabbalist Avraham Yagel noted that if Kabbalah was, as claimed, a divinely revealed tradition there should be no differences of opinion between its practitioners. The fact that kabbalists did, however, disagree, and that they appealed to reason and analysis to support their various opinions, implied that Kabbalah should be better described as a science.[1] This was the dawning of the scientific age, but not yet the death of magic and mystery.

Scientific awakening was not the only reason for Kabbalah's extensive popularity. Rome's fear of heresy was another. Although, as we have seen, knowledge of Kabbalah proliferated widely in the aftermath of the expulsion from Spain, the study topic of choice for most Jews remained the Talmud. When, in 1559, in an attempt to regulate theological thought, the Index of Prohibited Books was produced, the Jews of Catholic Europe found that the Talmud had been banned. And in the same year the ecclesiastical authorities in Cremona ordered all copies of the Talmud to be burned, just as had happened six years earlier in Venice and Rome.[2]

With the market in copies of the Talmud under siege, the Hebrew printers turned instead to Kabbalistic literature. They found eager customers. Whatever they had thought of Kabbalah before, the new literature offered an alternative, often refreshing, method of religious enquiry for those reeling from the loss of their Talmuds. The number and availability of Kabbalistic volumes burgeoned; in the aftermath of the Talmud's burning, nearly every significant work of medieval Kabbalah appeared in print. And a new wave of contemporary Kabbalistic literature emerged as well: sermons, commentaries and anthologies.[3] Italy's Jewish communities and Christian Cabalists found they had a wider choice of mystical texts to read than anyone had ever dreamed of.

As we have seen, the printing of the Zohar was not universally welcomed. A struggle broke out in the town of Pesaro between those who opposed printing because they believed Kabbalah should only be made available to the select few who fully understood it and those who thought that making it as widely available as possible was a good thing. One of the advocates of printing argued, somewhat patronisingly, that those who did not understand the complex passages in the Zohar would simply skip over them, paying attention only to the simple meaning of a few verses which are 'sweeter than honey and the comb'.[4]

The supporters of printing were not helped in their cause by a tendency among the Safed kabbalists to treat the Zohar as a magic talisman. Moses Cordovero recommended reading the Zohar even if one did not understand what one read; even uttering its language would bestow mental happiness. It is hard to argue in favour of printing a book if its only use is to be magical.

Elijah del Medigo, who had criticised Yohanan Alemanno's belief that Kabbalistic magic could be used to summon spiritual powers, objected not just to the printing of Kabbalah, but to the subject as a whole. He regarded the very idea of the *sefirot* as heresy and the suggestion that one could influence heaven through Kabbalah as a dangerous fantasy. He also rejected the idea that Shimon bar Yoḥai had written the Zohar. It was inconceivable, he argued, that the book could have been written so long ago and remained wholly concealed, not even alluded to anywhere. More damning still was the fact that many of the characters in its pages were not born until after bar Yoḥai's death. This, del Medigo asserted, was incontrovertible proof that the second-century rabbi could not have written it.

One of Elijah's descendants, Joseph del Megido, also penned critiques of Kabbalah. But since he wrote defences of the Kabbalah alongside his criticisms, all he really managed to accomplish was disagreement between later scholars about what he really stood for.

The grammarian and philologist Elia Levita, from whom Cardinal Egidio da Viterbo had learned Hebrew, queried the Zohar's antiquity, on the grounds that its grammar was much more modern than its supposed age would suggest. This was a charge repeated by Christian scholars including the Dutch classicist Joseph Scaliger and the French theologian Louis Cappel.

But of all who participated in the backlash against Kabbalah, none lashed back more than Leon of Modena.

Leon of Modena was born in 1571, in Venice, the city where he spent most of his life. He was ordained as a rabbi and spent 40 years doing a job he didn't enjoy, preaching, teaching and ministering to the Venetian community. Poorly paid and supplementing his income through proofreading and private tutoring, his fame came through the books he wrote.

Leon's most important book was the one he wrote in his old age. He called it *Ari Nohem*, or A Lion Roars. A lion, because of the convention in Jewish literature for a book title to be a pun on the author's name. Roaring, because at 68 years old, impoverished, sick and disillusioned, roaring was all he was able to do. His age and infirmity did nothing to lessen the power of the book.

His disillusionment stemmed from the ubiquity of Kabbalah, which permeated every aspect of his life. He was not a Kabbalist himself; far from it, Leon of Modena was a champion of science and rationalism. Had he not found himself hemmed in religiously, socially and even domestically by the enthusiastic presence of kabbalists and their books, he might never have fulminated against it. But that was never a possibility. Kabbalah was everywhere in Venice, a social force ever-present in the life of the city's Jews and passionately advocated even by those whom he held dearest. His favourite student, on whom he had pinned so many hopes, had turned into an enthusiastic Kabbalist. So had his son-in-law and cousin. To top it all, Menahem Azariah da Fano, a renowned Talmudist and legal authority who had guided him when he was young, was now posthumously revered as one of Italy's leading authors on Kabbalah. Leon of Modena was surrounded by Kabbalah. He could not get away from it. It made him roar.

It wasn't just emotion that turned Leon against Kabbalah. He had strong philosophical objections, too. He singled out three distinct themes for criticism. He objected to Moses Cordovero's assertion that the *sefirot* were the essence of Judaism and that anyone who did not accept them was a heretic. How could rejection of the *sefirot* be heresy, Leon wondered, when kabbalists themselves held differing views about their nature? As for the doctrine itself, Leon saw it as contradicting the principle of God's indivisibility. Not one God, but ten.

He similarly took exception to the claim made by an earlier Kabbalist, Meir ibn Gabbai, that Kabbalah was essential for the perfection of the soul. And he railed against the way kabbalists rejected the rationalist philosophy of Maimonides.[5]

Those were his intellectual motivations. But the goad, over and above everything else, that drove Leon of Modena's attack on Kabbalah, was what he saw as the wasted energies of his outstanding student, Joseph Ḥamitz. To Leon's mind, Ḥamitz should have typified the new generation of scientifically minded religious thinkers, who would eradicate superstition and cement their faith firmly on the pillars of philosophy and reason. Ḥamitz had studied medicine and philosophy at the University of Padua, Galileo's alma mater and one of the great European centres of learning. He received his doctorate in 1624 and was immediately ordained as a rabbi in Venice. It was to Leon's great chagrin that Ḥamitz fell under the lure of Kabbalah. Leon addressed A Lion Roars to Ḥamitz, in an attempt to steer him away from Kabbalah and back to philosophy.

Leon's book was not an intemperate rant against Kabbalah's ideas and influence. He was too smart for that. Instead, he argued against it point by point, building a case: roaring but not throwing a tantrum. He opposed the printing of Kabbalah, not on the grounds that there was something wrong with it, but because it was an esoteric subject, intended for a small number of eyes and not for public consumption. It was a similar argument to that used in Pesaro, and echoed the concerns of Isaac the Blind all those years before, except that Isaac tried to forbid the teaching of Kabbalah whereas Leon argued against its printing.

His central argument was directed against the age and authorship of the Zohar. Again, his criticism was subtle. He didn't condemn the Zohar; far from it, he was effusive in its praise. The stories themselves were 'pleasant to those who listen to them. How pleasant and how endearing! And that is why I praise and glorify the composition, the book of the Zohar ... more than any other work composed among our nation in the past three hundred years.'[6]

But the Zohar's elegantly composed narrative was not the butt of his criticism. His issue was the veneration of the book and the authority attributed to it, based on what he regarded as an incorrect assessment of its antiquity. He argued that Kabbalistic books regularly presented themselves as being older than they actually were, in order to gain greater authority for themselves. If the Zohar had been written by Shimon bar Yoḥai, who lived in the second century, why had it not had an impact then? Why did it take a thousand years before its ideas entered circulation? And, if Shimon bar Yoḥai possessed the esoteric secrets attributed to him in the Zohar, why were his opinions not accorded greater authority in the Talmud? Indeed, why were many of his legal opinions in the Talmudic literature ignored in the codification of Jewish law? Furthermore, how could he have written the Zohar while hiding in a cave?[7] He and his son were sustained in the cave by a miraculous carob tree and a spring of water, so where did they get pen and paper from, and how could they write if they were buried up to their necks in sand?

When he had finished demolishing the Zohar, Leon turned his fire on Kabbalah's promoters. He accused Israel Sarug, the man who brought Luria's Kabbalah from Safed to Italy, of being a charlatan, flattering wealthy Venetians by telling them they bore the soul of famous people from the past. He condemned Sarug for creating a cult of personality around the memory of Isaac Luria. The hostility between the two men was palpable, if gentlemanly. On one occasion Leon complained that at a festive meal Sarug had hurled a loaf at bread at him. He didn't give a reason, and Sarug later apologised.

Leon of Modena was not the first critic of Kabbalah, and he would not be the last.[8] Yet, of all of Kabbalah's critics, he was the only person to systematically reject its validity and antiquity. A Lion Roars was the first closely argued, sweeping assault both on the mythology of Kabbalah and on its principles.

Leon had written his book to try to wean his pupil Joseph Ḥamitz away from non-rational investigation and back to his scientific studies. It didn't work. After Leon's death, Ḥamitz drifted even further from the path his teacher had envisaged for him. He became a follower of the messianic pretender Shabbetai Zevi, the man who, as we shall now see, did more than many other in history to bring Kabbalah into disrepute. From that point of view, A Lion Roars was a failure.

PERMITTING THE FORBIDDEN

Populist movements have flourished throughout history, irrespective of the strength of the intellectual arguments hurled against them. This explains why Leon of Modena's campaign against Kabbalah

1. Manuscript of *Shaarei Orah*,
Gates of Light, c. 1400

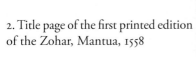

2. Title page of the first printed edition
of the Zohar, Mantua, 1558

3. Shabbetai Tzvi

4. Pages from manuscript
of Abraham Abulafia's
Sefer Hatsiruf

5. Title page from Knorr von Rosenroth's *Kabbala Denudata*

6. Amulet for a safe pregnancy

7. Page from Abraham
Abulafia's Sitrei Torah

8. Athanasius Kircher diagram
of the Names of God in *Oedipus
Aegyptiacus*, Egyptian Oedipus

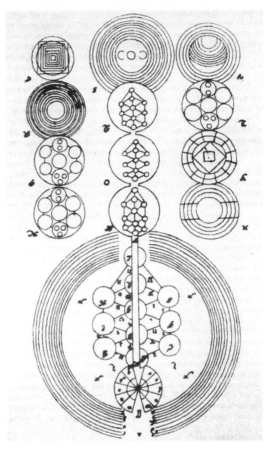

9. Diagram of the *sefirot* from Knorr von Rosenroth's *Kabbala Denudata*

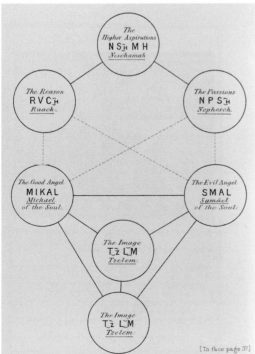

10. The Formation of the Soul, from *La clef des grands mystérès*, by Eliphas Lévi

11. Heinrich Cornelius Agrippa

12. Prayer following a circumcision. From *Book of the Secret of the Lord*, 1687 CE

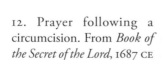

רִבּוֹנוֹ שֶׁל עוֹלָם כָּךְ מְקוּבָּל לְפָנֶיךָ כְּאִלּוּ

13. Eliphas Lévi, 1874

14. Tomb of Rabbi Shimon bar Yochai

15. Fantasy crowning of
Shabbatai Tzvi

16. Fourteenth-century
commentary on *Sefer
Yetsirah* by a student of
Eleazar of Worms

was doomed to failure. His rationalism was no match for the emotional promise that Isaac Luria's Kabbalah extended to the downhearted Jewish communities of the seventeenth century.

Many factors contributed to a sense of despondency among Europe's Jews. Even though the Spanish expulsion had taken place over a century earlier, a sense of exile remained palpable. This was, after all, a nation which was still grieving over its previous eviction from Jerusalem, the best part of two millennia earlier. They prayed daily to return to their original homeland, for the restoration of their Temple and their political independence. And even though it was a formal grief, the raw emotion having dissipated many generations ago, the more recent expulsion from Spain was more than enough to reignite a manifest sense of loss. The nation which had reminded itself daily for so long that it had once been dispossessed was now brutally exposed to the reality of a new exile, making all the more potent their craving for a restoration, their longing for redemption.

Isaac Luria's Kabbalah spoke to their sense of exile. It didn't matter that very few actually studied it, and that even fewer understood it in all its complexity. The basic myth was simple enough. A catastrophe at the time of the creation had caused a cosmic dislocation. The *Shechina*, the divine presence, was thrust into exile,[9] where she yearned to be restored to her male counterpart. Israel's homelessness on earth reflected this cosmic drama. She, too, yearned for an end to her exile. But while the divine presence had chosen to be a passive participant in this drama, Israel had no such option. There was a redemptive role she was obliged to play.

In order for the *Shechina* to return to her ordained place, and for the cosmos to be restored to perfection, the holy sparks trapped beneath the shards of the broken vessels had to be liberated, to ascend to the level from which they had fallen. Israel's purpose was to be the agent of this liberation. Their duty was to keep the commandments Moses had given them, repair the world in accordance with the teachings of the Kabbalah, hasten the coming of the Messiah and thereby bring an end both to their own exile and that of the *Shechina*.

The myth itself was simple but it wasn't the motivation for what was about to happen. Ending their exile was a worthy dream, but solving their daily problems was more urgent. Everyone had problems, even though not all Jewish lives were the same. The rural Jews of Poland were sunk in poverty, ill health and despair. Their co-religionists in the more prosperous cities of Europe lived materially better lives but were subject to religious persecutions, extraordinary and arbitrary taxations, restrictions on where they could live and the insecurity of wars and political events. The anxieties may have been different across the communities, but the melancholy was pretty much the same.

The final straw came in 1648, a year that some kabbalists had predicted would be when the messianic redemption would begin. They'd made similar predictions about 1492. The messianic hopes vested in that earlier year vanished when the Jews were expelled from Spain. The promise of 1648 fared no better. A Cossack uprising in the Ukraine, led by Bohdan Chmielnicki, blamed the Jews for the country's subjugation. A call went out to rid the land of its Jewish population. Tens of thousands were slaughtered, whole communities wiped out; countless refugees fled into Russia or the Crimea, where many were sold as slaves. Opinions are divided as to whether the Chmielnicki massacres were the direct cause of the astonishing events about to unfold or just one of the contributory factors. For the Kabbalist charlatan and messianic pretender Shabbetai Tzvi, it little mattered either way.

Shabbetai Tzvi was born in Smyrna, now Izmir in Turkey, on the ninth day of the Hebrew month of Av, in 1626. The ninth of Av is traditionally observed as the anniversary of the destruction of the two Jerusalem Temples, the first in 586 BCE and the second in the year 70 of the current era. It is also said to be the date upon which the expulsion decree was announced in Spain. Since optimism insists that sadness will be turned into rejoicing, it is also expected to be the day on which the Messiah will be born. Shabbetai Tzvi's parents, cooing over their ninth of Av baby, may never have announced to the world that he was the Messiah, but the thought cannot have been far from their minds. They called him Shabbetai, because he had been born on the Sabbath.[10]

As a child Shabbetai received a traditional religious education but seems to have abandoned his formal studies in his teens. Something of a loner, he shut himself away in a room in his father's house where he devoted himself to the study of the Zohar and a very limited selection of other Kabbalistic books. Studying alone, with no comrades or teacher, and apparently beginning to suffer from a form of bipolar disorder, he began experiencing visions. What he may or may not have seen is a bit hazy, largely because everything that we know about his early life comes from reports and testimonies recorded much later by his followers and opponents, often fanciful and frequently contradictory. But there is general agreement that during this early period of Kabbalistic study Shabbetai Tzvi believed that God had revealed himself to him, to proclaim him Messiah. And that the patriarchs Abraham, Isaac and Jacob had anointed him into the role.

One of the great paradoxes of Shabbetai Tzvi's life is that, despite his reclusive tendencies, he was a charismatic and charming personality, with a delightful singing voice which attracted people to him. Admirers warmed to him and easily fell under his sway. At some point he must have broken out of his self-imposed confinement in the family home for a small group of acolytes (disciples is probably too strong a word) gathered around him. This anonymous group were the first people with whom he developed his Kabbalistic ideas; ideas that defined his relationship with God.

In traditional Kabbalah the *sefirot* symbolise the divine forces that emanate from God and descend to the material world. But they are not God himself. God exists beyond the *sefirot*, unknowable, unimaginable and infinite. For want of a better word the kabbalists refer to this indescribable existence as *En-Sof,* 'endless'.

En-Sof was not Shabbetai Tzvi's God. Instead he believed that the God of the Bible, which he called the God of his faith, was the *sefira* known as *Tiferet,* or beauty. In the traditional Kabbalistic scheme *Tiferet* is the sixth *sefira.* In Shabbetai Tzvi's mind, however, *Tiferet* was elevated above all the other *sefirot*, making it the dominant force in the cosmic drama and effectively neutralising *En-Sof.*

From a traditional point of view this was a profoundly heretical idea, implying that the ultimate cause of existence lies not within the unknowable divinity but with a secondary force, derived from *En-Sof* but somehow superior to it. From another point of view, though, the idea that God is in some way knowable, that humans can have a relationship with a personal God, was attractive to people trying to make sense of their unhappy existence.

The details of Tzvi's thinking on this subject are not at all clear. He left no books or treatises behind, and in any event he may have deliberately concealed his mystical beliefs, leaving it to others to figure out what he was thinking. But the fact that Shabbetai Tzvi's religious outlook was rooted in Kabbalistic thought is inescapable. It would become even more pronounced as his career progressed.[11]

Believing himself to be the Messiah and tormented by the extremes of his bipolarity, Shabbetai Tzvi's behaviour became increasingly erratic. He married, but refused to consummate the union. The couple divorced and shortly afterwards he married again. Once again, he refused to sleep with his wife, and the marriage ended. The names of neither wife are known.

Sometimes he would make a public demonstration of offending against religious law, believing that he had been commanded to do so. At other times he would manically yell the secret name of God in the synagogues. Sometimes he appeared so badly stricken he could scarcely communicate. On the whole his community, recognising that he was unwell or possessed by demons, seems to have tolerated his eccentricities.

The toleration came under strain when Shabbetai began experimenting with Kabbalistic magic. On one occasion he gathered his friends together and took them out into the fields, telling them that they would make the sun stand still at midday. He hurled incantations at the sun, demanding that it halt in the sky. He insisted that his companions do the same. They tried, but soon became too embarrassed to continue. When the elders of the Smyrna community heard about his magical endeavours, they summoned Shabbetai to appear before them. He refused to attend, sending back a message daring them to excommunicate him and his associates.

The details of what happened next have not been recorded, but the outcome is certain. The extremes of his behaviour reached a point at which the community authorities could tolerate his presence in the city no longer. Some time between 1651 and 1654 he was expelled from Smyrna. With nowhere particular to go, he set off wandering from town to town.

Shabbetai's wanderings did nothing to normalise his odd behaviour. Shortly after his arrival in Salonika, he invited the leading rabbis in the city to a banquet. When they arrived, he erected a bridal canopy and had a Torah scroll brought in. He proceeded to perform a marriage ceremony between himself and the Torah. When the rabbis expressed their outrage, he declared that the book of Proverbs stated that everyone who loved the Torah could be considered its husband. The rabbis were not impressed and had him thrown out of the city.

He then travelled to Constantinople, where he purchased a huge fish, dressed it in the clothes of a baby and placed in a cradle. He explained that the redemption of Israel would take place under the sign of Pisces, the sign of the fish. The incident not being blasphemous, the townsfolk put his strange behaviour down to his illness. But when he celebrated the annual cycle of religious festivals all in the space of one week, and declared that certain ritual transgressions were now permitted, the rabbis began to worry. They feared his ideas and the passion with which he expressed them might lead people astray. The judicial authorities had him flogged and the rabbis forbade all members of their community from having any further contact with him.

Shabbetai Tzvi next made his way to Jerusalem, where he seems to have made a more favourable impression on those around him. He lived an ascetic life, spending all day in his room, occasionally wandering off to nearby caves. Fasting all week, he ate only on the Sabbath. He must have reignited his personal charm, for he was selected by the community to undertake a mission to Cairo to raise money to pay off an unexpected tax imposed by the Ottoman governor. While he was there he married once again. His new wife, Sarah, was almost as odd as he. Of the many stories circulating about her, the most intriguing was her insistence that she was destined to marry the Messiah. It is not certain whether they met in Cairo or whether Shabbetai had heard of her strange belief and sent for her. One way or another, they married. As before, the marriage was not consummated, until after two years Shabbetai finally consented to have intercourse with his wife.

Before then, while Shabbetai Tzvi was still chastely married to Sarah in Cairo, a young man in Gaza was beginning his Kabbalistic studies. His name was Nathan Ashkenazi. He'd acquired a reputation as an outstanding Talmudic student in Jerusalem, his dedication to his studies paying off when he was introduced as a prospective husband to the daughter of wealthy parents from Gaza. The couple married and Nathan moved to live with his wife's family. It was in Gaza that he began teaching himself the system of Kabbalah developed by Isaac Luria, a Kabbalistic approach in which Shabbetai Tzvi had never taken an interest, disdaining its complexities in favour of the earlier, less systematised approach of the Zohar.

During the course of his studies, Nathan experienced a mind-blowing revelation, one which would change not only his life but also the life of Shabbetai Tzvi and tens of thousands of Jewish families across the globe.

At the time, Nathan was locked away in solitude, mired in a lengthy period of fasting and meditation. As he prayed, a spirit came over him, his hair stood on end and his knees trembled. Before him there appeared a vision of the heavenly Chariot, the very throne to which the ancient mystics had ventured to descend so many centuries ago. Upon the side of the Chariot was engraved a face. In itself that was no surprise: everyone knew that etched onto the flank of the heavenly throne is the face of the biblical patriarch Jacob. But Jacob's was not the face that Nathan saw. In his vision, engraved on the heavenly Chariot Nathan Ashkenazi saw the face of Shabbetai Tzvi. A man he had never even spoken to.

The two men had never met, but they had lived in Jerusalem at the same time, part of the small Jewish community in that city. Comprising no more than two or three hundred families, they all dwelt within the same few streets. Shabbetai's strange way of life must have led him to be regarded as a local oddity, so that Nathan, who was bound to have passed him in the street, would have known exactly what he looked like. Shabbetai Tzvi may not have known Nathan Ashkenazi by sight, but Nathan certainly knew Shabbetai. And he knew that it was Shabbetai's face he had seen engraved upon the heavenly Chariot. As a result of his vision Nathan Ashkenazi, Nathan of Gaza as he became known, set off on a course which would lead him to become, in Gershom Scholem's words, 'the first great theologian of heretical kabbalism'.[12]

Nathan's life-changing vision led him to decide he should become a healer of souls. He took his cue from Isaac Luria, who, so they said, could read a person's sins on their face and intuit the actions necessary to erase them. Nathan began composing 'repairs' for the souls of penitents who approached him.[13] These took the form of heavy fasts and physical deprivations, prayers and meditations, all composed by Nathan but deriving from Luria's Kabbalah.

Reports of Nathan's newfound skill were received with excitement in Gaza. The news that a young prophet, the son-in-law of one of their wealthiest families, was curing souls, apparently with great success, spread through the town. Word spread south, to Egypt, where Shabbetai Tzvi was still fundraising for the Jerusalem community. He abandoned his mission and set off to obtain a repair for his own soul. When the two men met, Nathan flung himself on the ground and begged Shabbetai's forgiveness for not having paid homage to him sooner.

Had it not been for Nathan of Gaza, Shabbetai Tzvi would have gone down in history, if he had gone down at all, as a man of provocative behaviour, prone to delusions, whose early belief that he was the Messiah became so exaggerated that he eventually signed his letters 'I am the Lord your God, Shabbetai Tzvi'.[14] That he became the leader of a mass movement which at its peak attracted tens of thousands of supporters, split families, divided communities, spawned fierce opposition and reshaped Jewish life until this day owes far more to Nathan of Gaza's skills as a communicator and publicist than it does to Shabbetai Tzvi.

Nathan provided the theoretical justification for Shabbetai's claim to be the Messiah. Traditional Judaism already had a conception of how the Messiah would be recognised, and Shabbetai Tzvi, with his bizarre rituals and deliberate transgressions of religious law did not fit the model at all. Nathan's great success was to override the traditional view, offering an apparently coherent, Kabbalistic explanation which demonstrated that Shabbetai's messiahship was cosmically necessary and inevitable. His pronouncements eliminated any apprehension Shabbetai's followers may have had about the alleged Messiah's bizarre behaviour.

As for those who did not believe, they were of no importance. Nathan declared (having heard it from an angel) that belief in the Messiah required no proofs, signs or wonders; faith was all that counted. The souls of those who did not believe in Shabbetai's messiahship were tainted by evil inherited from former, rebellious generations. A precondition of their repair was faith, a quality they did not have. And without repair, they had no hope.

Nathan set out his Kabbalistic justification of why Shabbetai was the Messiah in a letter to Raphael Joseph, the leader of Egyptian Jewry, an active supporter of the new movement, a man whom Shabbetai knew well. In a long, convoluted and highly technical missive, Nathan explained that none of the sparks which had fallen to earth during the creation catastrophe remained in the demonic realm. The cosmos was repairing, redemption was at hand and the light of the *sefirot* were about to become visible on earth. He advised Joseph on the meditations that he should undertake and told him to forget the devotions formerly prescribed by Isaac Luria, as he had now been superseded by his former student, Hayyim Vital. Nathan went on to predict that within a year and some months Shabbetai would seize power bloodlessly from the Sultan, the ruler of the Ottoman Empire, master of all the lands Shabbetai and Nathan had ever known. All nations would submit to Shabbetai's rule.

Shabbetai's triumph over the Sultan would come about solely through the singing of hymns. When it was accomplished, Moses would be resurrected, Shabbetai would marry his daughter and his present wife would become her maidservant. Spectacularly, Jerusalem's temple would descend, ready-built, from above and the dead in the Land of Israel would be resurrected. Forty years later the remainder of the world's dead would also be reborn.

Needless to say, none of this came true.

THE MADNESS SPREADS

Looking back, it is hard to appreciate the scale or momentum of the Sabbatean movement. Within a year of Nathan and Shabbetai's first encounter, the whole of Jewish Europe, North Africa and the Near East was in the grip of messianic fever. Those fortunate enough to have survived the Chmielnicki massacres now realised the cosmic significance of those terrible years; they had been, in the words of the Talmud, 'the footsteps of the Messiah', the necessary apocalyptic prelude to the utopian age. Impoverished communities everywhere recognised that their generations of deprivation had all been for the good, penances paid in advance for their few sins, in order that they might enjoy the future in absolute bliss. From Hamburg to Yemen to Marrakesh came reports of people selling their possessions, donating their money to charity and preparing to travel to the Holy Land. The diarist Glückel of Hameln recalled how her father-in-law sent casks of dried food and linen to his family in Hamburg, to be kept in readiness for the day they would sail to the Holy Land. For three years the casks stood unopened, while her father-in-law waited for the signal to depart. Word never came and everything in the barrels rotted.[15]

In Israel itself, the flow of pilgrims was so great that the houses and courtyards could not contain them all; people slept in the bazaars and streets. In Nathan's shire of Gaza, there were 'two hundred and twenty penitents who were fasting for two days and nights, not to speak of those who fasted for even longer, and the women and children who fasted for single days only'.[16]

Popular interest in Kabbalah soared. It seemed as if mystical prophets could be found on almost every street corner. The most famous, Moses Suriel, who believed himself to be a reincarnation of Shimon bar Yoḥai, was reported to have composed a new Zohar, though nobody ever laid eyes upon it. Rabbis, penitents and admirers would gather around Suriel every evening, singing hymns to Shabbetai Tzvi and dancing ecstatically, the fervent atmosphere rising in a crescendo until the prophet fell to the ground in what may have been an epileptic fit. Speaking in Aramaic, the language of the Zohar, he would reveal new mysteries that were recorded by scribes sitting alongside him. When he recovered from his trance the scribes would read his revelations back to him, yet he could not understand a word that he had spoken. Like Nathan of Gaza and Isaac Luria, he could discern a person's past sins just by looking at their faces, and prescribe the appropriate penances

And yet there were siren voices. Many kabbalists and Talmudists railed against the hysteria. The signs by which a true prophet would be recognised were clear; they had been set out in the Torah and expanded upon in subsequent literature. According to these criteria, Nathan was no prophet. As for Shabbetai, he could be nothing other than a charlatan. No Messiah would transgress the commandments of the Torah, let alone pronounce Shabbetai's trademark benediction of 'he who permits the forbidden', which Hebrew speakers recognised as nothing more than a pun on the conventional blessing of God 'who releases the bound'.

Those who opposed Shabbetai did not have an easy time of it. Jacob Sasportas, one of Shabbetai's most fervent opponents, was forced to admit that the believers were in the majority, and that the movement's detractors were afraid to speak out. But he persisted, as did others. While many rabbis and scholars flocked to Shabbetai Tzvi during the few months that his star was in the ascendant, saner voices consistently refused to do so. Time would prove them right.

Convinced that he was about to be afforded the Sultan's crown, Shabbetai Tzvi divided the kingdoms of the earth among his most faithful supporters, naming each new ruler after a biblical king. Then he set off for Constantinople. The Sultan, trying to hold his vast and fractious empire together, was not excited to hear of his impending arrival. As far as he could tell, Shabbetai was no more than a Jewish madman whose followers expected him to take control of the kingdom. The Jews of the city of Constantinople were even less enthusiastic; their safety and security depended on maintaining good relations with the imperial authorities. The numerous conflicting reports of what happened next make it hard to reconstruct the details. Whether the Jews handed him over or the Turkish navy tracked his arrival into port may never be known. But, one way or another, on reaching Constantinople, Shabbetai Tzvi was arrested and thrown into gaol.

It was a setback for the movement but not a calamity; nobody ever expected the Messiah's path to be easy. But further calamity followed. In September 1666 the Sultan summoned Shabbetai to his presence. His followers were excited: this was bound to be the moment they had waited for, when the Messiah would remove the Emperor's crown and place it on his own head.

It wasn't. The Sultan listened to Shabbetai, and sentenced him to death.

The death sentence imposed on Shabbetai was accompanied by an offer of clemency. His life would be spared if, and only if, he agreed to convert to Islam. Shabbetai does not seem to have been conflicted. He chose to convert. The Jewish Messiah became a Muslim.

Although some insisted on seeing Shabbetai's conversion as a messianic stratagem, most realised it was not. It was an apostasy to save his life, one which would not be reversed. Shabbetai adopted his new faith. His followers were left leaderless, directionless and utterly perplexed.

Even after Shabbetai converted to Islam, messianic speculation remained rife. Shabbetai had proved to be an imposter but there was no shortage of others who believed themselves to be the real thing. Anxious to prevent another charismatic figure luring vulnerable followers through the misuse of Kabbalah, the rabbinic authorities put preventative measures in place. There had always been an understanding that mystical matters should only be studied by those of sufficient wisdom and learning; now they formalised a ruling adduced a few years earlier, that Kabbalah should not be studied until the age of 40.[17] Intended as a firm, and inviolable rule, it has always been honoured more in the breach than in the observance.

The rabbinic precautions were only partially effective. Other messianic pretenders did emerge. Jacob Frank caused the greatest stir. Although he was a minor figure in comparison to Shabbetai Tzvi, with far less charisma and an even more authoritarian attitude, he still managed to gather a considerable following around himself, until he, too, converted, along with his followers. In their case it was to Christianity.

Sixty years after Shabbetai Tzvi's conversion the renowned Kabbalist Moses Hayyim Luzzatto was accused of harbouring secret Sabbatean sympathies. The evidence against him was slim and superficial, but sufficient in the still febrile environment to impair his reputation severely. The rabbinic court in Venice exiled Luzzatto to Amsterdam and banned him from writing Kabbalistic works. Complying with their wishes, he turned his hand instead to composing ethical literature. His *Path of the Upright*, written in his Amsterdam exile, remains one of the most widely read works of Jewish ethics.

The Sabbatean crisis had been brief but its impact was devastating. Less than 16 months had elapsed between Nathan of Gaza's first meeting with Shabbetai Tzvi and the latter's conversion. It had been no time at all. But neither the Kabbalah nor even the Jewish world would ever be the same again.

Decline and Revival

LOSING ITS WAY

By the seventeenth century Christian Cabala had become so integrated into the broad spectrum of the occult that it was in danger of losing its unique identity. We have already mentioned Giovanni Agostino Pantheo, who used Cabala as a tool in his alchemical calculations, and Paracelsus, who harnessed it to magic, believing it would speed up his medical experiments. Other esoteric thinkers followed in their footsteps, introducing elements of Cabala into their particular systems.

The Jesuit scholar Athanasius Kircher inserted a 150-page treatise on the 'Kabbalah of the Hebrews' into his book *Oedipus Aegyptiacus* (Egyptian Oedipus). Kirchner believed that the mythical Hermes Trismegistus, who was supposed to have been a contemporary of Moses, had encoded his mystical doctrine within ancient Egyptian hieroglyphics. Kabbalah, Kircher asserted, was the key to deciphering these mysteries, although it needed to be backed up by various other esoteric tools including Pythagorean verses, Chaldean Oracles, Orphic hymns and Arabian magic.[1]

In his commentary on the biblical episode of the Golden Calf, the Protestant visionary Jacob Böhme claimed that the Ten Commandments had been written on a globe of black fire, in letters of white fire. He came across this image, a stark contrast with the stone tablets of the biblical version, in Johannes Reuchlin's *De Arte*

Cabalistica. It was just one of many Cabalistic allusions that he adduced in his writings, together with references to alchemy, magic and other esoteric arts.

Not every thinker succeeded in tempering their particular occult art with elements of Cabala. Sometimes the only thing they really knew about Cabala was its name, and its reputation as a repository of profound mysteries. Nevertheless, claiming that Cabala played a part in their thinking was a useful strategy designed to win respect. The publishers of two tracts which appeared in the early seventeenth century must have thought so. Their work caused great excitement, not least because it was said to partly rely on Cabala. Cabala was almost certainly a subject they only knew about because of the work of that misunderstood messianic hopeful, Elizabethan England's John Dee.

As we have seen, John Dee's career had not worked out as he hoped. He didn't turn out to be the Prophet of the Last Days and his intimacy with the angels, which he attributed to Cabala, was no more than a delusion. But his legacy was not one of complete failure. As he made his way back to England from his sojourns in Bohemia and Poland, he was visited by the alchemist Heinrich Khunrath. That he made a good impression on Khunrath is apparent from the fact that the alchemist drew on several of Dee's theories for his own endeavours. And, according to Francis Yates, it was the magical, alchemical and Cabalistic features that are so central to the work of both Dee and Khunrath which inspired the publishers of the two seventeenth-century tracts that made such an impression when they came to light. Tracts that laid the foundations for a strange movement so mysterious in its origins and obscure in what it stood for that, even today, scholars find it difficult to explain exactly what it was. It, too, claimed to be linked to Cabala. But exactly how is hard to say.[2]

The first of the two tracts was published in 1614 in the German town of Cassel. Entitled *Fama Fraternitatis*, or Report of the Brotherhood, and unattributed to any author, the pamphlet proclaimed the arrival of a new wisdom which would change the world. This wisdom had first come to light with the opening of

a tomb belonging to someone known only as 'Brother C. R.'.
Inside the tomb, or so it was claimed, were ancient books of
magic, alchemy and Cabala which C. R. had acquired during his
travels to the East. These books, and the mysterious, anonymous
brotherhood that they spawned, were claimed by the writers of the
pamphlet to herald the dawning of a new age for mankind.

A year later a second pamphlet was published, swelling the
excitement even further. *Confessio Fraternititatis* (Confessions of
the Brotherhood) gave the year of C. R.'s birth as 1378, stated that
he had lived for 106 years and that the tomb had lain undisturbed
for a further 120 until its opening in 1604.

Another year passed. A romantic novel, undoubtedly linked to
the two earlier manifestoes, appeared. Called *The Chemical Wedding
of Christian Rosenkreutz*, it was an alchemical allegory describing
the spiritual ascent of a man whose initials are C. R.

Today, almost everyone who has heard of him believes that
Christian Rosenkreutz, or Rose-Cross, was a mythical character.
Not so in the seventeenth century, when the anonymous reports
first emerged of the opening of his tomb and the Rosicrucian
brotherhood he was supposed to have founded. The Rosicrucian
name survives today, although the contemporary movement has
little in common with its seventeenth-century forebear.

It was never established who was responsible for writing or
circulating the Rosicrucian manifestoes, or what their intentions
were. Their message, too, is uncertain. Many different, often
competing interpretations of the pamphlets were published
claiming to be based at least in part on Cabala, but none actually
explaining how.

The first manifesto, Report of the Brotherhood, must have
been circulating in manuscript form for some years before it was
printed. For in 1610, four years before it appeared in print, Adam
Haslmayr, an Austrian schoolmaster and follower of Paracelsus,
wrote a response to it. In his response, Haslmayr called upon
the mysterious Rosicrucian brotherhood – whose unknown
members nobody had ever met – to hasten the Second Coming
by illuminating the troubled world with their wisdom. This

wisdom was composed of various elements, of which Cabala was one.

Haslmayr was in no doubt about Cabala's antiquity: in one passage he wrote about Cabalists who teamed up with St Paul to teach the esoteric secrets of Christianity to the world. Disappointingly, though, Haslmayr did not tell his readers what he believed Cabala to be, or what role it played either in Rosicrucian wisdom or Paul's secret teachings. The Christian Cabalist Robert Fludd offered a tiny bit more detail, explaining that the Rosicrucian brotherhood used Cabala to converse with angels.[3]

This vague and undefined use of the name Cabala was not confined to the Rosicrucian movement. The same happened throughout the occult world. No matter what the arcane enterprise, Cabala was likely to be cited as an ingredient. Rarely was any explanation given on how it had been used.

The name Cabala had become an emblem signifying profundity and wisdom; it added credibility to any theory with which it was associated. The reason was not hard to find. People could get away with using the word Cabala in a vague sense because Christian Cabala itself had become amorphous; its very nature had grown hazy.

Despite the work of people like Francesco Giorgi, Christian Cabala had barely evolved since the pioneering foundations laid by Pico della Mirandola and Johannes Reuchlin in the early sixteenth century. Whereas the traumas of exile and dispersion had continually invested Jewish Kabbalah with new insights, most notably in the mystical city of Safed, nothing comparable had happened to its Christian offshoot. Always a minority interest in Christianity, ordinary Christians had never known enough about it to seek answers from it to the disappointments of day-to-day life. Christian Cabala had been oblivious to the recent great upheavals in Christianity, the turmoil engendered by the advent of Protestantism and the religious wars that followed in its wake. Largely irrelevant in everyday life, Christian Cabala was only of real interest to those who wished to harness it to their occult cause.

What Christian Cabala needed was a reassessment of its core principles, a return to the texts and ideas which had given it its founding impetus. Fortunately, that is exactly what was about to occur. Christian Cabala received a new lease of life.

THE CABALA UNVEILED

'To the Reader, Lover of Hebrew, Lover of Chemistry, Lover of Philosophy': so begins the preface of *Kabbala Denudata*, or The Cabala Unveiled, the seventeenth century's most significant work of Christian Cabala. First published in 1677 and containing Latin translations of a selection of texts from the Zohar and Lurianic Kabbalah, it provided Christian readers with far greater and easier access to Kabbalistic texts than ever before.

The selection of texts in *Kabbala Denudata* were compiled and translated into Latin by Christian Knorr von Rosenroth, an alchemist who was employed as the Chancellor to Prince August of Sulzbach. Von Rosenroth had been born during the Thirty Years War, the devastating religious conflict which claimed more than eight million lives, sparked off a wave of religious persecutions and realigned the power structure of Central Europe. Working as political advisers in the wake of this trauma, von Rosenroth and his associate Francis Mercury van Helmont advocated an agenda of social reform. Kabbala and alchemy were their tools in this endeavour, alongside the more conventional disciplines of diplomacy and politics.

The incongruous juxtaposition of Hebrew, chemistry and philosophy in von Rosenroth's preface to the *Kabbala Denudata* shows just how closely all three disciplines were connected in his mind. It was through the coupling of mysticism and natural science that the political reforms he and van Helmont advocated would be achieved. Advances in science would heal the natural world, creating the conditions for a just and equitable society. Mysticism would produce the necessary cosmic repair, as outlined in Isaac Luria's Kabbalistic system. And just in case this partnership was not conveyed clearly enough in von Rosenroth's prefatory note, dedicating the book to the lovers of Hebrew, chemistry and philosophy, it was reinforced graphically in the book's frontispiece (Fig. 5).

As Allison Coudert explains, the maiden in the illustration represents the Kabbalah. In one hand she holds a scroll containing both Old and New Testaments. The keys dangling from her arm and the word *explicat* on the scroll indicate that she alone is able to unlock their mysteries. Ahead of her is the *Palatium Arcanorum*, the Palace of Secrets, the repository of natural sciences. The circles inside the sun are the *sefirot*. Kabbalah is depicted as the illuminating, unifying force, bringing together the cosmic and natural secrets.[4]

Von Rosenroth hoped that his Latin translation might heal the rift between Catholics and Protestants, which had led to the disastrous Thirty Years War. If members of both denominations were to read Kabbalah, which he believed to be the proof of Christianity, they might surely put their differences aside. To assist readers to gain as much benefit as possible from the selection of translated Kabbalistic texts, von Rosenroth, van Helmont and the English philosopher Henry More incorporated explanatory essays of their own into *Kabbala Denudata*.

Even more ambitious than von Rosenroth's hope that *Kabbala Denudata* would bring Protestants and Catholics together was his aspiration that it might assist in the task of converting Jews to Christianity. Now that he had translated Jewish texts for Christians to read, perhaps the Jews would reciprocate by reading Christian works. To give this aspiration greater traction he arranged for a new printing of the Zohar, in its original Aramaic, into which he inserted a Latin introduction. Believing the Zohar to be a proof of Christianity, he reasoned that providing the Jews with a copy introduced in a language they could read might encourage them to take an interest in his faith. He also arranged for copies of the New Testament in the ancient Syriac language, a close relative of Aramaic, to be printed in Hebrew characters.[5]

By giving his readers access to Kabbalistic texts that could be studied on their own, von Rosenroth helped remove Christian

Cabala from the occult patchwork into which it had been stitched, restoring it to a discipline in its own right.

Von Rosenroth's work proved popular. It was studied for the next two centuries, until Latin ceased to be Europe's common language of scholarship. Then, in 1887, Samuel Liddell MacGregor Mathers took up the baton, publishing English translations of sections from *Kabbalah Denudata*. His compendium, *Kabbalah Unveiled*, is still being printed today. Seven years later, von Rosenroth's version of the *Idra Rabba* or Great Assembly section of the Zohar was translated into French by Eliphas Lévi.

By the nineteenth century *Kabbalah Denudata* had become the normative gateway to Kabbalah for those who could not understand the original language of the Zohar. But its influence at the time of its original publication was arguably more important, if not as immediately obvious.

Allison Coudert has made a convincing case for the seminal influence of *Kabbala Denudata* on emerging social attitudes in the seventeenth century, underpinning the Enlightenment and helping shape contemporary Western culture. Within *Kabbala Denudata*, she argues, 'one can find the bases for the faith in science, belief in progress and commitment to religious tolerance'.[6]

Kabbalah Denudata's influence was boosted in no small measure by von Rosenroth's collaborator van Helmont, through his highly impressive network of seventeenth-century thought leaders. Among van Helmont's close friends was the mathematician and philosopher Gottfried Wilhelm Leibniz. Van Helmont collaborated with Leibniz on some of his astonishingly creative inventions, which included steam-powered fountains, shoes with springs on the soles for fast getaways and a coach that ran along a track at high speed.

Leibniz's religious philosophy betrays Kabbalistic influences, almost certainly the result of his exposure to *Kabbalah Denudata* and conversations held with van Helmont during the lengthy sojourns they shared in Hanover. Both men held highly unorthodox Christian views, even rejecting the idea of eternal hell and Jesus's essential role in salvation. Both views logically follow from Lurianic

Kabbalah. Luria's principle of reincarnation makes eternal hell redundant; if people are admitted into a cycle of reincarnation until they reach perfection, then there is no purpose in having a place of eternal punishment. And, since it is the responsibility of humans to repair the world in order to heal the cosmos, the role of Jesus or indeed any other Messiah in saving the souls of humanity, while potentially beneficial, is no longer essential.[7]

Another of van Helmont's friends, the political theorist John Locke, shared these views. Regarded as the first philosopher of the Enlightenment, Locke was unwell for much of his life. In in his later years he retired to the home of his friends Sir Francis and Lady Masham in Essex, where van Helmont was a frequent visitor.

Locke had many of the Kabbalistic and philosophical books written by van Helmont in his library. He also had a copy of *Kabbala Denudata*; it was one of the few books in his possession which he'd read closely enough to have made notes. He collated the notes he wrote on the book's final treatise into a collection he entitled *Doubts about Eastern Philosophy*. They demonstrate the depth of attention that he paid to the work, and although what he writes is somewhat critical it is obvious that he took the whole business of Kabbalah seriously.[8] It is stretching the point too far to argue that *Kabbala Denudata* was a core text in the formulation of Locke's scientific and political philosophy, but it almost certainly formed an important part of his intellectual arsenal.

Van Helmont also knew Isaac Newton, a man whose relationship with the occult has long interested biographers and researchers. Newton left behind a large body of alchemical writings, running to over one million words and including laboratory notebooks and lists of alchemical substances. The copy of *Kabbala Denudata* that van Helmont gave him is preserved in his library in Cambridge's Trinity College. It is evident from the book's dog-eared state that he perused it well.[9] He accepted the assertion that the Kabbalah was the product of the second-century sage Shimon bar Yoḥai, and from his writings it is clear that he had subjected its belief system to rigorous analysis. But he did not accept that Kabbalah was a proof of Christianity, nor did he believe it was valuable as a means of understanding the principles of Christian belief. Far from it; for Newton, Kabbalah was a Jewish error, the result of their contact with surrounding cultures. As part of what he termed the 'mystery of iniquity', he declared that Kabbalah was a gnostic heresy which had distorted early Christianity.[10]

Newton and Leibniz were bitter rivals. Both men claimed to have discovered the principles of mathematical calculus. They quarrelled over whether Leibniz had copied Newton or reached his conclusions independently. It is not beyond possibility that Newton's intellectual hostility to Kabbalah may have been influenced by his battle against Leibniz. Newton was a deeply religious man with a unique theological approach. He was too great a thinker to reject Kabbalah for anything other than theological reasons. But he would certainly have been aware that by criticising Kabbalah he was also implicitly criticising his adversary. Rejecting the factors which influenced Leibniz's religious philosophy would have been one way for Newton to undermine his opponent's credibility.

Despite Newton's criticisms, the accessibility and popularity of *Kabbala Denudata* ensured that the influence of Kabbalah contributed to the intellectual discourse shaping the new scientific Enlightenment. Things could hardly have been more different in Eastern Europe, far from the reach of the Enlightenment, in lands where Christian Cabala had barely penetrated. There Jewish families and communities were still reeling from the effects of Shabbetai Tzvi's failed messianic heresy, which had been fuelled so heavily by the misinterpretation of Kabbalistic doctrine.

Shabbetai Tzvi was finished, but Kabbalah most certainly was not. Indeed, it was about to enjoy arguably its finest hour. A new Kabbalistic faction was emerging. Known as Hasidism and still going strong today, it has turned out to be the longest-lasting of all modern Jewish religious movements. Inspired by kabbalists, and with Kabbalistic concepts underpinning its view of the world, Hasidism is the only movement that has incorporated Kabbalah wholeheartedly into its way of life.

Hasidism

THE GOOD NAME

A story is told of Rabbi Israel, son of Eliezer. A charismatic leader and sage, his days were filled dealing with the problems of villagers who came to him for assistance and advice. But at night, when his body lay asleep and his soul was free, it would ascend to heaven. When he arrived the angels would greet him, converse with him and conduct him through the heavenly halls. Each night he would progress a little further into the secret empyrean chambers, each time staying a little longer, returning ever more invigorated, ready to respond to the cries of those who depended upon him, to heal their wounds with his touch, solve their problems with his sound counsel.

One night his soul's heavenly odyssey was obstructed. A barrier arose before him; he could progress no further. He had reached the wall surrounding the Garden of Eden. The angel accompanying him said that he was free to enter the Garden, to experience its delights. But if he did decide to enter he would have to remain for eternity. Before he could be admitted he was required to make a declaration renouncing his earthly life. The decision was his alone.

It only took a moment for Israel to decide. He thought of his earthly life and realised just how unbearable the problems he dealt with day by day had become. He could not help but be affected by the misery afflicting those who came to him. And even here, outside the wall, he could smell the scent of the Garden of Eden, could almost taste its delights. Why hesitate? His soul began to speak, 'I renounce my earthly ...'

In a village on the steppes of Poland a woman is bending over the sleeping body of a man. His complexion is pale, there is not a flicker of movement in his face. Concerned, she touches his face. It is as cold as ice. 'Israel!' she screams.

On the far side of eternity her cry reaches the soul. He breaks off in the middle of his declaration. Hurling himself into the waiting arms of the angel, the soul of Israel son of Eliezer speeds back home, to his body and his sobbing wife. This is his life, the life he was placed on earth to lead, the destiny he is obliged to fulfil. Never again did he venture heavenward at night.[1]

Israel, son of Eliezer, is generally considered to be the founder of Hasidism, although it is more likely the movement emerged organically from a Pietist circle in which he was the leading light.[2] He is colloquially known as the *Besht*, an acronym of his full nickname, Ba'al Shem Tov, meaning Master of the Good Name. A Master of the Name, or Ba'al Shem, is a saintly, practical Kabbalist who, through skilful use of the divine names and by means of amulets, incantations and a primitive knowledge of medicine, is able to heal an illness, foretell the future, summon or cast out a spirit, revoke a curse, subdue an enemy or achieve some other practical effect of consequence.

Several practical kabbalists have been referred to as Masters of the Name. Perhaps the most interesting was Hayyim Falk, the Ba'al Shem of London. Also known as Dr Falcon, he arrived in London in 1742, apparently penniless, an escapee from Germany, where he had been accused of sorcery. Within a few years he had transformed himself into a wealthy Londoner, whose charitable fund is still being distributed today. Fantastic legends circulate around him. He could, apparently, fill his cellar with coal by uttering a prayer, redeem goods left with a pawnbroker simply by commanding them to return and on one occasion was said to have saved the Great Synagogue from fire by inscribing four Hebrew letters on its doorpost. He even established a so-called Kabbalistic laboratory on London Bridge, where he carried out alchemical experiments. Charlatan, magician or Kabbalist, Dr Falcon's life was hardly that of a typical Ba'al Shem.

Nor indeed was Israel ben Eliezer typical. His very title sets him apart. All the others were Masters of the Name. Israel was the only one referred to as the Master of the *Good* Name. The Ba'al Shem *Tov*, or alternatively just *The* Ba'al Shem.

The facts of his life are far from certain. Much scholarly work has been done in recent years to piece together his life history. Nevertheless, we cannot escape the fact that much of what is believed to be known about the *Besht* comes from hagiographies composed by his disciples, or from legends which, as the account of his nightly heavenly excursions shows, are frequently fanciful.

The *Besht* was born around 1700 and died in 1760. One of his younger contemporaries recalled that when he was a child his father had pointed the *Besht* out, saying he was a reincarnation of the Zohar's supposed author, Shimon bar Yoḥai.[3] Isaac Luria, the great Kabbalist of Safed, was also said to have borne Shimon bar Yoḥai's soul, yet he and the *Besht* were scarcely alike. Both men were eulogised for their Kabbalistic piety and both wrote very little, their teachings being transmitted by their followers. That is as far as the comparison goes. Unlike Luria, the *Besht* was neither an innovator nor theoretician of Kabbalah. He knew the works of Abulafia, took an interest in the traditions describing journeys to the heavenly Chariot and paid particular attention to the *Book of the Angel Raziel,* a medieval volume about Kabbalistic magic. Books of Lurianic Kabbalah do not seem to have been on his reading list.

Nevertheless, his followers regarded the *Besht* as the man who reinvigorated Kabbalah and made it relevant for their time. They believed he was possessed of mystical powers, a worker of miracles, a man as much at home in the higher worlds as he was on earth. His disciple and successor, Dov Baer of Mezeritch, eulogised his mystical potency. 'His holy disciples revelled in the dust of his feet, thirstily drinking in his words … With every gesture, movement and action he revealed the precious source of the glory of this wisdom ... the customs of the upper world and its unification with the lower world.'[4]

Despite such adulation it seems that the *Besht* came up with little in the way of insights into the workings of the *sefirotic* world. He developed no new theory of the cosmos, nor any explanation for the existence of evil. Neither does he seem to have gazed into people's eyes to discover which reincarnated soul was occupying their body. As for the question of how the infinite and transcendent God created physical matter, it does not seem to have bothered him at all.

The *Besht* did not inspire the Hasidic movement by dwelling on such questions. They were not the subjects that drew his disciples to him. His magnetism lay in the effect he had on ordinary people. He changed lives through his profound spirituality, charismatic presence, all-consuming sense of joy and sheer force of personality. His great innovation was to divest Kabbalah of its elitism, making it accessible to all. Simple faith, enthusiasm, song, dance and rapture were all a humble soul needed to experience mystical absorption within God.

There was no question of the *Besht*'s followers trying to match his depth of spirituality. That just was not possible. What counted above all else was their purity of thought, and the strength of their mystical faith. Over a hundred years after the *Besht* died, this idea was expressed in a homily. It was said that when the *Besht* was faced with a difficult problem to resolve he would go with his followers to a certain place in the woods. There they would light a fire, stacking the wood in a particular way so that the flames would ascend in a direct column. They would sing songs, dance and utter a prayer. As if of itself, the problem would be resolved.

After the *Besht* died, his disciple Dov Baer, 'the Preacher of Mezeritch', encountered a similar problem. He took his followers to the same place in the forest. But they had forgotten how to stack the wood to light the fire. So they sang the song, danced the dance and uttered the prayer. Once again, the problem was solved.

The same happened in the next generation. But now, as well as not knowing how to light the fire, they had forgotten the prayer. So they went to the woods, sang the song and danced the dance, and all became well.

The following generation didn't even recall the song to sing or the dance to be danced. But they went to the same place in the forest and everything worked out for the best.

As for today's generation, they don't even know where to go in the forest. All they can do is tell the story. And as long as they tell it with the right intention, all will be well.

The *Besht* revealed his mystical character in a letter to his brother-in-law Abraham Gershon, living in the Land of Israel. The *Besht* had entrusted the letter to his disciple, Jacob Joseph of Polonnoye, to deliver to Abraham. However, Jacob Joseph's plans to journey to the Holy Land fell through and the letter was never delivered. We only know about it because it was eventually published by Jacob Joseph in his book of sermons and biblical commentary.[5]

In the letter the *Besht* describes an 'ascent of the soul' that he undertook on the Jewish New Year in September 1746. He said that he saw wondrous things which were impossible to describe. But he did describe his encounter with a large number of deceased souls, many belonging to people he had known.

They were more than could be counted and they ran to and fro, from world to world, through the path provided by that column known to the adepts in the hidden science [i.e. the Kabbalah]. They were all in such a state of great rapture that the mouth would be worn out if it attempted to describe it, and the physical ear too indelicate to hear it. Many of the wicked repented of their sins and were pardoned, for it was a time of much grace. All of them entreated me, to my embarrassment, saying 'the Lord has given Your Honour great understanding to grasp these matters. Ascend together with us, therefore, so as to help and assist us.' Their rapture was so great that I resolved to ascend together with them.

The letter continues with the *Besht* describing the ascent he took together with the souls he had met. He entered the palace of the Messiah, where

> I witnessed great rejoicing and could not fathom the reason
> for it, so I thought that, God forbid, the rejoicing was over my
> own departure from the world. But I was afterwards informed
> that I was not yet to die, since they took great delight on high
> when, through their Torah, I perform unifications here below.

These unifications are Kabbalistic techniques intended to draw the individual soul towards its heavenly root and facilitate the process of reuniting the world with its Creator. They are performed by harnessing the spiritual forces contained in the letters of the Hebrew alphabet. Although this is a difficult Kabbalistic concept to grasp, the *Besht* was in no doubt that it was one his brother-in-law was familiar with:

> Whenever you offer your prayers and whenever you study, have
> the intention of unifying a divine name in every word and
> with every utterance of your lips. For there are worlds, souls
> and divinity in every letter. These ascend to become united one
> with the other and the letters are combined in order to form
> a word so that there is complete unification with the divine.
> Allow your soul to be embraced by them at each of the above
> stages. Thus all worlds become united and they ascend to that
> immeasurable rapture and the greatest delight is experienced.[6]

Unifications are deeply mystical concepts which most people have little interest in. They were not the reason he won the heart of the masses. Rather, it was the *Besht*'s emphasis on rapture, ecstasy and merrymaking that attracted idealistic young people and made Hasidism so popular. Such heightened emotions provided a psychological escape from the physical harshness of life in the Jewish villages of Poland. A century had passed since the Chmielnicki massacres, but life had got no easier. It wasn't just poverty. Pogroms, violent attacks on villages and communities, happened with alarming regularity.

Superstition had it that the orgies of killings, rapes and forced conversions were the work of Samael, the avenging angel. In his letter the *Besht* described an encounter he had on high with Samael. He challenged the angel, demanding to know why he permitted such horrors to take place on earth. In particular, he wanted to know why so many Jews who had been forced to convert to Christianity were subsequently killed by their captors. Samael replied that this was a deliberate policy on his part, carried out for the sake of heaven. His intention was to show others that since they were going to be killed anyway, there was no point in also relinquishing their faith. The *Besht* seemed satisfied with this strange reply, noting that shortly afterwards a pogrom had occurred in which many had been killed but none apostatised.

His encounter with Samael leads into the oddest feature of the *Besht*'s letter. Having concluded his account of the spiritual elevation he made in 1746, the *Besht* described a second ascent of the soul he made three years later. (That two events, so far apart in time, are recounted in the same letter was due to the difficulties of sending international mail, a problem the *Besht* bewailed at the beginning of his letter. Much of the letter summarised things he had written about in earlier dispatches, none of which his brother-in-law had received. Ironically, this letter was not delivered either.)

During this later ascent the *Besht* was forewarned about a horrific pogrom about to take place. He tried to prevent it by resorting to a tactic attributed to the biblical King David, in the book of Kings. David had sinned and as a result his nation was about to suffer divine retribution. He was given a choice: the retribution could come about through either war or a plague: it was up to him. In a famous response David declared, 'Let us fall into the hand of the Lord, and do not let me fall into the hand of man[7]'.

The *Besht* repeated David's entreaty, word for word. The pogrom was stayed but a catastrophic epidemic broke out. When the *Besht* tried to intercede on behalf of the sick the angels told him that his prayers were forbidden. He had made his choice, and, as an accuser, he could not now change roles and become a defender.

REFASHIONING SOCIETY

The *Besht* and his circle transformed Jewish life in Eastern Europe. Their innovations, transmitted through an expanding network of disciples and followers, provided a joyous, emotionally charged alternative to the legal formalism of traditional Judaism. They reshaped the role of Kabbalah in daily life, offering unlettered people a glimpse of the mysteries of creation. In place of the elitism of early Kabbalah, accessible only to those who had been schooled in its symbols, techniques and complexities, Hasidism was open to all.

For the *hasidim*, as the *Besht*'s followers are known, the world is infused with divine vitality; the divine presence is everywhere, within reach of everyone. The simple pleasures of dance and song, perhaps the earliest example of 'soul music', sensitised the Hasidic spirit to a constant devotion to God. As Louis Jacobs explains, when the Hasid confronts the divine he loses all sense of personal identity. The ego, humiliated by the grandeur of the divine essence, seeks to be absorbed into its all-embracing, infinite presence. This state of mind is known in Hasidic terminology as 'the renunciation of being'; it led some *hasidim* to try to eradicate all self-centred thought, even to the extent of avoiding the pronoun 'I'. The renunciation is best achieved at times of prayer, when God is in one's thoughts and the mind wholly absorbed.[8]

Some systems of Hasidic thought took the idea of fusing the self with the divine essence even further. They declared that there is no distinction between the material and spiritual worlds, that the whole of existence dwells within God.[9]

As with all Kabbalah, the mystical ideas that underlie Hasidism are not always easy to grasp, but that doesn't make it hard to be a Hasid. Far from it: one of the great innovations of the Hasidic revolution was to enable ordinary people, unversed in Kabbalistic theory and too busy staying alive to immerse themselves in study, to nevertheless reap the rewards of mystical contemplation. They did not know how to enter into ecstatic communion with God themselves. But they knew a man who could.

This was the most revolutionary aspect of the new Hasidic movement. Among the *Besht's* circle were several other spiritually charged figures, each of whom attracted talented followers of their own. Independent Hasidic circles developed, evolving in time into clans led by the spiritual heirs of the original leaders. Within a few decades the Hasidic world was comprised of dozens of dynasties, geographically dispersed, each with their own local customs, traditions and distinct identities.

The most innovative feature of the dynastic system was that the leader of each Hasidic grouping acted as a spiritual conduit for his followers. In traditional Judaism each individual has a direct, personal relationship with God. The innovation of Hasidism was that the *tsaddik*, as the dynastic head is known, acted as an intermediary between his *hasidim* and God. Nearly four centuries later the same system holds; the Hasidic world continues to thrive, composed of various dynastic sects with a *tsaddik* at the centre of each.[10]

The *tsaddik* is far more than just a remote, guru figure. He is a role model for how life should be lived. Dov Baer, known as the Preacher of Mezeritch, was a leading disciple of the *Besht*, succeeding him as leader of the early movement. One of his own followers is said to have declared that he did not visit his master to learn interpretations of the Torah, but to see how he tied his shoelaces. Dov Baer himself, when he first visited the *Besht*, is said, in one legend, to have been disappointed by all the talk of horses. Until, that is, the *Besht* summoned an angel and Dov Baer realised that the frivolous chatter had been a mask for the profound meditations his master was performing on a deeper level.

As an oracle, the *tsaddik* is infallible. His followers are just as likely to turn to him for advice on personal or work-related matters as they are to seek an audience with him to receive his blessing. In extreme cases he is even believed to have power over death, for his prayers can overturn a heavenly decree. When he has finished eating at one of the large communal meals over which he presides, the *Hasidim* sitting closest to him will make a grab for the crumbs left on his plate, to benefit from the spiritual bounty they contain.

The *tsaddik* can be a fount of blessing even after death. Rav Naḥman of Bratslav, one of the most charismatic and mystically inspired of all *tsaddikim*, is still venerated two centuries after his demise. Each Jewish New Year, tens of thousands of his Bratslav *hasidim* from all over the world make the pilgrimage to the site of his grave in the Ukrainian town of Uman.

The Kabbalistic idea underpinning that of the *tsaddik* is that the physical world is suffused with sparks of divinity. Most of us do not possess sufficient spiritual insight to perceive these sparks. Only a small number of highly sensitive, spiritually enriched people are endowed with the gifts to sense the divine aspect of reality. Only such a person can be a true *tsaddik*. It falls to them to channel the spiritual energy they receive so that it flows through them to their followers.

It is no easy matter to become a *tsaddik*. There are only three possible ways. The most common route is through direct descent, with the son inheriting his father's spirituality. Another way is the rebirth of someone who had been a *tsaddik* in an earlier life, sent back into the world to continue what he had already started. Such a person is likely to manifest himself as the highest-flying student of the *tsaddik* he will eventually succeed. Finally, in very fortunate circumstances, succession can take place when a newborn child is given the current *tsaddik*'s name. Whichever the route, the *tsaddik* will only succeed to his position as head of dynasty on the death of his predecessor. At least, that is the theory. On several occasions in contemporary Hasidic communities a leader who has been passed over for succession has set himself up as the *tsaddik* of a breakaway group, sometimes even establishing a new dynasty.[11]

The Hasidic way of life is grounded in Kabbalah, yet it does not follow the ways of the earlier kabbalists. For them, the divine world was remote and mystical speculation was esoteric. They were interested in profound ideas: *sefirot*, the nature of evil, Primordial Man, the transmigration of souls, unification of the cosmos with the divine and so much more that lies beyond the scope of this book. Hasidism, which sees God as accessible and available to ordinary people, is conscious of those matters but less exercised by them. It is more interested in what God and people have in common, particularly words, letters and language. The divine and human aspects of speech stand at opposite ends of the causeway that connects the hidden and manifest worlds.

This does not, however, mean, as has sometimes been argued, that Hasidism presents a less intellectual approach to Kabbalah. The best-known Hasidic book, Shneur Zalman of Liadi's *Tanya*, is a spiritual guide based on Kabbalistic principles. Aimed at a Hasid of average piety, the book can only be understood fully by those with a good Kabbalistic education. An 'average' Hasid, at least in Shneur Zalman's Ḥabad movement, was no ignoramus.

OPPOSITION

Some scholars maintain that the rapid growth of Hasidism in the eighteenth and nineteenth centuries was due to the failure of the popular but doomed Sabbatean cult.[12] On this view Hasidism was a revivalist movement that aimed to retain the elements of Kabbalah which appealed to the masses, while neutralising the dangerous messianic mania which drove the Sabbatean revolution and led to its spectacular and demoralising collapse.

Whether or not this is so, it is quite likely that the opposition which dogged Hasidism during its early years was due to a fear that this was another destructive populist cult in the making. More than a century had elapsed since Shabbetai's death but the memory of his heresy was still raw. For many observers, Hasidism's popular appeal echoed Shabbetai Tzvi's seduction of the masses. Devout kabbalists resented the popularisation of their arcane science. Talmud traditionalists were outraged by what they considered to be the lax religious innovations of the new movement. The fences so painstakingly erected over previous centuries around religious law were now proving vulnerable to breach.

Those who resisted Hasidism became known, unimaginatively, as the Opponents. They fought the *hasidim* on three fronts: political, social and religious. When vibrant Hasidic communities began to vie for control of communal institutions and funds, challenging the established leadership and confronting local rabbis, the Opponents retaliated by issuing bans of excommunication. When that failed, they called in the secular authorities. Shneur Zalman of Liadi, a disciple of the Preacher of Mezeritch and the leading Hasidic Kabbalist of his generation, was twice imprisoned because of denunciations laid against him by his enemies.

Skirmishes were fought over religious law. The most divisive was a dispute over the specially sharpened knife introduced by the *hasidim* for the kosher slaughter of animals. Superficially the argument was about the manufacture of a knife, but in reality the dispute went far deeper. The *hasidim* argued that the instrument which had been traditionally used was too blunt and heavy to be efficient. The Opponents maintained that the new, thin, ultra-sharp knife might snap, injuring the animal and rendering the meat ritually ineligible. In truth the dispute had very little to do with religion, and much to do with politics and economics. Politically, it was a contrived dispute, to establish who had the right to license butchers and therefore where legal authority in the community lay. Economically the argument was more personal, with the new Hasidic butchers setting up in competition against existing traders, threatening their livelihoods.

Of all the quarrels between the *hasidim* and the Opponents, the most famous is rooted in Kabbalah. It was a dispute shaped by the towering intellect of Elijah, the outstanding rabbinic scholar of Vilna, now Vilnius, in Lithuania. There was nothing political or economical about Elijah's opposition to Hasidism. His condemnation of them was wholly concerned with religion. It stemmed from his encyclopaedic knowledge of the Talmud, and his profound grasp of the minutiae of Kabbalah.

Known as the *Gaon*, or Excellency, of Vilna, Elijah was a reclusive figure. Immersed in his books, snatching half an hour's sleep here and there, he never slept more than two hours in a night, his feet sunk into a bowl of cold water to keep him awake. He is said to have written more words on the Kabbalah than all his Hasidic contemporaries put together, including possibly 30 different commentaries on the Zohar.[13]

Acclaimed as the spiritual leader of Vilna's large Jewish population, which comprised a majority within the town, Elijah rarely involved himself in the community's day-to-day issues. He made an exception of this when it came to fighting the *hasidim*.

The city of Vilna had never been a bastion of Hasidism. When, in the early 1770s, a Hasidic leader began running a prayer group in the town, he and Shneur Zalman of Liadi paid a courtesy visit to Elijah, to calm any fears he may have had. Elijah slammed the door in their face.

Backed by Vilna's communal leaders, Elijah circulated a pamphlet denouncing Hasidism. Shneur Zalman and his colleagues were 'heretics, deserving the punishment of death'. He instructed his followers to 'catch them, run after them, minimize their influence and banish them with full vigour'.[14]

The tactic backfired. Elijah's pamphlet was publicly burned, and he received death threats. His supporters retaliated by beating and excommunicating local supporters of the *hasidim*. A local rabbi who accused Elijah of lying was hauled before the courts and forced to apologise. Another of Elijah's abusers was imprisoned for a week before being clamped in the stocks.

Hasidism remained uncowed. In 1781, Jacob Joseph of Polonnoye published his book of sermons and commentaries, including the *Besht*'s letter that had never been delivered to his brother-in-law. It was a work that contributed hugely to the spread of Hasidism, by introducing its teachings to those who knew nothing of it. The book's immense popularity stimulated Elijah to renew his attack, but with a change of emphasis. Instead of condemning Hasidic teachings he focused on the social disruption spread by the growing movement, and the recurring fear that it was a reincarnation of Sabbatean licentiousness.

Unlike those who succeeded him, Elijah held back from involving the state authorities in his assault on Hasidism. He was already dead when Shneur Zalman of Liadi was thrown into gaol. Shneur Zalman, perhaps regretting the demise of an old opponent, stated that he knew such a thing could never have happened during Elijah's lifetime. No matter how egregious he believed the offence to be, Elijah would never, on principle, said Shneur Zalman, bring the matter to the attention of the government.

Elijah's ideological disagreement with the *hasidim* was rooted in Kabbalah. It was a profoundly theological argument, which might never have blown up as it did if it had been merely an academic dispute, and not one which resulted in the social and political upheaval of Hasidism.

The disagreement hinged on the concept of *tzimtzum,* the theory that in order to create the world God had to withdraw into himself, leaving a void in which creation could take place. Shneur Zalman of Liadi, who articulated the fullest but most radical Hasidic position, maintained that, rather than withdrawing from the world, God had merely screened himself from human perception. In other words, God is still present in the whole of creation, dwelling within all. Taken to its extreme, this view comes dangerously close to equating God with nature, a suggestion that was rank heresy in Elijah's mind. Elijah's more conventional understanding of *tzimtzum* was that God had withdrawn into himself, as if occupying a separate space, wholly beyond this world, so that he could only be perceived through his actions.

Some commentators interpret the dispute between Elijah and the *hasidim* as one which centres on what it means to perceive God. The Hasidic heresy in Elijah's eyes was the belief that all is in God and that, through annihilation of the ego, one must renounce any sense of having an existence outside of him. This contrasted with Elijah's own view that humans must acknowledge their own limits and not seek to transgress the impermeable boundaries between themselves and God.[15] These are arcane arguments, but they hinge on the different Kabbalistic outlooks of Elijah of Vilna on the one hand and Hasidism on the other, particularly as expressed in the thought of Shneur Zalman of Liadi.

The nineteenth century was Hasidism's golden age, giving Kabbalah a new lease of life. But Hasidism was far from being Kabbalah's only nineteenth-century incarnation. In Western Europe, a world away from the centres of Hasidic life, the Kabbalah experience felt very different. The occult was enjoying something of a revival. Once again, Kabbalah stood at its heart.

The Occult Revival

THE MISUNDERSTOOD TAROT

Unlike its Christian offshoot, Jewish Kabbalah did not find itself drawn into the world of the occult. Very few Jewish kabbalists took an interest in in the occult sciences, or in its practitioners. The same held true in reverse. Hayyim Vital did tinker with alchemy before he settled in Safed, but gave it up as soon as he took an interest in Kabbalah. For all we know, Judah Loew and John Dee might have passed each other on a bridge in Rudolf II's Prague, or even stood alongside each other at a market stall. If they did, neither man mentioned it. They may not even have known who the other was; they certainly paid no attention to each other's work. Only the strange Dr Falcon, operating his alchemical-Kabbalistic laboratory on London Bridge, spanned the mystical divide.

Kabbalah and the occult: two esoteric streams, diverging from the same source, each peering beyond and studiously ignoring the existence of the other. It was not until the nineteenth century that the two systems found some sort of rapprochement.

Adolphe Franck, the first thinker to approach Kabbalah from an academic perspective, also took an active interest in the occult. He did not believe in it, but he did welcome the revived interest it enjoyed during his lifetime; he said that it represented the first steps towards natural science and acted as an antidote to the pessimism and atheism which he felt dogged his world.[1] Frank kept up to date

with the various occult journals that circulated in France. Noting
that each of them displayed an awareness of Kabbalah, he made
a point of insisting that he did not undertake 'to guarantee the
correctness with which it is expounded'.[2]

Born into a French Jewish family in 1809, Franck was on track
to become a rabbi before he was distracted by philosophy. In
1843 he wrote a treatise outlining the philosophy and principles
of Kabbalah, which he believed occupied a unique position
in the history of human thought. His book, *The Kabbalah or
The Religious Philosophy of the Hebrews*, which Moshe Idel has
described as contributing 'more to the knowledge of Kabbalah in
modern Europe' than any other work until the twentieth-century
researches of Gershom Scholem, was translated into German,
Hebrew and English.[3]

For Franck, the only things that mattered about Kabbalah were
its philosophy, creeds and ideas. He was disparaging about its
'fantastic procedures', such as the permutation of letters and words
to find hidden meanings in the biblical text. These were just its
'gross envelope' surrounding 'the profound and original ideas, the
bold creeds ... and the striking views' which Kabbalah has instilled
'into the foundations of every religion and morality'.[4]

Despite Kabbalah's great antiquity, its only books that he
considered to be of value were the *Sefer Yetsirah* and the Zohar.
He regarded the Safed kabbalists with disdain, insisting that both
Cordovero and Luria lacked the gift of originality. He was less
harsh on Cordovero than he was on Luria, accepting that at least
Cordovero kept close to the meaning of the original Kabbalistic
writings. Unlike Luria, who, Franck said, almost always deviated
from the true text in order to give free rein to his reveries. Yet these
reveries were nothing more than 'dreams of a diseased mind'.[5]

Franck believed that the origins of Kabbalah lay in a universal,
primordial religious consciousness. Although it had matured in a
Jewish environment, he maintained that its roots lay elsewhere,
possibly in Persian Zoroastrianism.

This conception of a 'universal Kabbalah' originating in a
non-Jewish environment was shared by another Frenchman of

Franck's generation. The two men had much in common. But whereas Franck was only interested in the philosophical aspects of Kabbalah, and had no time for its techniques and symbolism, his contemporary, who went under the name of Eliphas Lévi, took a diametrically opposed view.

Eliphas Lévi's birth name was Alphonse-Louis Constant. He was born in 1810 into a poor Parisian family. Like Adolphe Franck he studied for the ministry, in his case the Catholic Church. But he fell in love with one of his students, and although the relationship did not develop he realised he could never live the celibate life of a priest. Abandoning the Church, he began teaching for a living and was drawn into politically radical circles, where he met the feminist socialist activist Flora Tristan. It was as a result of her influence that in 1843 he published his first book, *The Bible of Liberty*, a radical socialist interpretation of Scripture. The French authorities seized almost the entire print run on the day of the book's publication and Constant, as he was still known, was sentenced to eight months in prison.

Over the next few years Constant wrote further incendiary publications and was sentenced to more spells in prison. His life could easily have continued along this track had he not come into contact with Jósef Höené-Wronski, a Polish visionary who, like Constant himself, believed in the imminent return of the Holy Spirit. His encounters with Wronski set Constant off on the spiritual journey which would transform him into Eliphas Lévi, a Hebraised version of the name Alphonse-Louis. It was a journey for which he endowed himself with the title Professor of High Magic, and which established his reputation as the most significant Kabbalist-occultist of the nineteenth century.

Unfortunately, it is hard to obtain a clear, definitive understanding of Lévi's mystical beliefs. As Christopher McIntosh describes it, his work was incoherent, his writings rambled, he wasn't a great scholar and he tended to get things wrong.[6] Nevertheless, he was trenchant when it mattered. 'All true dogmatic religions stem from the Kabbalah ...' he wrote in 1896, '... all that is scientific and grandiose in the religious dreams of all illuminated ones ... is taken from the Kabbalah.'[7]

During the course of 1890 and 1891 the occult journal *Initiation* published ten letters written by Lévi to one of his pupils, a Monsieur Montaut. Collected together under the title *Elements of Kabbalah* and intended as a ten-part course, these letters are probably the best, perhaps the only, way of understanding his somewhat chaotic interpretation of Kabbalah.[8]

In his first lesson Lévi states that only three occult sciences are based in reality rather than dreams. They are Kabbalah, Magic and Hermeticism. Magic, according to Lévi, is the knowledge of the hidden forces of nature, while Hermeticism is the science of nature, the search for the principle of life, encoded within the Egyptian hieroglyphics and other ancient symbols. Kabbalah can be thought of as the 'mathematics of human thought. It is the algebra of faith … It gives to ideas the clarity and rigorous exactitude of numbers; its results, for the mind, are infallibility … and for the heart, profound peace.'[9]

He continues by explaining, in highly convoluted language, that Kabbalah's mathematical properties are contained in 32 paths, made up of the 22 letters of the Hebrew language and the ten numerals. The 32 paths are an ancient Kabbalistic metaphor first found in the *Sefer Yetsirah* and based on the first chapter of Genesis. Genesis states that God created the world through ten Hebrew statements, each beginning with the words 'Let there be …'. He spoke in Hebrew, a language with a 22 letter alphabet. Ten statements and 22 letters, making 32 paths altogether.

Sefer Yetsirah lists the powers that each letter has in the created world. The tenth letter, for example, rules over the constellation Virgo, the Hebrew month of Elul, the left hand, and the aspect of Action. Other letters rule over planets, emotions or physical elements. Lévi, in his *Elements of Kabbalah*, draws on this system but attaches 'ideas' instead of physical elements to the letters and numerals. He maintained that each 'idea' flowed logically from the preceding one.

The example he uses is based on the first seven Hebrew letters, which he associates, for reasons unstated, with Father, Mother, Nature, Authority, Religion, Liberty and Ownership, in that order.

The way that they flow together is that 'Man is the son of woman, but woman comes out of man as number comes out of unity. Woman clarifies nature, nature reveals authority, which creates religion, the basis for liberty, which makes man master of himself.'

The next stage in Lévi's ten-lesson course on the Kabbalah is even more perplexing. He digresses into a discussion of Tarot cards, which he claims were linked to Kabbalah and of a similar antiquity.

As Lévi saw it, the cards in a Tarot deck represent the Kabbalah's 32 paths. There are 22 trump cards, corresponding to the 22 letters of the Hebrew alphabet and there are four suits each containing ten numbered cards, similar to those in a conventional deck of playing cards. The deck of Tarot cards, with its arrangement of 22 and ten, does indeed seem to bear a schematic resemblance to the 32 paths designated by *Sefer Yetsirah*, which lie at the heart of Eliphas Lévi's Kabbalistic system. This might imply that Tarot has profound, ancient mystical properties which could be used, as Lévi explains in his magnum opus *Dogma and Ritual of High Magic*, for magical and divinatory purposes.

The connection between Kabbalah and Tarot appears very neat. Unfortunately, any relationship is probably no more than fortuitous. The current scholarly view on the history of Tarot cards is that they have no connection whatsoever either with the ancient world, or with the occult, or indeed with the Kabbalah. A letter dated 1449 states that they were invented by Duke Visconti of Milan and that the first deck was painted by the artist Michelino da Besozzo. The cards had been a gift for Isabella, Queen of Anjou, and were used for playing games. The earliest extant set of Tarot cards comes from northern Italy and was made in the first half of the fifteenth century.[10]

An early set of Tarot cards was painted for another Duke of Milan, Francesco Sforza. Sforza was an ally of Cosimo de' Medici, the ruler of Florence whose interest in the Hermetic mysteries contributed to the birth of the Renaissance and made possible Christian interpretation of the Kabbalah. Kabbalah had been known in Italian Jewish circles since the time of Abraham Abulafia over 200 years earlier, and there was well-established intellectual contact between small numbers of Christians and Jews in Italy. It is possible that Kabbalistic concepts were already beginning to be discussed among the Italian intelligentsia when the first Tarot cards were devised, even before Pico della Mirandola put Kabbalah onto the Renaissance map at the beginning of the sixteenth century. Even so, it is unlikely that the earliest packs, of which only remnants have survived, contained 22 trumps, thus undermining the suggestion that the Tarot was modelled on *Sefer Yetsirah*'s pattern. And there is certainly no evidence that the Tarot was an ancient hieroglyphic system, as Eliphas Lévi claimed. He remains the only source for the belief, which still persists today, that the Tarot is an ancient system of divination.

IMAGINED HISTORIES

Various reasons have been suggested to explain the revival of the occult in the nineteenth century. Some say it was a reaction against advances in the natural sciences, with their emphasis on reason rather than supernatural powers. Others hold it may have been the opposite, that occult was actually a quest for a rational explanation of those matters which the science of the day had so far failed to penetrate. It may also have been driven by archaeological finds in Egypt, sparking an interest in the mysterious hieroglyphics, so obscure that they could only be arcane. Equally, it could simply have been the result of publicity given to a few charismatic magi, spiritualists and theosophists, of whom Eliphas Lévi had been just one.

Whatever the reasons, the occult revival was real, even if much of its subject matter was not. Its disciplines continued to be blended one with the other, even more than in the past, creating new occult schools and esoteric streams. In New York, the mysterious and controversial Madame Blavatsky founded the Theosophical Society, in the wake of a lecture she gave in 1875 on the 'Kabbalah of the Egyptians'. Blavatsky saw Kabbalah as a key to the ancient mysteries, but insisted that, since the time of Moses de León, Kabbalah in both its Jewish and Christian forms was merely a remnant of an earlier, deeper but now lost Chaldean mysticism. The surviving remnant was all that the Syrians, Chaldeans and ex-gnostics of the thirteenth century wanted to reveal. It was, she wrote, hardly worth studying.[11]

The Hermetic Order of the Golden Dawn, a British fraternity founded in 1887 whose founders forged documents to make it appear far older, drew on many occult disciplines for its rituals. One of its three founding members, or 'Chiefs', was Samuel Liddell MacGregor Mathers. We met him earlier: he was the man who translated Knorr von Rosenroth's *Kabbala Denudata*, enabling an English readership to study extracts from the Zohar for the first time.

The Order of the Golden Dawn defined itself as a 'Hermetic Society whose members are taught the principles of Occult Science and the Magic of Hermes'. Its doctrines were based on the mysteries supposed to have been transmitted by Christian Rosenkreutz, which were themselves a 'new development of the older wisdom of the Qabalistic Rabbis and of that very ancient secret knowledge of the magic of the Egyptians into which Moses had been initiated ... for the Hebrews were taught at one time by the Egyptians and later by the Chaldees of Babylon'.[12] The Order was rigidly structured. New initiates into the society advanced up a hierarchical system of grades and ranks, supposedly based on the Kabbalistic Tree of Life. The third and highest grade is that of the Order's Great Rulers, who 'represent the Supernal Triad of the Sephiroth and are shrouded and unapproachable to the profane and to all others but the Chiefs of the Adepts'.

Within a few years of its founding, Golden Dawn fell victim to factional infighting, scandal and criminal trials. Laura Horos, who passed herself off as one of the fictitious Rosicrucians mentioned in the documents forged by the movement's founders, was exposed as an imposter. She and her husband Theo were tried for rape and fraud, and gaoled. The Order never recovered. Today several variants of the Hermetic Order of the Golden Dawn can be found on the internet. Any connection they may have with the original order is uncertain.

SGT. PEPPER'S FAVOURITE KABBALIST

The Hermetic Order of the Golden Dawn's most famous member was the Irish poet W. B. Yeats. Its most notorious, who was only a member for two years before failing in an attempt to seize control, was Aleister Crowley. At his death in 1947 Crowley was condemned in the popular press as, at the very least, an egotistical exhibitionist, black magician, sexual orgiast, drug-soaked derelict and sadistic, satanical anarchist.

Crowley's star began to shine more brightly after his death. In the late 1960s the priests of psychedelia and evangelists of the counter-culture adopted him as an oracle. The Beatles put him on the cover of *Sgt. Pepper*, David Bowie sang about him in his seminal album *Hunky Dory* and the vinyl of *Led Zeppelin III* was overprinted with his aphorism 'Do What Thou Wilt'. A generation later he became the subject of university tutorials, academic research and Ph.D. theses. Much of his literary oeuvre was republished for a contemporary audience, together with commentaries. In 2002 he came 73rd in a BBC poll of the 100 Greatest Britons.[13] In death he enjoys a status of cult figure never afforded to him in life.

Crowley's vision was more ambitious than that of the occultists who preceded him. Like them he incorporated diverse occult sciences into a unified system, but the range of disciplines he drew upon was wider and his end goal was greater than merely explaining and manipulating the supernatural and paranormal. He propounded a new religion, which he named Thelema. It was a religion based on individual liberty unconstrained by ancient moral codes, whose chief principle was that every individual has a higher purpose or essence, which remains hidden from most people. Everyone has their own True Will, their Higher Guardian Angel. The sole Law of Thelema was the phrase which had captivated Led Zeppelin just as flower power's bloom was fading: Do What Thou Wilt.[14]

Like Eliphas Lévi, Crowley regarded the Kabbalah as the key to mystical understanding. Lévi had written of Kabbalah as the mathematics of human thought and the algebra of faith. Crowley, in his typically verbose and convoluted prose described it as:

> a science that, properly understood by the initiated mind, is as absolute as mathematics, more self-supporting than philosophy, a science of the spirit itself, whose teacher is God, whose method is simple as the divine Light, and subtle as the divine Fire, whose results are limpid as the divine Water, all-embracing as the divine Air, and solid as the divine Earth ...[15]

Despite the exuberant language, there was nothing original about Crowley's understanding of Kabbalah. He drew connections linking what he called the data of mysticism, including Kabbalistic concepts, Hebrew letters, names of angels and of God, with a wide range of natural, occult and religious systems. These embraced the attributes of Tarot, colours, planetary elements, Egyptian, Scandinavian, Roman and Greek gods, Hindu deities, Buddhist meditations, plants, animals, precious stones, magical words, weapons, perfumes, drugs, supernatural powers, concepts from Tao, geometrical figures and so much more.

Crowley's tables of correspondences display a cornucopia of connections, but the relation between the basic Kabbalistic concepts and this expansive testimony to humanity's mystical and religious imagination appears spurious at best, if not wholly random. Does the fifth letter in the Hebrew alphabet (pronounced H and written ה) really correspond to the Egyptian god Men Thu, the Bloody Corpse of Buddhist Meditation, the Greek goddess Athena, a Ram, an Owl and a Tiger Lily? Maybe it does.

There is no doubt that Crowley knew the principles of traditional Kabbalah. Unfortunately, no matter how useful his Kabbalistic knowledge may have been to the development of the occult as it entered the twentieth century, it did nothing to enhance the study of Kabbalah itself. For that, Kabbalah had to go back to its own Hebrew roots, and to the man whose scholarship paved the way for the contemporary, twenty-first-century popularisation of Kabbalah as a system for growth and personal development. His name was Yehuda Ashlag. He, like so many kabbalists before him, had to advance his studies in an intellectual environment that opposed Kabbalah and considered it of little worth.

Towards Modernity

AN EMBARRASSMENT

Not everybody in the nineteenth century considered Kabbalah to be an ancient mystical philosophy deriving from the hoary wisdom of the vanished civilisations of Egypt, Babylon or Persia and preserved within the Jewish tradition. Some, particularly rationally minded Jews schooled in the Western European, scientific method, saw Kabbalah as a primitive, embarrassing superstition that sullied the grandeur and dignity of Judaism. Heinrich Graetz, the great pioneering historian of the Jews, declared that Kabbalah 'rests upon nothing else than delusion'; it is 'a caricature that distorts the Jewish and philosophical ideas in an equal degree'.[1] He was no more generous about the work of the sixteenth-century Safed kabbalists: 'When Europe beheld the dawn of a new day, the darkness of medievalism settled upon Jewry.'[2]

Less vituperatively, Simeon Singer, the English translator of the Jewish Prayer Book, simply omitted prayers of Kabbalistic origins. Even Adolf Jellinek, who had translated Adolphe Franck's *The Kabbalah or The Religious Philosophy of the Hebrews* into German, and was not unsympathetic to Kabbalah as a subject of scholarly interest, declared that as a religious approach it was utterly alien to the Judaism of his day.[3]

It was not alien, however, to the *hasidim* of Eastern Europe, for whom Kabbalah was central to their religious outlook. Nor was it looked upon disparagingly by the Jews of North Africa and the Middle East, where kabbalists had been venerated as holy men, and their prayers, amulets and blessings had been an indispensable part of Jewish life ever since Kabbalah had been forced out of Spain at the end of the fifteenth century.

Kabbalah had remained strong in the Holy Land, too, where it had been studied continually since the days of the Safed kabbalists. But now it looked as if even there it might become vulnerable to the same criticisms as those levelled at it by Western European intellectuals. During the 1920s in Jerusalem, Ariel Bension began work on a book in which he portrayed his father, who had died in 1897, as the last of the kabbalists. The book, which he never finished, was intended to be a history of Jerusalem's renowned Kabbalist academy, *Bet El*. The academy was, according to Bension, in a state of terminal spiritual decline matching that of Kabbalah itself, its building derelict and decaying.[4] Other accounts written at the time painted a similar picture of the last hours of Kabbalah.

Accounts of the college's demise, and of the waning of Kabbalah in Jerusalem, were grossly exaggerated. The college had indeed passed beyond its heyday, but it was still actively functioning. New Kabbalistic colleges were also being established in the city. The perceived decline of Kabbalah in Jerusalem resonated with the then fashionable notion of Kabbalah as a medieval superstition unfit for the modern age. But the decline was more imagined than real.

The occult movements of the nineteenth century had accelerated a subtle shift in Kabbalah that had been gathering pace ever since Isaac Luria first directed its focus towards the human soul. Kabbalists were growing more interested in human processes on earth, and less concerned with divine activity in heaven. Accentuating the psychological dimension of Kabbalah was a trend that would continue into the twenty-first century, and perhaps beyond. It was psychology together with a sprinkling of politics that rescued Kabbalah in Jerusalem from its threatened decline.

A SPLENDID TYPE OF MYSTIC

Abraham Isaac Kook was no ordinary Kabbalist. Indeed, Kabbalah was only one of his many fields of interest. As chief rabbi of the Jewish community in Palestine under the British Mandate, Kook's reputation rests as much on his communal leadership, his ethical and spiritual outlook, breadth of vision and intellectual acuity as it did on his Kabbalistic insight. 'Vision and poetry, thought and speculation, theological reflection and observations – all would pour forth from him in an unending stream.'⁵

Kook's 'unending stream' of thought did not transcribe easily onto the printed page. Much of his writing, particularly his mystical work, consists of brief passages of inspiration, jotted down as thoughts occurred to him and not necessarily arranged in a systematic format. His knowledge of the vast body of Kabbalistic literature was immense, yet his approach was highly original. Gershom Scholem described it as 'the last example of productive Kabbalistic thought of which I know'. Kook, for Scholem, was 'a splendid type of Jewish mystic'.⁶

Kook's Kabbalistic thought is based on his premise that we all only perceive particular aspects of reality, and are blind to everything else. We see the world in a fragmented and chaotic way, and do not appreciate that beneath the 'garments' of reality lies a true, unified essence. We reject those aspects of existence that we cannot see, and react negatively to them when we do encounter them. The result is conflict. Mysticism, in contrast, enhances our perception of reality. By its nature it 'penetrates to the depth of all thought, all feelings, all tendencies, all aspirations and all worlds'.⁷

Kook wasn't the first to explain Kabbalah in terms of human perception; that distinction belongs to the eighteenth-century Hasidic thinker Baruch of Kosov.⁸ But the psychological dimension of Kabbalah became increasingly important as the twentieth century wore on, and Kook is the thinker to whom this trend can be ascribed. Kook reinterpreted Isaac Luria's dramatic metaphor of the catastrophic breaking of the divine vessels at the moment of creation. In Luria's depiction this resulted in divine light being trapped in a material world, beneath the fragments of the broken vessels. Kook saw it the other way round. The breaking takes place, not in heaven, but within people. Humanity cannot absorb the great divine love bestowed upon them, without breaking and longing to be healed by returning to God. The structure of the metaphor is similar to Luria's, but for Kook the action takes places here on earth, not in the cosmic realms.[9] Kabbalah becomes a process of healing the human personality, rather than the cosmos. From here it was only a short step to the modern-day idea of Kabbalah as a tool for self-improvement and personal development.

Unlike some religious thinkers, Kook had a positive attitude to science. He admired Darwin's theory of evolution, and not just because it made scientific sense. The concept of evolution, describing a process of constant improvement in nature, sits in perfect harmony with the Kabbalistic ideal of elevating the divine sparks to bring repair to the world.

Nevertheless, despite all his originality, Kook is rarely considered first and foremost as a Kabbalist. He is remembered for his religious, political and social outlook. In this sense he was very different from his younger contemporary, Yehuda Ashlag, a Kabbalist through and through, who ushered Kabbalah into the second half of the twentieth century, towards its encounter with the cultural radicalism that would become known as the New Age. There it would become embroiled in a whole new set of disputes and controversies.

ALTRUISTIC COMMUNISM

Yehuda Ashlag always refused to name the person who had taught him Kabbalah as a young man in Warsaw. This obligation, presumably imposed upon him by the anonymous teacher, may have been influential in shaping his own attitude once he moved to Jerusalem in the 1920s. Reacting against the clandestine environment in which he had been taught, Ashlag determined to take Kabbalah out of its closed, esoteric world where it could only be understood by those immersed in its arcana. He resolved to explain it in such a way that even those who were not schooled in its mysteries could understand and benefit from it.

Ashlag was the most influential Kabbalist thinker of the twentieth century. Like Kook, he explained Kabbalah in psychological terms, but he added a political dimension. In Ashlag's interpretation of Kabbalah, God is characterised by the desire to give, bestowing divine favour upon a cosmos defined by the desire to receive. The process of bestowing and receiving culminated in the creation of human beings, who are endowed with egos that only wish to receive.

The human desire to receive is profoundly inferior to the divine desire to give. But as people we have the opportunity to draw closer to spiritual perfection by exercising our ability to transform ourselves, eradicating our wishes to receive, and drawing closer to the divine quality of wishing to bestow.

As we become givers rather than takers, we are able to perfect our relationships with people and with God and we improve the communities in which we live. This leads to a perfected society in which all are able to give according to their abilities and to receive according to their needs. Ashlag called this 'altruistic communism', a pure form of socialism based on Kabbalah rather than on Marx.

As part of his mission to make Kabbalah accessible to a wide audience, Ashlag translated the Zohar from the complex and idiosyncratic dialect of Aramaic in which it had been written into a far more accessible, contemporary Hebrew. He published the translation in a new edition of the Zohar, which he supplemented with a new commentary. Complaining that all previous commentators on the Zohar had ignored its many difficult passages, and that the interpretations of the few passages they did address were often less intelligible than the original text, he strove to make his commentary fully comprehensive, straightforward enough to be easily followed by the average reader. Known as *HaSulam*, or The Ladder, it has become the most widely used of all Zohar commentaries. As yet, only extracts have been published in English.

THE UNCONSCIOUS ARCHETYPE

It is unlikely that the Swiss psychoanalyst C. G. Jung, the man who drew the most explicit connection between Kabbalah and psychology, had ever heard of either Abraham Isaac Kook or Yehuda Ashlag, even though they had preceded him in showing how Kabbalah could be used to explain aspects of the human mind. That Jung was unaware of it is no surprise: for all his interest in Kabbalah he knew very little about the vast majority of kabbalists, whether ancient or modern. His knowledge of Kabbalah came almost exclusively from Knorr von Rosenroth's *Kabbala Denudata*. And it appears that he was almost at the end of his career when he began to realise how closely Kabbalah mirrored the psychological theories he had already developed.

In 1944, when he was 68 years old, his reputation as an outstanding theorist of psychotherapy long established, Jung broke his foot. The accident was swiftly followed by a heart attack, as a result of which Jung spent several feverish months slipping in and out of consciousness. He experienced hallucinations. In his memoirs he described one particularly vivid vision:

> Everything around me seemed enchanted. At this hour of the night the nurse brought me some food she had warmed for only then was I able to take any, and I ate with appetite. For a time it seemed to me that she was an old Jewish woman, much older than she actually was, and that she was preparing ritual kosher dishes for me. When I looked at her, she seemed to have a blue halo around her head. I myself was, so it seemed, in the *Pardes Rimonim*, the garden of pomegranates, and the wedding of Tiferet with Malchut was taking place. Or else I was Rabbi Shimon bar Yoḥai, whose wedding in the afterlife was being celebrated. It was the mystic marriage as it appears in the Cabbalistic tradition. I cannot tell you how wonderful it was. I could only think continually, 'Now this is the garden of pomegranates! Now this is the marriage of Malchut with Tiferet!' I do not know exactly what part I played in it.

At bottom of it was I myself: I was the marriage. And my
beatitude was that of a blissful wedding.[10]

The pomegranate garden in which Jung found himself is the title of
Moses Cordovero's most famous book, his systematic exposition of
the Kabbalah.[11] The wedding of the two *sefirot*, *Malchut* and *Tiferet*,
is the idealised state at the end of time when cosmic harmony will
be restored. It is quite clear from Jung's account that by 1944 he
was familiar with some basic concepts of the Kabbalah, although
he may not have been aware that identifying himself with Shimon
bar Yoḥai was hardly original, Moses Suriel and Isaac Luria, among
others, having long preceded him in this.

In his psychological writings Jung frequently referred to
alchemy, and even more often to the ancient system of religious
thought known as Gnosticism, which Gershom Scholem argued
was closely connected to Kabbalah. He considered these disciplines
to contain important metaphors about the human psyche. Jung
had known Scholem and his work since the 1930s and must have
long been aware of the putative connection between Kabbalah and
Gnosticism. Yet he remained silent about any connection between
Kabbalah and his theories until 1954, ten years after he experienced
his vision in the pomegranate garden.[12]

It is a silence which has puzzled many. Perhaps it was due to his
flirtation with fascism during the pre-war period, a flirtation which
he later deeply regretted. As early as 1928 he had written that it
would be 'quite an unpardonable mistake to accept the conclusions
of a Jewish psychology as generally valid'.[13] Kabbalah, with its
Jewish roots, was not a system Jung cared to acknowledge. At least,
not until the final decades of his career.

Things changed when, in 1952, Jung began to recognise a
connection between Kabbalah and his theories of psychology. That
year, in response to a question from his long-term correspondent
James Kirsch, Jung wrote that although Judaism did not believe
God's incarnation in Christ, the *sefira* known as *Tiferet* symbolised
the same notion in Kabbalah.[14] Two years later he wrote to another
correspondent about the 'remarkable idea' in Lurianic Kabbalah.

'Man is destined to become God's helper in the attempt to restore the vessels which were broken when God thought to create a world. Only a few weeks ago, I came across this impressive doctrine ... I am glad that I can quote at least one voice in favour of my rather involuntary manifesto.'[15]

In the same year Jung published his last major work, *Mysterium Coniunctionis*. Ostensibly a treatise on alchemy, the book was replete with Kabbalistic symbols. These symbols were to become defining metaphors in the final development of his theory of psychology.

Buried deep within the unconscious mind of all of us, according to Jungian psychology, are ancient categories of concepts and beliefs. Styled as archetypes in Jung's terminology, they stem from the earliest stages of human development. He believed that our loss of contact with these primitive archetypes was the cause of psychological trauma and neurosis.

Jung considered the symbols of Kabbalah to be metaphors for these archetypes. Primordial Man, for example represents the unconscious Self; the ten *sefirot* which emanate from him are the values through which humankind was created. Psychological transformation, the reintegration of values within the Self, is analogous to the reunification of the *sefirot*. In a similar way the breaking of the vessels at creation and the sparks that need to be elevated to restore the cosmos symbolise the psychological process required to restore and unify the Self.[16]

Jung was not the first to appreciate that Kabbalah could be interpreted as a window onto the human soul. He was well aware that the *hasidim* had preceded him, although it is hard to say exactly when this realisation dawned. He appears to have known nothing about Hasidism in 1933, when his outstanding student Erich Neumann strongly condemned his teacher's apparent flirtation with Nazism and his negative attitude to Jews. Neumann castigated Jung for knowing everything about India 2000 years ago, yet nothing of the *hasidim* only 150 years earlier.[17]

How much of a role this criticism played in Jung's subsequent investigation of Hasidism may never be known. What we do know, however, is that in 1955, during an 80th birthday interview, he confessed, 'Do you know who anticipated my entire psychology in the eighteenth century? The Hassidic Rabbi Baer from Meseritz, whom they called the Great Maggid. He was a most impressive man.'¹⁸ Jung was speaking of the *Besht*'s successor, the Preacher of Mezeritch.

Jung was a student of Kabbalah, but it would be hard to categorise him as a Kabbalist. Even so, his contribution to the future of Kabbalah was seminal. Like von Rosenroth, Leibniz and van Helmont before him, he introduced Kabbalah into the intellectual discourse of his time. It became a topic of interest among those who might previously have dismissed it as superstitious nonsense, irrelevant at best.

The Kabbalah that Jung knew was medieval in character, reflecting Isaac Luria's teachings in sixteenth-century Safed. It would need to be modernised if it was to have any relevance in the rapidly changing post-war world. Jung didn't know it but the process of modernisation had begun; Abraham Isaac Kook and Yehuda Ashlag may not have considered themselves modernisers, but that is what they turned out to be.

All that was needed now was for the new person-centred terms in which they expressed Kabbalah to converge with the psychological respectability that Jung had given it. Change was in the air. Once again, Kabbalah was about to set off in a new direction.

The New Age

KABBALAH FOR A CHANGING WORLD

Yehuda Ashlag's clear and accessible explanations of Kabbalah found a receptive audience in the mid-twentieth century, even though the appeal of his socialism diminished as times changed. His most direct legacy, and that of Abraham Isaac Kook, is now to be found in Kabbalistic circles in Israel, where the founding of the Jewish state has cast a new light on the old themes of exile and redemption.

Classical Kabbalah regards the exile of the Jewish people from their ancestral homeland as the earthly manifestation of the estrangement of the *Shechina*, the divine presence, the *sefira* in closest contact with the created world. With the creation of the Jewish state and the return of the Jews to their patrimony, it was possible to imagine that the estrangement of the *Shechina* was also coming to an end. In Kabbalistic terms, its reunification with the upper *sefirot* had begun.

Abraham Isaac Kook, who lived before the State of Israel was founded, stressed that this redemptive process was driven by a small mystical elite whom he called *tsaddikim*, the same title as is applied to the heads of Hasidic dynasties. The devotional power of this elite is able, according to Kook, to influence the entire world. Kook seems to have seen their mystical power as the engine behind the nationalist Zionist movement, driving their efforts to establish the Jewish state. Unfortunately, like so much of the material he wrote, his views on nationalism are often opaque. The difficulty in understanding them is compounded by the fact that some of his most pertinent unpublished writings were concealed by his followers after his death. Those works they did release were often censored. Scholarly research is continuing to throw new light on his beliefs. Generally, though, Kook seems to have been reticent about the need to create a politically independent state because of the military threat. Yet at the same time he considered the mystically generated, emerging political power of the nation to be a messianic portent.[1]

Some of Kook's more radical followers have exploited his ideas about the mystical nature of power and nationalism to foster a more radical agenda. They use Kabbalistic vocabulary and metaphors to express partisan views. Opposing political positions are characterised as satanic and evil. Enemies of the state are portrayed as the husks of the broken cosmic vessels, entrapping the divine sparks of nationalism. In this new strain of power-mysticism, Kabbalistic myth has become an allegory for political and military intransigence.

In the 1980s Israeli extremists hatched a plot to blow up the Al Aqsa Mosque and the Dome of the Rock on Jerusalem's Temple Mount, the site holy to both Jews and Muslims. The extremists expressed their intentions in Kabbalistic terms, claiming that they were engineering an 'awakening from below'. This is a rather obscure idea based on the dubious principle that by precipitating events the divine will can be bent to accommodate human desire. They planned to speed up the process of redemption by making it impossible for the divine will to do anything other than respond positively to their action. The absurd incongruity of trying to manipulate divine favour through a criminal act of terror seems not to have entered their minds. When the plot was rumbled and they were brought to trial, they were condemned by kabbalists and non-kabbalists alike. Nevertheless, they had demonstrated, as if anyone needed reminding, that Kabbalah, like nearly every other religious and ideological system, can be harnessed in the service of any political position however extreme, wrong or mad it may be.[2]

Nationalism is not the only manifestation of Kabbalah in contemporary Israel. In recent decades a small number of venerable, other-worldly kabbalists have become cult figures, their blessings, amulets and protective charms sought by the sick and needy, by politicians and those hoping for success in a new venture or enterprise. Kabbalah has become trendy; the bazaars, galleries and market stalls of Safed display Kabbalistic art, created in every conceivable medium. Within secular Israeli society an infiltration of New Age ideas and concepts has led to Kabbalah's blending with other forms of mystical speculation. Spiritually questing groups blend Kabbalah with tai chi or Chinese medicine. Israeli youth travel to India for spiritual inspiration, and study there with teachers of Kabbalah whom they might have met more easily at home. Kabbalistic healers offer alternatives to stress-filled lives. Authors try to demonstrate an affinity between science and Kabbalah.[3]

The popularity of Kabbalah as a New Age phenomenon in Israel demonstrates that, although the *Shechina*'s exile may not be over in theological terms, the establishment of a Jewish state with a Western cultural ethos has largely eliminated the yearning for redemption, other than among the strictly religious. Kabbalah has been transformed into a route towards self-enlightenment. Whether the different trends in Kabbalah in twenty-first-century Israel will coalesce into a single new mystical philosophy or whether we are witnessing another round of fragmentation within the spectrum of Kabbalistic thought is a question only time can answer.

The New Age is a product of the optimism which galvanised the West as the social and economic recovery from the Second World War gained momentum. This optimism expressed itself in the early 1960s with the belief that the world was entering the Age of Aquarius, an idealised, utopian era in which peace, love and harmony would reign. In Kabbalistic terms, it would be when the long-awaited repair of the cosmos would be brought about.

The Aquarian priests knew very little about Kabbalah, but here and there among the psychedelic vibes a Kabbalistic voice could be heard. In California, a group of Jewish hippy poets immersed themselves in Abraham Abulafia's mysticism. One of them, David Meltzer, published *Tree* magazine, a counter-cultural excursion into Kabbalistic art, poetry and texts.[4] Kabbalistic symbols and allusions also appeared in *Semina*, Wallace Berman's eclectic, hand-bound magazine. Around the same time two young rabbis, Shlomo Carlebach and Zalman Schachter, opened the House of Love and Prayer, a Kabbalistic-Hasidic synagogue in San Francisco, the capital city of the hippy revolution.

Responding to the allure of Eastern mysticism which had attracted disproportionate numbers of young Jews during the 1960s and 1970s, the saintly leader of Ḥabad Hasidism, Menaḥem Mendel Schneerson, created a highly successful outreach programme, drawing thousands of young Jews into his movement's orbit. Another young rabbi, Aryeh Kaplan, published a guide to Jewish meditation and translated several Kabbalistic texts, including *Sefer Yetsirah*, to which he appended an extensive and detailed commentary.

And in Israel, one man was embarking on a personal mission that would ultimately propel Kabbalah far beyond its core religious constituency. Claiming to be Yehuda Ashlag's mystical heir, the organisation he founded has attracted critics as rapidly as it has enthusiasts. His name was Philip Berg. His brainchild is now known as the Kabbalah Centre.

THE KABBALAH CENTRE

Among the students who gathered around Ashlag was his brother-in-law, Yehuda Tzvi Brandwein. Born into a Hasidic family, and ordained as a rabbi by Abraham Isaac Kook, Brandwein was a builder by trade who confined his Kabbalah studies to the hours when he was not working. This did not impede his prolific literary activity. Among his various books, his magnum opus was a 14-volume edition of Isaac Luria's teachings.

After Ashlag died, Brandwein completed his brother-in-law's commentary on the Zohar. He set up a small academy to disseminate Ashlag's teachings and, sharing a similar political outlook, chaired the religious affairs committee of Israel's trade union movement. Yet, distinguished scholar as he was and natural successor to Yehuda Ashlag, Brandwein would have gone down in history as just one Kabbalist among many had it not been for one of his own students. A student who for a while would be the husband of his niece, an insurance salesman from Brooklyn, Shraga Feivel Gruberger, later to be known as Philip Berg.

Philip Berg met Yehuda Tzvi Brandwein in Israel in 1964. On the face of it, the two men had something in common. Both had been ordained as rabbis, yet both decided not to follow vocational careers. But whereas Brandwein had continued his studies, and was now regarded as one of the leading kabbalists of his generation, Berg's thirst for mystical insight was as yet not satiated. Studying with Brandwein changed his life, and laid the foundations for Kabbalah's most recent controversy, albeit almost certainly not the last.

Returning to New York after meeting Brandwein, Berg opened the National Institute for Research in Kabbalah, with the intention of distributing his teacher's books and raising funds to support his academy. In 1969, when Brandwein died, Berg claimed that he'd sent him a letter, appointing him as the academy's head. This claim was contested, both by Brandwein's other students and by those of Ashlag's son and successor, Baruch. One of Baruch's pupils stated flatly that 'Berg did not study Kabbalah with any true Kabbalist; you can ask Ashlag or Brandwein about it'.[5]

Berg was not deterred by challenges to his self-proclaimed status. Adopting the mantle of Brandwein's successor, he expanded the activities of the National Institute, first producing English translations of Ashlag's writings and eventually his own popularised books on Kabbalah. He left his wife and eight children, setting out with his new wife, Karen Mulnick, to find their own students to teach. They were looking for young, secular Jews whom they would encourage to return to their ancestral faith. They intended to achieve this by teaching their particular perspective on Kabbalah, based on Ashlag's teachings but with a New Age outlook emphasising personal development and wellbeing, while minimising religious obligation and duty.

By the 1980s, having enjoyed a certain amount of success, Karen and Philip Berg decided to expand their constituency. Taking advice from marketing experts, they refined their vocabulary so as to appeal to North American audiences unfamiliar with traditional Jewish and Kabbalistic terminology. No longer focusing on young secular Jews, they reached out as widely as possible, to men and women, young and old. They introduced a range of products for sale, including audio tapes and beginners' guides to Kabbalah. They rebranded as the Kabbalah Centre and embarked on a more assertive proselytising programme.

In 1997 the comedian Sandra Bernhard introduced the singer Madonna to the Bergs. By this time there were 14 Kabbalah Centres, including eight in the USA and three in Israel, all small and undistinguished. Madonna embraced the Bergs' project with gusto, her enthusiastic promotion of the brand proving a turning point in the Kabbalah Centre's fortunes.

Madonna's name and active support acted as a magnet to the wealthy and famous. Celebrities arrived in their dozens, some just to dabble, others to peer intensely behind the mystical veil of secrecy that had parted for their benefit. Elizabeth Taylor, Roseanne Barr, Demi Moore, Mick Jagger, Gwyneth Paltrow, Ashton Kutcher and Donald Trump's ex-wife Marla Maples were just some of those said to have been associated with the Kabbalah Centre. In most cases their affiliation was easy to spot; on their wrists they wore the band of red thread that the Kabbalah Centre had adopted as its identifying icon, an ordinary piece of string mystically transformed into a status symbol.

There were warning signs. In the same year that Madonna joined the Kabbalah Centre, an article by the anti-cult campaigner Rick Ross quoted former members complaining of the opulent lifestyles enjoyed by the Bergs, along with accusations of abuse and exploitation. 'They say the Bergs decide "everything connected to the lives of the crew ... [Berg] is asked whether it is permissible to become pregnant, and Karen [Berg] is asked how to have sexual relations." One former follower admits, "I felt it was a great *mitzvah* [meritorious act] for me to clean Karen's washrooms. I used to clean her slippers with a toothbrush." '6

Nevertheless, such criticisms did nothing to lessen the Kabbalah Centre's popularity. The murmurings of a few apparent malcontents counted as little when compared to the spiritual bounty assured to those who immersed themselves in the Kabbalah Centre's teachings. The Bergs' charismatic leadership, Kabbalah's mystique and the allure of a star-studded cast of visitors propelled the Centre to heights that even Philip Berg could not have begun to contemplate when he was still Feivel Gruberger, a struggling insurance salesman with eight, soon to be abandoned, children.

New centres opened in France, Mexico and London. Although doubt continued to be cast upon the Bergs' motives during this period of rapid expansion, it seems fairly clear that the majority of people they employed to run the centres believed they were participating in a life-affirming, global mission to spread Kabbalah as widely as possible.

For some years the Kabbalah Centre appeared glamorous and dazzling. It was not to last. The early warning signs grew more and more ominous. The most damaging incident was when Madonna, with Philip Berg's son Michael, raised $18 million to found a school in Malawi. When it was discovered that, of the funds raised, $3 million had been spent on the Kabbalah Centre in Los Angeles, Madonna sacked Michael Berg and the rest of the school's board, and the Centre came under investigation for tax fraud.

The complaints and criticisms multiplied. Anti-cult organisations cited the products sold by the Kabbalah Centre, including bottles of mystically endowed 'Kabbalah water' and highly priced lengths of red string to be worn as bracelets to ward off the Evil Eye, as evidence that the organisation was more interested in money than spirituality. They quoted testimonies from people who had been asked to make large financial donations to the Centre or its staff, ostensibly to cure an illness or resolve a crisis. Today the Cult Education Institute's website carries over 300 critical media reports, many of which describe family breakups, financial destitution and sex scandals allegedly linked to the Kabbalah Centre.[7] According to the *Los Angeles Times*, the Kabbalah Centre was accused of taking more than $600,000 for the Centre from a widow with dementia.[8]

The media focused on sex scandals, probes by the tax authorities and criminal charges. When reporting on the Kabbalah Centre they invariably mentioned some of the celebrities who had been involved with it, more often than not Madonna. An investigation by *Radar* magazine produced a wave of accusations against the centres. These included 'bizarre scientific claims made by the Centre's leaders on behalf of Kabbalah Water, ranging from its ability to cleanse the lakes of Chernobyl of radiation, to its power to cure cancer, AIDS, and SARS' and their 'use of cult-like techniques to control members, including sleep deprivation, alienation from friends and family, and Kabbalah-dictated matchmaking'.

The scandals, combined with the vagaries of fashion, precipitated a celebrity exodus from the Centre. Speaking of the Kabbalah Centre in 2005, Sandra Bernhard said: 'I think they are a little bit lost on their own spiritual path right now. I think they've been overwhelmed by celebrity and that's always a corrupting experience.'[9]

When Philip Berg died in 2013 leadership of the organisation passed to Karen Berg and their sons. Things are quieter these days; the glamour has gone and the Evil Eye seems to have been tamed, at least for now. In 2017 the Kabbalah Centre was reported to be buying new premises in Los Angeles, the epicentre of their many lawsuits and investigations. Occupying an area of 58,000 square feet, the building was said to be costing them $60 million.

SCANNING

Although nominally based on Yehuda Ashlag's teachings, the Kabbalah Centre's model diverges in important ways. One of the most prominent differences lies in the Bergs' focus on a matrix of letters from which 72 three-lettered divine names can be derived.

The names can be found encoded in three successive biblical verses describing the parting of the Red Sea. Each verse, when written in Hebrew, comprises 72 letters.[10] By writing out the three verses, one above the other, with the second verse written backwards, one ends up with 72 columns of three letters. Each column is considered to constitute a divine name.

The 72 names are mentioned in the *Bahir* and in the Zohar, but neither book deals with them in any great depth. Neither do they feature significantly in Ashlag's Kabbalah. But they receive extensive treatment in the Bergs' system, where they are considered a 'very powerful spiritual technology'. Indeed, they become the very tools that Moses used to part the Red Sea. As the Kabbalah Centre puts it:

> The formula Moses used to overcome the laws of nature has been hidden in the Zohar for 2000 years. This formula is called the 72 Names of God. Not names like Betty, Bill and Barbara, but rather 72 sequences composed of Hebrew letters that have the extraordinary power to overcome the laws of nature in all forms, including human nature ... The 72 Names are each 3-letter sequences that act like an index to specific, spiritual frequencies. By simply looking at the letters, as well as closing your eyes and visualising them, you can connect with these frequencies.[11]

Making use of the 72 names in this way turns them into meditation aids, that can be used to 'recalibrate the day' when feeling stressed or negative. Each name offers a 'unique vibration', encompassing a wide range of emotional, spiritual and psychological needs. These include subduing the ego, releasing negative energy and even contacting departed souls. Their powers can be invoked simply by passing one's eyes over the three letters of the appropriate name, with the intention of drawing upon their energy.[12]

Known as 'scanning', this technique invented by the Kabbalah Centre requires no knowledge of the Hebrew alphabet. All that is needed is the ability to concentrate on the shapes of the letters.

And it is not just the 72 names that can be scanned. The Kabbalah Centre also encourages scanning of the Zohar. Cryptic in meaning, and obscure even in translation, Kabbalah's primary text is not an easy book to study. Yet the Kabbalah Centre believes that its letters contain energy, and that this energy can be released through scanning. The Centre publishes a chart showing, for each week of the year, the sections of the Zohar that should be scanned by the eyes, together with additional passages that can be subjected to the same process in case of special need, for example to assist with an easy childbirth, achieve financial success or find the right partner.

The technique of scanning owes something of a debt to an exhortation by the sixteenth-century Safed Kabbalist Moses Cordovero to read the Zohar, even if one doesn't understand it.[13] The big difference is that Cordovero assumed that his readers could understand Hebrew. After all, that was the language in which he was writing to them. Hebrew is a similar language to the Aramaic of the Zohar; with effort a Hebrew speaker can make sense of Aramaic. Cordovero's intention was that, even if people didn't understand the language of the Zohar on first reading, by going over the same passage again and again they would begin to make sense of it. It's a far cry from what the Bergs had in mind.

Commenting on the Kabbalah Centre's claims that one needed no knowledge of Hebrew to plumb the depths of Kabbalah, that scanning alone would suffice, Rabbi Barry Marcus of London's Central Synagogue commented, 'These ridiculous claims are tantamount to being told at school that you do not require a basic understanding of arithmetic and science in order to master quantum physics.'[14]

IS THE KABBALAH CENTRE LEGITIMATE?

There is no precedent in classical Kabbalah for the technique of scanning, or for the belief that each of the 72, three-letter names governs a distinct psycho-spiritual property. But precedent is not a necessary condition for Kabbalah. Throughout its history Kabbalah has been endowed with innovative ideas. In earlier times, classical kabbalists immersed in the traditions of the Zohar and Isaac Luria paid little attention to these innovations. Isolated in inward-looking communities, in an age when there was little meaningful communication between different faiths, very few of them had even heard of Christian Cabala, of the fusion of Cabala with the occult sciences, or of Kabbalah's role in the early Enlightenment. There were occasional moments of cooperation between Christian and Jewish kabbalists, collaboration during the printing of the Mantua edition of the Zohar being one such example. But these instances of contact were few and far between. And the few classical kabbalists who had heard of Christian Cabala or the occult did not consider these innovations to be a threat. They were too far removed from their realm of experience.

Today, in an age of enhanced communication, even the most isolated Kabbalist has heard mention of the Kabbalah Centre. And although the Kabbalah Centre has universalised its message in recent decades, unlike Christian Cabala it is unashamedly rooted in the Jewish tradition. It's understandable therefore that to a traditional Kabbalist living in the twenty-first century the Kabbalah Centre appears as a more disturbing development than did Christian Cabala to his forebears in the sixteenth.

This explains why classical kabbalists and even traditional Jews with no Kabbalistic leanings have reacted so strongly to the Kabbalah Centre, accusing it of being a cult, of trivialising Kabbalah and distorting it for their own ends. They condemn the Centre for teaching people unversed in the complexities of Talmudic traditions, who do not have the tools to appreciate its intricacies or the necessary training to defend themselves against the Kabbalah's perceived perils. Numerous rabbis have warned their communities about the Kabbalah Centre, describing it as 'shallow and unimportant', 'a blatant distortion, leading students to believe they have attained high spiritual levels when in fact they have been sold a fantasy' and, most disparagingly, 'a dangerous sect'.[15]

As early as 1993 the Chief Rabbi of South Africa, Cyril Harris, issued a statement alerting all congregants to avoid it. Ten years later, when the Kabbalah Centre in London embarked on a high-profile recruitment campaign to mark the opening of its new £3.7 million centre, Jewish leaders responded forcefully. The United Synagogue issued a statement advising the Jewish community that the Centre did not fall 'within the remit of the Chief Rabbinate or any other recognized Orthodox authority in the UK'.[16] An article in *The Times* reported that a businesswoman in her late 30s had been urged to donate £65,000 to cleanse her parents' souls. When confronted with this and other complaints, Yehuda Berg, another of Philip Berg's sons, laid the blame on the 'jealous and sceptical'.[17]

In January 2005 a BBC documentary brought the controversies surrounding the Kabbalah Centre to a wider audience. One of its leading teachers told an undercover reporter that the Holocaust could have been avoided if the Jews had used Kabbalah. Another reporter was offered a package of remedies against cancer, for £860.[18]

It is not just traditional kabbalists who rail against the Kabbalah Centre. As we have seen, most of the controversies have had less to do with esoteric theories than with the traditional scandals of money, power and sex.

However, charges of impropriety, unethical conduct and exploitation of the vulnerable are of a different nature to those alleging misrepresentation of the Kabbalah. Accusations of unethical behaviour do not necessarily mean that the Kabbalah Centre's method is illegitimate. Indeed, of all the charges laid at the Kabbalah Centre's door, that of illegitimacy seems to be the hardest for its accusers to defend.

There has long been a Kabbalistic tradition that bears no relation to either Judaism or Christianity. It manifested itself, as we have seen, in alchemy and the occult. Whatever they may say to the contrary, the leaders of the Kabbalah Centre can only imagine themselves as belonging to this external tradition. There is no other credible way to explain some of the statements that they make. The historical fiction headlined on the front page of Kabbalah.com that the Kabbalah Centre was founded by Yehuda Ashlag in 1922 (rather than Philip Berg in the 1980s) is a deliberate misrepresentation, an attempt to equate their approach with that of Ashlag, rather than it being a rather distant derivative, as it truly is. It is unlikely that they would make this claim if they truly saw themselves as part of the Jewish Kabbalistic tradition, a tradition which accepts Ashlag but rejects them. Similarly, the tautology that they are a 'spiritual community that lives within Jewish traditions that are in harmony with Kabbalistic principles' can only be understood if it means that they regard Kabbalah and Judaism as distinct from each other.[19]

The Kabbalah Centre belongs to the long tradition of Kabbalah that lies outside Judaism. Nor does it have any connection with Christian Cabala. But nobody has proprietary rights to the name Kabbalah; it means too many things to too many different sorts of people. As such, it is difficult to condemn their system as inauthentic or as a distortion, even though it bears less than a shadow of resemblance to any system of Kabbalah that preceded it. All one can say is that the Kabbalah Centre's approach is closer to a New Age philosophy than it is to classical or traditional Kabbalah. This does not make it illegitimate. Nor, of course, does it in any way excuse the more serious charges of which it has been accused.

THE FUTURE OF KABBALAH

The history of Kabbalah has been one of continual development and change. Driven as much by the spirit of the age as by the demands of religion, Kabbalistic ideas and techniques have been used, among other things, to fuel mystical trips to heaven, reveal ideas concealed deep within the biblical text, symbolise the mysteries of creation, uncover the mystical roots of Christianity, magically change lives and objects, provide a theoretical foundation for community building, promote messianic dreams, achieve psychological and spiritual harmony, open a gateway to the supernatural and help the pious to draw closer to the Divine.

Largely perceived as superstition, Kabbalah fell out of favour among Western Jews during the nineteenth and early twentieth centuries. It continued to be nurtured within oriental and Hasidic communities, which were more insulated from cultural trends in the West. But even here, its centrality to daily life diminished. It was not until the 1920s that Kabbalah's profile began to recover, largely through the work of Yehuda Ashlag and Abraham Isaac Kook. The academic community began to take an interest in the mid-twentieth century, driven mainly by the pioneering work of Gershom Scholem. Now Kabbalah studies are on the curriculum in universities across the world.

Nearly 80 years ago Gershom Scholem predicted that the story of Jewish mysticism had not ended, that it had not yet become history. The secret life it holds, he said, could break out tomorrow, although under which aspects it would surface again, one could not tell.

Scholem was right on all counts. He was right that the history of Kabbalah had not ended, and nor has it yet. He could not have predicted the Kabbalah Centre, or the New Age, nor could he have foreseen the harnessing of Kabbalah by right-wing nationalist groups in Israel. The only constant, which was by no means certain when he made the prediction in the dark days of 1941, has been the use of Kabbalah by strictly orthodox Jews. Even in those circles, not wholly unresponsive to the zeitgeist, Kabbalah has started to play a more prominent role in the study programmes of young rabbinical students; the taboo against studying it before the age of 40 now largely ignored.

Today Kabbalah is a household word, although there are signs that its mention no longer commands the same veneration that it did a few years ago. The Kabbalah Centre may still be investing in expensive buildings, but it appears to have passed the peak of its popularity. The New Age is morphing into a twenty-first-century cultural norm and right-wing Israel nationalism is subject to the transience that affects all political ideologies. Were Scholem to be making his prediction today, it would be pretty similar to when he first made it. Kabbalah has a future, of that there is little doubt. What that future holds, for Kabbalah, as for the rest of us, is anybody's guess.

Appendix: A Very Brief Outline of the *Sefirot*

Kabbalah grapples with the problem of how the diverse and flawed material world can be created by an infinite God who has no limits and no imperfections, who is devoid of all contradictions and diversity and who is in no way tangible or material. In Kabbalistic terminology this infinite Creator is called *En-Sof*, meaning 'without end'. *En-Sof* is absolutely unknowable, to the extent that it can neither be contemplated nor be the object of any thought. It is utterly transcendent, incomprehensible and unreachable.

Yet there is an aspect of God which manifests itself to the world. It is through this process of manifestation that the universe was created. Drawing on the theories of a Greek philosophical school called Neoplatonism, the kabbalists describe this process as a series of emanations of divine power that issued from *En-Sof*. What instigated these emanations is unknowable, but the emanations themselves act as a sort of bridge between the infinite and finite.

These emanations are called *sefirot* (singular *sefira*). The word originally meant numbers but was later given other meanings: spheres, powers or lights. There are ten *sefirot*, which descend hierarchically from each other, divine benevolence flowing between them. The *sefirot* have names which allude to the divine powers contained within them. They are sometimes designated as

parts of God's body, for although the kabbalists know that God
has no body, they also know that humanity was created 'in God's
image'.[1]

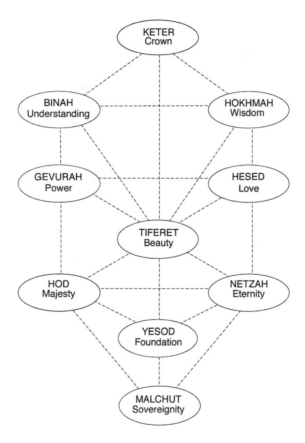

The idea of humanity being created in the divine image is
alluded to by a common portrayal of the *sefirot* in the shape of a
human being. The shape can also be visualised as a tree, hence the
designation of the *sefirot* as the Tree of Life.

The uppermost *sefira*, *Keter* or Crown, represents the divine will
for volition. This desire results in the will to create, which flows
into the next two *sefirot*, Wisdom and Understanding. These three
sefirot collectively represent the divine 'thought' which is necessary
to design the process of creation.

The lower seven *sefirot* derive from the top three and represent divine qualities. Those on the left, the side which tends towards judgement, balance those on the right, the side of mercy. The central *sefirot* act as a harmonising principle between the two sides. In this way *Gevurah*, or Power, on the left-hand side, is balanced by *Hesed*, or Love, on the right. Both, if left uncontrolled, might engulf all. Standing between and below them, *Tiferet* reconciles and harmonises the two.

The lowest of the ten *sefirot* is *Malchut*, or Sovereignty. Also known as *Shechina*, this *sefira* can be perceived in the physical world as the divine presence. However, the *Shechina*, which is feminine in nature, is in exile, cast adrift from the unity of the other *sefirot*. In the later Kabbalah, which is unashamed to express ideas in terms of sexual imagery, the goal of human endeavour is to restore *Shechina* to her original place among the *sefirot*, elevating her until she unites with the male waters of *Tiferet*.

Just as *En-Sof* is unknowable and may not even be imagined, so speculation on the upper three *sefirot* is also discouraged. The vast majority of Kabbalistic investigation is directed at the lower seven *sefirot*, the Children as they are often termed, of Wisdom and Understanding; Wisdom being the father and Understanding being the mother.

In a variant of this scheme, the *sefirot* occupy each of four worlds. The upper world is known as the World of Emanation. Beneath that is the World of Creation, then the World of Formation and finally the divine source of the domain we occupy, the World of Action. These four worlds became significant in the more complex Kabbalistic system devised by Isaac Luria, some 300 years after the Zohar.

In Luria's system a fundamental question is to explain how the infinite God could create the finite universe. How can infinity find the space to create something new? The answer is mooted through the doctrine of *tzimtzum*, in which God withdraws into himself, leaving a void within which the world can be created. However, the void is not wholly empty. A ray of divine light remains in the void, containing the infinitely small points that will expand to become the *sefirot*. The ray of light is called Primordial Man. Light streamed from the eyes of Primordial Man to form *Keter*, the uppermost *sefira*. The light flowed backwards and forward between *Keter* and Primordial Man to form the next two *sefirot*. Primordial Man constitutes a world of its own, above the four worlds mentioned above.

The ten *sefirot*, the worlds, the letters of God's name, their numerical values and other even more complex clusters of divine entities can all be infinitely combined with each other by skilled kabbalists. In performing their complex combinations and unifications these skilled kabbalists fulfil humanity's ordained role in the universe's essential and ongoing process of creation, restoration and repair.

This is a far from complete outline of the Kabbalistic system. It is not necessary to understand it in order to read this book. But it may be useful for reference from time to time.

Glossary

Ari or *Ha-Ari*: 'Lion' or 'The Lion'. The name by which Isaac Luria is usually known, based on an anagram formed from the first letters of his name.

Ari Nohem: 'Roaring Lion' or 'A Lion Roars'. Seventeenth-century critique of Kabbalah by Leon of Modena.

Ars Magna: 'Great Art', thirteenth-century mystical book by Catalan philosopher Ramon Llull.

Baal Shem: 'Master of the Name'. A title given to masters of practical Kabbalah who might, for example, write amulets, compound elixirs or exorcise demons.

Bahir: The first truly Kabbalistic book, of unknown authorship, first referred to in twelfth-century Provence.

Besht: The popular name for Israel ben Eliezer, the putative founder of Hasidism. Formed as an acronym from the initial letters of his honorific *Ba'al Shem Tov*: Master of the Good Name.

Cabala: The traditional spelling used to denote Christian Kabbalah.

Conclusiones: The name of Pico della Mirandola's thesis in which he tried to draw together 900 universal philosophical statements.

Conversos: Spanish and Portuguese Jews who converted to Christianity, usually as a result of pressure from the Inquisition.

Corpus Hermeticum: A magical-mystical collection of writings from the early Christian era which were mistakenly believed to have been composed by a mythical priest-magician, Hermes Trismegistus, in ancient Egypt.

De Verbo Mirifico: 'On the Miraculous Word', the first Cabalistic book written by Johannes Reuchlin.

Devekut: 'Clinging'. The mystical state of approaching God with the intention of communing with, or cleaving to, him.

Dybbuk: A spirit or demon believed to have taken possession of someone, inducing a state of madness.

Golem: An artificial human, made from clay and animated through Kabbalistic rituals and incantations.

Hasidim, sing. *Hasid*: Literally meaning pious people; generally used to denote members of the religious-Kabbalist movement originating in eighteenth-century Eastern Europe and still flourishing today.

Hechalot, sing. *Hechal*: Literally meaning palaces, temples or halls. Used to describe the literature that deals with mystical voyages to the heavenly halls, and the mystics who undertook these voyages.

Hechalot Rabbati: 'The Great Hechalot' or 'Great Palaces'. The most important text of the *hechalot* literature.

Idra Rabba: 'The Great Assembly'. A section of the Zohar describing an important gathering at which the deepest mysteries were revealed.

Kabbala Denudata: 'Cabala Unveiled'. Title of a seventeenth-century anthology of earlier Cabalistic texts, translated into Latin by Christian Knorr von Rosenroth.

Kavod: 'Glory', used in a Kabbalistic sense to designate a divine quality flowing from heaven to earth.

Maggid: 'Storyteller'. A skilful preacher, usually in the Hasidic community. Can also mean a heavenly voice that communicates exclusively with a specific person.

Malchut: 'Kingdom'. The tenth and lowest *sefira*, also known as *Shechina*. Symbolises the divine presence on earth.

Merkavah: 'Chariot'. The heavenly throne in Ezekiel's vision. The destination for those who aspire to travel mystically to heaven.

Midrash: The ancient Jewish technique of expounding the biblical text. Also the name of a genre of Hebrew Bible commentary, written mainly in the first millennium CE.

Pardes: 'Orchard' or 'Garden'. A synonym for heaven. Of Persian origin, related to the word Paradise.

Rabad: Acronym by which Rabbi Abraham ben David of Posquières was known.

Ramban: Acronym by which Rabbi Moses ben Naḥman was known.

Raza Raba: 'The Great Mystery'. Ninth-century Jewish-Babylonian tract which formed the basis of the book *Bahir*.

Sefer Hasidim: 'Book of the Pious'. Thirteenth-century moralistic book written by Judah the Pious in Germany.

Sefer Yetsirah: 'Book of Formation'. Written prior to the tenth century, a mystical book from an anonymous author that hints at the use of letters and digits in the creation of the world.

Sefira, pl. *Sefirot*: 'Number'. One of the ten divine emanations that form the basis of Kabbalistic theory. See Appendix.

Shechina: The divine presence, represented by the lowest of the ten *sefirot*, also known as *Malchut*.

Shiur Komah: 'Measure of Stature'. A book from the *Hechalot* period that purports to describe the dimensions and proportions of God's body.

Shoah: The Holocaust.

Sitra Aḥra: 'The Other Side'. The domain of evil, a mirror image of the *sefirotic* realm.

Talmud: Compendium of Jewish law, ethics, legend and faith. The central text of rabbinic Judaism, containing over a million words in 35 volumes. Completed by sixth century.

Tiferet: 'Beauty'. The sixth *sefira*, reconciling the *sefirot* of Power and Love.

Torah: The Five Books of Moses, believed to have been revealed to Moses in the Wilderness.

Tsaddik: 'Righteous'. The head of a Hasidic dynasty.

Tzimtzum: 'Contraction'. The process of God's withdrawal into himself to form the void in which the cosmos was created.

Notes

PREFACE

1 The molecular structure of Kabbalah water: http://news.bbc.co.uk/1/
   hi/4158287.stm. Sandra Bernhard: Emalie Marthe, Why Celebrities
   Stopped Following Kabbalah, *Broadly*, May 2017, https://broadly.
   vice.com/en_us/article/mbqvmy/why-celebrities-stopped-following-
   kabbalah. Big bang: Myers, 2011.

INTRODUCTION

1 Genesis 1.3.
2 Yates, 1972.

THE ORIGINS OF KABBALAH

1 The phrase 'cut the shoots' is obscure. But Elisha ben Abuya is best
   known as a learned rabbinic scholar who abandoned his religion. In
   Talmudic literature he is often referred to as 'the other one'. Cutting
   the shoots seems to be an extension of the *Pardes*–garden metaphor.
2 Tosefta Hagigah 2.2.
3 Babylonian Talmud, Hagigah 14b.
4 The prohibition is set out in Mishnah Hagigah 2.1: 'The mystery of
   creation is not explained to two people, nor the heavenly Chariot to
   one. Anyone who enquires into these four things, it would be better
   that they were not born: What is above, what is below, what is before
   and what is behind.'

5 Hekhalot Zutarti §408, Schafer, 1981.

6 Swartz, 2011.

7 Exodus 24.10

8 Isaiah 6.1–4.

9 Ezekiel I.

10 Ezekiel 29.3.

11 Schafer, 1981, §314.

12 1 Kings 18.42.

13 Schafer, 1981, §206.

14 B. M. Lewin, *The Iggeret of Rav Sherira Gaon*, Haifa, 1921.

15 For example, the *kedushot* of Kallir (Elbogen, 1993).

16 In Talmud Nazir 48b Ishmael is called the High Priest. In Berachot 7a he describes how he was ministering as High Priest when he saw a divine manifestation which asked for his blessing. In Berachot 51a Suriyel advises him how to avoid snares set by destructive angels.

17 Babylonian Talmud Sanhedrin 90b and elsewhere.

18 Genesis 5.24.

19 A parasang is an ancient Persian measurement indicating the distance a person can walk in an hour.

20 Probably meaning a drop of semen.

21 Adapted from Chavel, 1983.

22 Schafer, 1981, §108.

23 Ibid., §120.

24 *Hechalot Rabbati* 31.4.

25 Talmud Hagigah 15a.

26 Exodus 15.6.

27 For example, Ishmael's aphorism 'The Torah speaks in human language'; see above, p. 20.

28 The *targumim*, as these Aramaic translations were known, relied on the concept of *memra*, a sort of divine manifestation that could perform the physical acts that the Bible had attributed to God.

29 Moses of Taku, *K'tav Tamim* in *Otzar Nehmad*, Vol. 3, ed. R. Kirchheim, Vienna, 1860, pp. 54–99.

30 *Yad, Hilchot Teshuva* 3.7. For a fuller discussion see Jacobs, 1964, pp. 121ff.

31 Friedman, 2007.

32 Georges Ifrah, *The Universal History of Numbers: From Prehistory to the Invention of the Computer*, New York, 2000.

33 Cohen, 1985.
34 Scholem, 1946.
35 In Hebrew the letters are also numerals. So every word has a numerical value. This technique, known as *gematria*, is used frequently in Kabbalah.
36 Song of Songs 5.11–13.
37 Dan, 2006.
38 Jackson, 2000.
39 For Maimonides see *Teshuvot HaRambam*, ed. A. Freiman, Jerusalem, 1934, No. 373; for Moses of Taku, *K'tav Tamim* in *Otzar Nehmad*, Vol. 3, ed. R. Kirchheim, Vienna, 1860, pp. 54–99.
40 Sanhedrin, 65b, 67b.
41 Dan, 1998.
42 The Hebrew word *blima*, which we have translated as 'without substance', literally means 'without what'. It comes from Job 26.7, where it is used to mean nothingness, empty space: he suspended the earth upon *blima*.
43 *Sefer Yetsirah* 1.4. The standard text edition of *Sefer Yetsirah* is Hayman, 2004. A detailed English commentary, but which does require some familiarity with orthodox Jewish principles, is Kaplan, 1997.
44 Ibid. 1.7
45 Ibid. 4.13.

OUT OF THE EAST

1 In a 1963 article in the journal *Tarbiz*, Israel Weinstock argued that a magic manuscript in the British Museum had been composed by Abu Aharon. In a rejoinder in the same issue of the journal, Gershom Scholem forcefully disagreed. I. Weinstock, Discovered Legacy of Mystic Writings by Aaron of Baghdad, *Tarbiz* 32, 1963, pp. 153–9; G. Scholem, Has a Legacy Been Discovered of Mystic Writings Left by Abu Aaron of Baghdad? ibid, pp. 252–65.
2 Robert Bonfil draws a connection between Abu Aharon's subduing of the lion in Baghdad and his restoration of the Spaniard's son in Gaeta. The donkey is the common motif which connects the two tales, and Bonfil takes the second tale to mean that by restoring the natural order of things, Aba Aharon had begun the process of atonement for his earlier offence. Bonfil, 2009.

3 Bonfil, 2009.

4 Babylonian Talmud, Sanhedrin 95b.

5 *Megillat Ahimaatz*, ed. B. Klaar, Jerusalem, 1944, p. 12.

6 Eleazar's claim that the family were relocated by Charlemagne himself has been modified by modern historians, who believe that it must have been his descendant Charles the Bald. If Charlemagne had commanded the family to move north, it could only have been before his death in around 814. Aaron is supposed to have arrived in Italy in 870, by which time Charlemagne was long dead. His grandson Charles II, known as Charles the Bald, seems a much more likely candidate for the bussing of the Kalonymus family from Italian to German soil.

7 From 'I Will Tell Belet's Story', published in *Penguin Book of Hebrew Verse*, ed. T. Carmi, Harmondsworth, 1981.

8 Dan and Kiener, 1986.

9 The historical name for the movement is *Hasidei Ashkenaz*. I have tried, wherever possible, to minimise the use of non-English terminology unless there is a compelling reason to do so.

10 Exodus 24.16.

11 Ezekiel 3.23.

12 For example, Psalm 45.14, All the glory of the king's daughter is inward.

13 For examples of how some of these techniques were applied see chapter 5, The Mystical Piety of Rabbi Eleazar of Worms in Jacobs, 1977.

14 Introduction to *Sefer HaRokeach*, Lemburg, 1859. The *gematria of* אלעזר and רקח are both 308.

15 Alexander, 1995.

16 Dan, 1993, p. 101.

17 *Sefer Hasidim*, No. 323, ed. A. A. Price, Toronto, 1960. The verse from Proverbs is 17.5.

18 Dan, 1993.

19 Dan, 1966.

THE BEGINNING OF KABBALAH

1 Thomsett, 2011, p. 81.

2 Thomsett, 2011.

3 Elior, 2006.

4 Meroz, 2002.

5 Scholem, 1987.

6 Scholem, 1987, Meroz, 2002.

7 The relationship between *Bahir* and Catharism has been explored by Shulamit Shahar in Catharism and the Beginnings of the Kabbalah in Languedoc — Elements Common to the Catharic Scriptures and the Book 'Bahir', *Tarbiz*, 40, 1971, pp. 483–507.

8 Shahar, 1971.

9 *Book of the Two Principles*, quoted in Shahar, 1971. The *Book of the Two Principles* was published by A. Dondaine in *Un traité néo-manichéen du XIIIe siècle: Le Liber de Duobus Principiis, suivi d'un fragment de rituel cathare*, Rome, 1939. An English translation is at http://gnosis.org/library/cathar-two-principles.htm

10 *Bahir*, 102, All quotations from Bahir are adapted from Aryeh Kaplan's 1979 translation, with occasional amendments to clarify context.

11 Kaplan 1979, pp. 123–4.

12 Ibid., p. 95.

13 Abraham ben David of Posquières, *Tamim Deim #113*, Lvov, 1812.

14 The glosses, known as *hasagot haravad*, are printed in every good edition of Maimonides's *Mishneh Torah*. Like all rabbinic acronyms, Rabad's is made up of the initial letters of his title and name, **R**abbi **A**braham **b**en **D**avid, with vowels added to assist pronunciation.

15 For a thorough examination of Maimonides's closely reasoned philosophy, which seems wholly antithetical to mystical speculation, see Kellner, 2006. But see also Louis Jacobs, Attitudes of the kabbalists and *hasidim* towards Maimonides, in *The Solomon Goldman Lectures*, Vol. 5, ed Byron L. Sherwin and Michael Carasik, Chicago, 1990, pp. 45–55, accessible on http://louisjacobs.org/articles/attitudes-of-the-kabbalists-and-hasidim-towards-maimonides/

16 Lobel, 2006.

17 For Abraham Maimonides see Russ-Fishbane, 2015. Scholem's comment is in Scholem, 1987.

18 Scholem, 1987, p. 394.

19 Ibid., p. 253.

20 Ibid., p. 394. It is in this letter that Isaac mentions that his ancestors never let a word of Kabbalistic doctrine cross their lips (above, p. 55).

21 Graetz, 1919.

22 Scholem, 1987, p. 43.

23 The Disputation at Barcelona, as it is known, is discussed in detail in R. Chazan, 1977, C. Chavel, 1983 and Freedman, 2014.

24 Naḥmanides, *Introduction to Commentary to the Torah*, Rome, 1480.

25 Naḥmanides commentary to Deuteronomy 33.1.

26 The most important are *Meirat Einayim* by Isaac of Acre and *Keter Shem Tov* by Shem Tov ibn Gaon.

27 Peter Burke, *Secret History and Historical Consciousness: From the Renaissance to Romanticism*, Brighton, 2016.

RADIANCE

1 B. Talmud Shabbat 33b.

2 The implication is derived by Boaz Huss in Huss 2016, based on a comparison of B. Talmud Yevamot 49b, Sanhedrin 97b and Sukkah 45b.

3 Zohar I, 11a–11b. Tishby and Lachower, 1989, translated by David Goldstein, pp. 154–5. All quotes from the Zohar are taken from this three-volume work. According to Tishby, bar Yoḥai's cryptic remark at the end means 'I would not be at the high level of experience I attained in the cave'.

4 Tishby and Lachower, 1989.

5 Scholem, 1946 enumerates 18 distinct sections.

6 Fishbane, 2011.

7 Scholem gives the example of R. Haggai in Zohar III 158a who lived at least 150 years after Shimon bar Yohai. Scholem, 1946.

8 Abrams, 2009.

9 Liebes, 1993, Meroz, 2007.

10 Above, p. 64.

11 Zohar II 15b-16a *Midrash ha-ne'elam*, Tishby and Lachower, 1989, pp. 672–3.

12 For the apple see, for example, Song of Songs 2.3; for the willow, Leviticus 23.40; and for hyssop, Exodus 12.22.

13 Exodus 3.1–4.17.

14 Zohar III 152a, Tishby and Lachower, 1989, pp. 126–7. The phrase 'soul of the soul' is a common Kabbalistic allusion to levels of deeper concealment which lie behind that which is already concealed.

15 Numbers 12.8.

16 Zohar III 132b.

17 Zohar III 79b. Boaz Huss's argument is set out in detail in Chapter 1 of his book Huss, 2016a, pp. 12–35.

18 Wolfson, 2011.

19 Hames, 2007.

20 Ibid., introduction.

21 Abraham Abulafia, *Book of the Life of the World to Come*, translated in Scholem, 1946, p. 136. I have modernised the somewhat archaic English of the translation.

22 Idel, 2011.

23 Idel, 1988.

24 Freedman, 2014.

25 Bava Batra 17a. For Aaron's death see Numbers 33.38, for Moses, Deuteronomy 34.5.

26 Recanati, Commentary to the Torah, Genesis 49.33.

27 Bereshit Rabba 1.1.

28 Yohanan Alemanno, Collectanea MS Oxford, Bodleiana 2234, fol. 164a, quoted in Idel, 2011, p. 183.

29 Idel, 2011.

CHRISTIAN CABALA

1 Yates, 1979. Chapter 1 contains a brief, clear discussion of Ramon Llull's *Ars Magna* with reference to Christian Cabala.

2 Yates, 1964.

3 Plato and Jeremiah were not contemporaries: they lived at least a century apart. The myth that Plato was a pupil of Jeremiah was known to Ambrose but refuted by Augustine. Nevertheless, it persisted into the Renaissance and is still cited today in certain ahistorical religious circles.

4 Borghesi, Papio and Riva, 2012.

5 Wirszubski, 1989.

6 Wirszubski wonders whether Lancilloto of Faenza, of whom Mithridates unashamedly boasts in his translations, is the same young boy whom he demanded in return for teaching Pico Aramaic. Ibid., p. 73.

7 Ibid.

8 Borghesi, Papio and Riva, 2012.

9 'Nulla est scientia quae nos magis certificet de divinitate Christi quam magia et cabala.'

10 Russell Kirk in Introduction to Pico della Mirandola, 1956, p. xi.

11 Pico della Mirandola, 1956, pp. 7–8.

12 Ibid., p. 48.

13 Ibid., p. 65.

14 Song of Songs 1.2. For Recanati's understanding of death by a kiss see above, p.85.

15 Wirszubski, 1989.

16 Arnold, 2011.

17 Price, 2010.

18 Zika, 2003.

19 For an excellent history of the Reuchlin Affair see Price, 2010.

20 Johannes Pfefferkorn, *Ajn mitleydliche claeg*, Cologne: 1521, fol. H2r, accessed at http://www.library.illinois.edu/rbx/exhibitions/Reuchlin/essay-section7.html

21 Dan, 1997.

22 Price, 2010.

23 Yates, 1979, p. 29.

24 Idel, 2014.

25 Reuchlin, 1993, p. 241, quoted in ibid., p. 36.

26 The difference between the two schools comes across most clearly when we look at how they interpreted the Bible. The early Jewish sources used wordplay and creative literary techniques to read new ideas into the text of the Bible. This was a technique which ran all the way through early Jewish Bible intepretation; it was not new to Kabbalah. The kabbalists relied on these same techniques, backed up by their own mystical experiences, to find hints in the Bible that alluded to the structure of the cosmos and the secret processes within the divine realms. Joseph Dan argues that Reuchlin failed to understand this. Rather than being a tool for understanding the cosmos, in Reuchlin's mind the techniques became the purpose of Cabala and were overemphasised.

An example of this occurs in the way that Exodus 14.19–21 was interpreted. Each of the three sentences contains 72 letters. The Jewish kabbalists believed that each sentence was attributed to one of the *sefirot* and that these three sets of 72 letters comprised the secret name of God. They wrote out the three sentences, each on a different line, but reversed the order of the second sentence, so that it became meaningless. They then read downwards to compose 72 words, each of three letters. All these three-letter words were meaningless, but each was considered to be an aspect of the divine name. The whole purpose of the exercise was to illustrate the basic Kabbalistic idea that the letters in the Torah are themselves the name of God, expressed in a complex permutation.Reuchlin, however, in Joseph Dan's analysis, missed this point. He understood how to derive the the 72 three-letter words, but treated them as the names of angels, which could be called upon for magical purposes. Whereas the kabbalists had viewed these three sentences in a mystical context, Reuchlin, not versed in the traditional subtleties of word and letter substitition, introduced an element of magic. See Dan, 1997.

THE CITY OF MYSTICS

1 Tishby and Lachower, 1989, Vol. I, p. 34.
2 Fine, 2003.
3 Zohar III 144a-b. Translation from Tishby and Lachower, 1989, Vol. I, pp. 158–9. The ten companions represent the ten *sefirot*. The three who ascend to heaven are the upper three, unknowable *sefirot*; those who remain in Rabbi Shimon's house are the lower seven, which act more directly upon the world. Rabbi Shimon himself represents the *sefirah* of *Binah*, understanding, which is the seventh from the bottom and from which all other *sefirot* flow. Hence everything depends on him.
4 Scholem, 1946.
5 For Lemmlein as a kabbalist see Scholem, 1973, p. 18, n. 15.
6 For examples see Shlomo Brody, *Halakha and Kabbalah: Rabbi Joseph Karo's Shulchan Aruch and Magid Mesharim.* http://text.rcarabbis. org/halakha-and-Kabbalah-rabbi-joseph-karos-shulchan-aruch-and-magid-mesharim-by-shlomo-brody/. Also Dwek, 2011, p. 76, on Karo's inclusion of the Zohar as an authoritative source in *Bet Yosef*; see also footnotes on Karo's ruling on wearing tefillin (leather boxes containing biblical passages, worn for prayer) during festivals.
7 Alkabetz's letter is printed in the introduction to Joseph Karo's diary *Maggid Mesharim*. This translation is taken from Jacobs, 1977, p. 126.
8 Jacobs, 1974, p. 11.
9 Fine, 2003.
10 Schechter, 1908.
11 Huss, 2016a.

12 Introduction to *Pardes Rimonim*, written by Moses Cordovero in 1548, published Kraków, 1591, Munkacs, 1906.

13 Liebes, 1993.

14 Fine, 2003.

15 *Sefer Hakavanot Uma'asim Nisim*, Constantinople, 1720, cited in Schechter, 1908.

16 Scholem, 1973, pp. 27–8.

17 Fine, 2003.

18 Saadia Gaon, *Sefer Emunot v'Deot*, New York, 1970, quoted in Scholem, 1991, p. 198.

19 For example, Kaplan, 1979, Section 155: 'But when Israel is wicked, [then I will bring] seed that has already been in the world. It is thus written (Ecclesiastes 1.4), "A generation goes and a generation comes."'

20 Fine, 2003, p. 337, quoting Hayyim Vital, *Sefer Hahezyanot*, ed. A. Z. Aeshcoly, Jerusalem, 1954, p. 143.

21 Scholem, 1946.

CABALA AND THE OCCULT SCIENCES

1 Idel, 2011. The two most important books were the *Sefer HaPeliyah and Sefer HaTemunot*. Idel regards these as originating among the exiles in Byzantium, although there are other scholarly opinions as to their origins.

2 O'Malley, 1968.

3 Busi, 1997.

4 For Halfon's attitude to non-binding the nature of Jewish law on non-Jews see his responsum printed (in Hebrew) at the end of D. Kaufmann, Elia Menachem Chalfan on Jews Teaching Hebrew to Non-Jews, *Jewish Quarterly Review*, Vol. 9, No. 3, April 1897, pp. 500–08, available at www.jstor.org/stable/1450681. For more on Henry VIII's appeal to Jewish law in his 'Great Matter' see Freedman 2014.

5 *Letters and Papers, Foreign and Domestic, Henry VIII*, Vol. 5, *1531–1532*. Originally published by Her Majesty's Stationery Office, London, 1880. Accessed at http://www.british-history.ac.uk/letters-papers-hen8/vol5/pp199-217

6 Hanegraaff, 2015.

7 Yates, 1979.

8 Reichert, 1997.

9 Petry, 2004, p. 158.

10 Ibid., p. 9.
11 Yates, 1964.
12 Parry, 2015.
13 Yates, 1979.
14 Scholem, 2015, p. 7.
15 Forshaw, 2013.
16 Michael Toxites, *Onomasticum*, quoted in ibid., p. 379.
17 Yates, 1979.

GOLEM

1 Eugene Newman, *Life and Teachings of Isaiah Horowitz*, London, 1972.
2 Sherwin, 1982.
3 *Sefer Niflaot Maharal im Hagolem*, Yudl Rosenberg, Piotrkow, 1909.
4 Sanhedrin 65b.
5 The Hebrew phrase is רבא ברא גברא. The Hebrew word for a limb is אבר.
6 Alternative translations: 'a third-grown calf' and 'was created for them'.
7 For a full discussion of these and other ancient early attempts to create living beings see Butler, 1993, and Idel, 1990. The discussion in the rest of this section is based on Idel's *Golem*.
8 *Hiddushei Aggadot*, Vol. 3, p. 166, Bene Berak, 1980, quoted in Idel, 1990, p. 108.
9 For arguments in favour of a connection between the golem and the homunculus see Scholem, 1996, p. 197, LaGrandeur, 2013, p. 66. For the counter-argument see Idel, 1990, pp. 185–6.
10 Idel, 1990, p. 102. The verse about Abraham and Sarah occurs in Genesis 12.5.

GOOD, EVIL AND THE LIFE OF THE SOUL

1 Elior, 2008.
2 The exorcism ceremony is described in detail in Elior, 2008, and the sources she quotes on p. 104, n. 54.
3 The Hebrew title is *Iggeret Sod Hageulah*. Never printed, a microfilm of the manuscript can be accessed at http://web.nli.org.il/sites/NLI/Hebrew/digitallibrary/pages/viewer.aspx?presentorid=MANUSCRIPTS&docid=PNX_MANUSCRIPTS000089059-1

4 B. Gittin 68a–b.
5 Lilith is long-haired in B. Eruvin 100b, winged in B. Niddah 24b and the seductress par excellence in B. Shabbat 151b.
6 This legend about Lilith is first mentioned in the eleventh-century *Alphabet of Ben Sira*.
7 Genesis 8.21.
8 For an expanded discussion on the Kabbalistic theories on the Descent of the Soul see Vol. 2 of Tishby and Lachower, 1989.
9 Idel, 1988, p. 67, cites a parallel in the *Katha Upanishad* IV:15. See also the sources he cites on p. 306, nn. 63 and 64.
10 Naḥmanides, Commentary to Deuteronomy 22.11.
11 Quoted in Idel, 1988, p. 68.

CRITICS AND CRISIS

1 Avraham Yagel, *Beit Ya'ar Halevanon* 47b, cited in Ruderman, 1988.
2 For the story of the banning and burning of the Talmud, which regularly occurred from the thirteenth to the sixteenth century, see Freedman, 2014.
3 Dwek, 2011.
4 R. Moses Basola, Introduction to Mantua edition of *Tikkunei Hazohar*, quoted in Huss, 2016a, p. 197.
5 Huss, 2016a.
6 *Ari Nohem*, ed. Nehemiah Leibowitz, Jerusalem, 1929, pp. 68–9, quoted in Dwek, 2011, p. 62.
7 Above, p. 68.
8 For examples of this debate see Ruderman, 1988, pp. 128ff.
9 The earlier Kabbalistic myth, that the *Shechina* was exiled when Adam and Eve were expelled from the Garden of Eden, is modified in Lurianic Kabbalah; she fell to earth with the holy sparks, where she remains, awaiting redemption.
10 There have been many studies of Shabbetai Tzvi, his biography, messianic movement and mystical theology. The classic treatment is Scholem 1973. Although some of his conclusions have since been challenged, it remains the fullest and most comprehensive work on the subject.
11 For discussions and various views on this subject see Scholem, 1973, Idel, 1998, Liebes, 1993.
12 Scholem, 1973, p. 208.

13 The technical Hebrew term for such repairs, whether of an individual or the whole world, is *tikkun*, plural *tikkunim*.
14 Scholem, 1973, p. 235.
15 Goodman, 2017.
16 Jacob Sasportas, *Tzitzat Novel Tzvi*, ed. Y. Tishby, Jerusalem, 1954, p. 142, quoted in Scholem, 1973, p. 261.
17 The rule was proposed by Shabbetai HoKohen, in his commentary on *Shulchan Arukh*, the legal code compiled in Safed by Joseph Caro (Siftei Kohen, *Shulchan Arukh, Yoreh Deah* 346.6).

DECLINE AND REVIVAL

1 Stolzenberg, 2004.
2 For John Dee's influence on the Rosicrucian movement see Yates, 1972. For a contrary view see Goodrick-Clarke, 1999.
3 Tilton, 2015.
4 For a fuller, more detailed explanation see Coudert, 2011, and her lecture The Kabbalah, Science, and the Enlightenment available at http://www.magia-metachemica.net/uploads/1 /o/6/2/10624795/coudert_-_Kabbalah_and_enlightenment.pdf
5 Huss, 2016b.
6 Coudert, 1997, p. 151.
7 For a detailed examination of Leibniz's relationship with Kabbalah see Coudert, 1995.
8 Nuovo, 2011.
9 John Harrison, *The Library of Isaac Newton*, Cambridge, 1978.
10 For an explanation of Newton's analysis and rejection of Kabbalistic theory see Goldish, 1994.

HASIDISM

1 Adapted from Buber, 1955.
2 For an up-to-date summary of contemporary research into the origins of Hasidism, and the *Besht*'s role, see Biale et al., 2018.
3 Rosman, 1996.
4 Dov Baer of Mezeritch *Maggid Devarav L'Yaakov*, ed. Shlomo of Lutsk, Koretz, 1781, quoted in Biale et al., 2018, p. 62.
5 Yaakov Yosef ben Zvi Hirsch HaCohen of Polonnoye *Ben Porat Yosef* Korets, 1781.

6 Jacobs, 1977, pp. 183–7.
7 2 Samuel 24.14.
8 Jacobs, 1972.
9 This belief is known as panentheism. It is a view held to a greater or lesser extent in all Hasidic mysticism although it can be distinguished most clearly in Habad hasidism. It differs from pantheism, which holds that God is in everything. In panentheism, the cosmos is contained within God, yet the two are separate. Jacobs, 1966.
10 Some sects, most notably Habad and Bratslav, no longer have a living *tsaddik*. Instead they venerate their departed leaders.
11 Biale et al., 2018.
12 Scholem, 1946.
13 Stern, 2013.
14 Mordekhai Wilenski, *Hasidim uMitnagdim*, Jerusalem, 1990, quoted in Stern, 2013, p. 86.
15 For a fuller treatment of this subject see Alan Nadler, *The Faith of the Mithnagdim: Rabbinic Responses to Hasidic Rapture*, Johns Hopkins University Press, Baltimore, 1999, pp. 11–20 and Alan Brill, The Mystical Path of the Vilna Gaon, *Journal of Jewish Thought and Philosophy* 3:1, 1993, pp. 131–51.

THE OCCULT REVIVAL

1 Hanegraaff, 2010.
2 Franck, 1926, p. xxiv. The journals he discussed included *Lotus*, *Dawn* and *Initiation*, which described itself as a 'Philosophic and Independent Review of the Higher Studies'.
3 Idel, 1988, p. 8.
4 Franck, 1926, p. xl.
5 Ibid, p. xxix.
6 For fuller details of Lévi's biography and thought see McIntosh, 2011.
7 Eliphas Lévi, *Dogma et rituel de la haute Magice*, 1896, cited in McIntosh, 2015.
8 *L'Initiation: Revue Philosophique des Hautes Études,* Vols 7 and 8, Paris, 1890–91, accessed at http://www.iapsop.com/archive/materials/l_initiation/
9 Ibid, Vol. 9, No. 3, December 1890, p. 194.
10 Farley, 2009.

11 H. P. Blavatsky *The Kabalah and the Kabalists*, Theosophical Publishing House, Adyar, 1919.

12 Historic Lecture – Golden Dawn, by V. H. Frater Sapere Aude (Dr W. Wynn Westcott), accessed at http://www.sacred-texts.com/eso/historic.htm

13 Churton, 2011.

14 Bogdan, 2015.

15 Aleister Crowley, The Temple of Solomon, *The Equinox* Vol. 1, No. 5, March 1911, p. 71.

TOWARDS MODERNITY

1 Graetz, 1919, Vol. 3, p. 332.

2 Ibid., Vol, 4, p. 442.

3 Idel, 1988.

4 Meir, 2016.

5 S. Y. Zevin, *Ishim ve-Shittot*, Tel Aviv, 1958, p. 232, quoted in Kaplan and Shatz, 1995, p. 2.

6 Scholem, 1946, pp. 354 and 18.

7 Abraham Isaac Kook, *Orot HaKodesh* 1.9, quoted in Fine, 1995.

8 Biale et al., 2018.

9 Fine, 2003.

10 Jung, *Mysterium Coniunctionis*. C. G. Jung *Collected Works*, Vol. 14, 1955, p. 294.

11 Above, p. 112.

12 In a letter to Rev. Erastus Evans, 17 February 1954. Jung, *Letters*, Vol. I and II, 1973.

13 C. G. Jung, *The Relations between the Ego and the Unconscious.*, *Collected Works*, Vol. 7, translated by R. F. C. Hull, Princeton, 1966. Cited in Drob, 1999.

14 Classical kabbalists would profoundly disagree.

15 Jung, *Letters*, Vol. 2, 1973, p. 157, quoted in Drob, 1999.

16 For a fuller description of Jung's application of Kabbalah to psychology, see the work of Sanford L. Drob, particularly Drob, 1999, and the website dedicated to his work, www.newkabbalah.com

17 *Analytical Psychology in Exile: The Correspondence of C.G. Jung and Erich Neumann*, ed. Martin Liebscher, 2015.

18 Quoted in *C.G. Jung Speaking: Interviews and Encounters*, ed. William McGuire and R. F. C. Hull, 1977, pp. 271–2.

THE NEW AGE

1 For a fuller discussion of Kook's nationalism, and the way it has been harnessed by his followers see Garb, 2009.

2 Garb, 2009.

3 Ibid. Garb's overview of the current state of New Age and Kabbalah mysticism in Israel is both thorough and incisive.

4 Christine A. Meilicke, The Forgotten History of David Meltzer's Journal 'Tree'. *Studies in American Jewish Literature*, 22, 2003, pp. 52–71. Christine A. Meilicke, Abulafianism among the Counterculture kabbalists, *Jewish Studies Quarterly*, 9(1), 2002, pp. 71–101.

5 For the claim of a letter see *History of the Kabbalah Centre*, https://Kabbalah.com/history. For the refutation see Michael Laitman, *Authentic Kabbalah or Authentic Business?* http://laitman.com/2008/07/authentic-Kabbalah-or-authentic-business/. Less partisan accounts of the origins and issues surrounding the Kabbalah Centre can be found in Altglas, 2011, and Myers, 2008.

6 Rick Ross, Has Madonna Joined a Cult? Cult Education Institute, December 1997, accessed at https://www.culteducation.com/group/1008-kabbalah-centre/11736-has-madonna-joined-a-cult.html

7 https://www.culteducation.com/group/1008-Kabbalah-centre.html

8 Emalie Marthe, *Why Celebrities Stopped Following Kabbalah*, Broadly, May 2017, https://broadly.vice.com/en_us/article/mbqvmy/why-celebrities-stopped-following-kabbalah

9 Naomi Pfefferman, Sandra Bernhard Talks about Kabbalah: Queen of Acerbity Takes on the World. Excerpted from the *Jewish Journal*, 11 March 2005, accessed at https://www.culteducation.com/group/1008-kabbalah-centre/11596-sandra-bernhard-talks-about-kabbalah.html

10 Exodus 14.19–21

11 The 72 Names of God. https://livingwisdom.Kabbalah.com/72-names-god

12 Open the Door: How to Connect to the Creator Through Meditation https://livingwisdom.Kabbalah.com/open-door-how-connect-creator-through-meditation

13 Above, p. 158.

14 Rabbi Barry Marcus, Kabala – So What's The Big Attraction? *South African Jewish Observer*, 2005.

15 'Shallow and unimportant': Rabbi Adin Steinzaltz, quoted in http://jewishjournal.com/culture/arts/8644/; 'a blatant distortion': Rabbi

Abraham Greenbaum, http://www.azamra.org/Kabbalah/FAQ/21. htm; 'a dangerous sect': Responsum of Bet Din Tzedek quoted in http://www.yadleachim.co.il/?CategoryID=111&ArticleID=125.
16 Statement from the Office of the Chief Rabbi, the London Beth Din and the Rabbinical Council of the United Synagogue, 25 March 2004.
17 *The Times*, 3 April 2004.
18 *Sweeney Investigates: The Kabbalah Centre*, BBC2, 13 January 2005.
19 https://Kabbalah.com/history

APPENDIX: A VERY BRIEF OUTLINE OF THE *SEFIROT*

1 Genesis 1.27.

Bibliography

Abrams, D. (2009). The Invention of the Zohar as a Book: On the Assumptions and Expectations of kabbalists and Modern Scholars. *Kabbalah*, 19, 7–142.

Alexander, T. (1995). Rabbi Judah the Pious as a Legendary Figure. In K. E. Grözinger (ed.), *Mysticism, Magic, and Kabbalah in Ashkenazi Judaism: International Symposium Held in Frankfurt am Main 1991* (pp. 123–138). Berlin: Walter de Gruyter.

Altglas, V. (2011). The Challenges of Universalizing Religion: The Kabbalah Centre in France and Britain. *Nova Religio: The Journal of Alternative and Emergent Religions*, 15(1), 22–43.

Arnold, J. (2011). *The Great Humanists: An Introduction*. London: I. B. Tauris.

Biale, D., et al. (2018). *Hasidism: A New History*. Princeton, NJ: Princeton University Press.

Bogdan, H. (2015). Aleister Crowley. In C. Partridge, *The Occult World* (pp. 293–302). London: Routledge.

Bonfil, R. (2009). *History and Folklore in a Medieval Jewish Chronicle: The Family Chronicle of Aḥima'az Ben Paltiel*. Leiden: Brill.

Borghesi, F., Papio, M., and Riva, M. (2012). *Pico della Mirandola: Oration on the Dignity of Man: A New Translation and Commentary*. New York: Cambridge University Press.

Buber, M. (1955). *The Legend of the Baal-Shem*. (M. Friedman, trans.) New York: Harper & Row.

Busi, G. (1997). Francesco Zorzi, A Methodical Dreamer. In J. Dan (ed.), *Symposium, The Christian Kabbalah: Jewish Mystical Books & their Christian Interpreters: A Symposium* (pp. 97–119). Cambridge, MA: Harvard University Press.

Butler, E. (1993). *The Myth of the Magus*. Cambridge: Cambridge University Press.

Caputo, N. (2007). *Maimonides in Medieval Catalonia; History, Community and Messianism*. Notre Dame, IN: University of Notre Dame Press.

Chavel, C. B. (1983). *The Disputation at Barcelona*. New York: Shilo.

Chazan, R. (1977). The Barcelona 'Disputation' of 1263: Christian Missionizing and Jewish Response. *Speculum*, 52(4), 824–42.

Churton, T. (2011). *Aleister Crowley: The Biography*. London: Watkins Publishing.

Cohen, M. S. (1985). *Shiur Komah: Texts and Recensions*. Tübingen: Mohr Siebeck.

Coudert, A. (1995). *Leibniz and the Kabbalah*. Dordrecht, Boston and London: Kluwer Academic Publishers.

— (1997). Leibniz, Locke, Newton and the Kabbalah. In J. Dan (ed.), *The Christian Kabbalah: Jewish Mystical Books & their Christian Interpreters: A Symposium* (pp. 149–79). Cambridge, MA: Harvard University Press.

— (2011). Christian Kabbalah. In F. E. Greenspahn (ed.), *Jewish Mysticism and Kabbalah: New Insights and Scholarship* (pp. 159–74). New York: New York University Press.

Dan, J. (1966). The Beginings of Jewish Mysticism in Europe. In C. Roth (ed.), *The World History of the Jewish People: The Dark Ages – Jews in Christian Europe 711–1096* (pp. 282–90). London: W. H. Allen.

— (1993). Was There Really a Hasidic Movement in Medieval Germany?. In P. Schafer, and J. Dan (eds), *Gershom Scholem's Major Trends in Jewish Mysticism, 50 Years After. Proceedings of the Sixth Annual Conference on the History of Jewish Mysticism*. Tübingen: Mohr Siebeck.

—(1997). The Kabbalah of Johannes Reuchlin and Its Historical Significance. In J. Dan (ed.), *The Christian kabbalah: Jewish mystical books & their Christian interpreters: a symposium* (pp. 55–97). Cambridge, Mass.: Harvard University Press.

— (1998). *Jewish Mysticism – Late Antiquity*. Northvale, NJ: Jason Aaronson.

— (1999). *The Unique Cherub Circle: A School of Mystics and Esoterics in Medieval Germany*. Tübingen: Mohr Siebeck.

— (2006). *Kaballah: A Very Short Introduction*. Oxford: Oxford University Press.

—, and Kiener, R. C. (1986). *The Early Kabbalah*. New York: Paulist Press.

Drob, Sanford L. (1999). Jung and the Kabbalah. *History of Psychology*, No 2, pp. 102–108.

Dwek, Y. (2011). *The Scandal of Kabbalah: Leon Modena, Jewish Mysticism, Early Modern Venice.* Princeton NJ: Princeton University Press.

Elbogen, I. (1993). *Jewish Liturgy: A Comprehensive Histor.* (R. P. Scheindlin, trans.) Philadephia, PA: The Jewish Publication Society.

Elior, R. (2006). *The Mystical Origins of Hasidism.* (S. Carmy, trans.) Oxford and Portland, OR: Littman Library of Jewish Civilization.

— (2008). *Dybbuks and Jewish Women in Social History, Mysticism and Folklore.* (J. Linsider, trans.) Jerusalem and New York: Urim Publications.

Etkes, I. (2004). *The Besht: Magician, Mystic, and Leader.* Hanover, NH: University Press of New England.

Farley, H. (2009). *A Cultural History of Tarot: From Entertainment to Esotericism.* London: I. B. Tauris.

Fine, L. (1995). Rav Kook and the Jewish Mystical Tradition. In L. J. Kaplan, and D. Shatz, *Rabbi Abraham Isaac Kook and Jewish Spirituality* (pp. 27–40). New York: New York University Press.

— (2003). *Physician of the Soul, Healer of the Cosmos: Isaac Luria and His Kabbalistic Fellowship.* Stanford, CA: Stanford University Press.

Fishbane, E. P. (2011). The Zohar: Masterpiece of Jewish Mysticism. In F. E. Greenspahn (ed.), *Jewish Mysticism and Kabbalah: New Insights and Scholarship* (pp. 49–67). New York: New York University Press.

Fishman, T. (1999). The Penitential System of Hasidei Ashkenaz and the Problem of Cultural Boundaries. *The Journal of Jewish Thought and Philosophy*, 8, 201–29.

— (2011). *Becoming the People of the Talmud.* Philadelphia, PA: University of Pennsylvania Press.

Forshaw, P. J. (2013). Cabala Chymica or Chemia Cabalistica – Early Modern Alchemists and Cabala. *Ambix*, 60(4), 361–89.

Franck, A. (1926). *The Kabbalah, or the Religious Philosophy of the Hebrews.* (I. Sossnitz, trans.) New York: The Kabbalah Publishing Company.

Freedman, H. (2014). *The Talmud: A Biography: Banned, Censored and Burned, The Book They Could Not Suppress.* London: Bloomsbury.

Friedman, S. (2007). Anthropomorphism and Its Eradication. In W. Asselt, P. Geest, D. Müller and T. Salemink, *Iconoclasm and Iconoclash – Struggle for Religious Identity* (pp. 157–78). Leiden: Brill.

Garb, J. (2009). *The Chosen Will Become Herds: Studies in Twentieth Century Kabbalah.* (Y. Berkovits-Murciano, trans.) New Haven, CT: Yale University Press.

Goldish, M. (1994). Newton on Kabbalah. In J. Force, and R. Popkin (eds), *The Books of Nature and Scripture: Recent Essays on Natural Philosophy* (pp. 89–103). Dordrecht: Springer.

Goodman, M. (2017). *A History of Judaism.* London: Penguin.

Goodrick-Clarke, N. (1999). The Rosicrucian Prelude: John Dee's Mission in Central Europe. In R. White, *The Rosicrucian Enlightenment Revisited* (pp. 73–98). Hudson, NY: Lindisfarne Books.

Graetz, H. (1919). *History of the Jews.* (A. Rhine and A. Harkavy, trans.) New York: The Hebrew Publishing Company.

Hames, H. J. (2007). *Like Angels on Jacob's Ladder: Abraham Abulafia, the Franciscans and Joachinism.* Albany, NY: State University of New York Press.

Hanegraaff, W. J. (2010). The Beginnings of Occultist Kabbalah: Adolphe Frank and Eliphas Levi. In B. Huss, M. Pasi and K. von Stuckrad, *Kabbalah and Modernity: Interpretations, Transformations, Adaptations* (pp. 107–29). Leiden: Brill. S.

— (2015). Heinrich Cornelius Agrippa. In C. Partridge (ed.), *The Occult World* (pp. 92–8). Abingdon and New York: Routledge.

Hayman, A. P. (2004). *Sefer Yeṣira: Edition, Translation and Text-critical Commentary.* Tübingen: Mohr Siebeck.

Herrmann, K. (1993). Re-Written Mystical Texts: The Transmission of the Hekhalot Literature in the Middle Ages. *Bulletin of the John Rylands Library,* 75, 97–116.

Huss, B. (2005). All You Need Is LAV: Madonna and Postmodern Kabbalah. *Jewish Quarterly Review,* 95(4), 611–24.

— (2010). 'The Sufi Society from America', Theosophy and Kabbalah in Poona in the Late Nineteenth Century. In B. Huss, M. Pasi and K. von Stuckrad, *Kabbalah and Modernity: Interpretations, transformations, adaptations* (pp. 167–96). Leiden: Brill.

— (2016a). *The Zohar: Reception and Impact.* (Y. Nave, trans.) Portland: Littman Library of Jewish Civilisation.

— (2016b). Translations of the Zohar: Historical Contexts and Ideological Frameworks. *Correspondences* 4, 81–128.

Idel, M. (1987). Differing Conceptions of Kabbalah in the Early 17th Century. In I. Twersky, and B. Septimus, *Jewish Thought in the Seventeenth Century* (pp. 137–200). Cambridge, MA: Harvard University Press.

— (1988). *Kabbalah: New Perspectives.* New Haven, CT: Yale University Press.

— (1990). *Golem: Jewish Magical and Mystical Traditions on the Artificial Anthropoid.* Albany, NY: State University of New York Press.

— (1998). *Messianic Mystics.* New Haven, CT and London: Yale University Press.

— (2011). *Kaballah in Italy 1280–1510: A Survey.* New Haven, CT: Yale University Press.

— (2014). Johannes Reuchlin: Kabbalah, Pythagorean Philosophy and Modern Scholarship. In H. Tirosh-Samuelson and A. W. Hughes, *Moshe Idel: Representing God* (pp. 31–55). Leiden: Brill.

Jackson, H. M. (2000). The Origins and Development of 'Shi' ur Qomah' Revelation in Jewish Mysticism. *Journal for the Study of Judasim in the Persian, Hellenistic and Roman Period,* 31(4), 373–415.

Jacobs, L. (1964). *Principles of the Jewish Faith.* London: Vallentine Mitchell.

— (1966). *Seeker of Unity: The Life and Works of Aaron of Starosselje.* London: Vallentine Mitchell.

— (1972). *Hasidic Prayer.* London: Routledge & Kegan Paul.

— (1974). *The Palm Tree of Deborah.* (L. Jacobs, trans.) New York: Hermon Press.

— (1977). *Jewish Mystical Testimonies.* New York: Shocken Books.

— (1985). *The Talmudic Argument: A Study in Talmudic Reasoning and Methodology.* Cambridge: Cambridge University Press.

Jellinek, A. (1855). *Bet HaMidrash* (Vol. 3). Leipzig.

Kahana, M. I. (2006). The Halakhic Midrashim. In S. Safrai, Z. Safrai, J. Schwartz and P. J. Tomson, *The Literature of the Sages: Second Part* (pp. 3–106). Amsterdam: Fortress Press.

Kaplan, A. (1979). *The Bahir.* New York: Weiser.

— (1997). *Sefer Yetzirah: The Book of Creation in Theory and Practice.* San Francisco, CA: Weiser.

Kaplan, L., and Shatz, D. (1995). *Rabbi Abraham Isaac Kook and Jewish Spirituality.* New York: New York University Press.

Kellner, M. (2006). *Maimonides' Confrontation with Mysticism.* Oxford: Library of Jewish Civilization Littman.

Krakotzkin, R. (2007). *The Censor, the Editor, and the Text: The Catholic Church and the Shaping of the Jewish Canon in the Sixteenth Century.* Philadelphia, PA: University of Pennysylvania Press.

LaGrandeur, K. (2013). *Androids and Intelligent Networks in Early Modern Literature and Culture: Artificial Slaves.* New York and London: Routledge.

Liebes, Y. (1993a). *Studies in Jewish Myth and Jewish Messianism*. (B. Stein, trans.) New York: State University of New York Press.

— (1993b). *Studies in the Zohar*. Albany, NY: State University of New York Press.

Lobel, D. (2006). *A Sufi-Jewish Dialogue: Philosophy and Mysticism in Bahya ibn Paquda's 'Duties of the Heart'*. Philadephia, PA: Pennsylvania University Press.

Marcus, I. (1981). *Piety and Society: The Jewish Pietists of Medieval Germany*. Leiden: Brill.

McIntosh, C. (2011). *Eliphas Lévi and the French Occult Revival*. Albany, NY: State University of New York Press.

— (2015). Eliphas Lévi. In C. Partridge (ed.), *The Occult World* (pp. 220–30). Abingdon: Routledge.

Meir, J. (2016). *Kabbalistic Circles in Jerusalem (1896–1948)*. Leiden: Brill.

Meroz, R. (2002). On the Time and Place of Some of Sefer ha-Bahir [Hebrew]. *Da'at*, 49, 137–80.

— (2007). The Middle Eastern Origins of Kabbalah. *The Journal for the Study of Sephardic and Mizrachi Jewry*, 39–56.

Myers, J. (2007). *Kabbalah and the Spiritual Quest*. Westport, CT: Praeger Publishers.

— (2008). The Kabbalah Centre and Contemporary Spirituality. *Religion Compass*, 2, 409–20.

— (2011). Kabbalah at the Turn of the 21st Century. In F. E. Greenspahn, *Jewish Mysticism and Kabbalah – New Insights and Scholarship*, pp. 174–190. New York, NY: New York University Press.

Nuovo, V. (2011). *Christianity, Antiquity, and Enlightenment: Interpretations of Locke*. Dordrecht, Heidelberg, London and New York: Springer.

O'Malley, J. W. (1968). *Giles of Viterbo on Church and Reform: A Study in Renaissance Thought*. Leiden: Brill.

Parry, G. (2015). John Dee. In C. Partridge, *The Occult World* (pp. 107–16). London: Routledge.

Petry, Y. (2004). *Gender, Kabbalah and the Reformation: The Mystical Theology of Guillaume Postel*. Leiden: Brill.

Pico della Mirandola, G. (1956). *Oration on the Dignity of Man*. (A. R. Caponigri, trans.) Chicago, IL: Henry Regnery.

Price, D. H. (2010). *Johannes Reuchlin and the Campaign to Destroy Jewish Books*. Oxford: Oxford University Press.

Rapaport-Albert, A., and Kwasman, T. (2006). Late Aramaic: The
  Literary and Linguistic Context of the Zohar. *Aramaic Studies*,
  4(1), 5–19.
Reichert, K. (1997). Kabbalah in the Seventeenth Century. In
  J. Dan (ed.), *Symposium, The Christian Kabbalah: Jewish Mystical
  Books & their Christian Interpreters: a* (pp. 127–43). Cambridge,
  MA: Harvard University Press.
Reuchlin, J. (1993). *On the Art of the Kabbalah: De Arte Cabalistica.*
  (M. Goodman, and S. Goodman, trans.) Lincoln, NE: University of
  Nebraska Press.
Rosman, M. J. (1996a). *Founder of Hasidism: A Quest for the Historical
  Ba'al Shem Tov.* Berkeley, CA: University of California Press.
— (1996). *Founder of Hasidism: A Quest for the Historical Ba'al Shem Tov.*
  Berkeley, CA: University of California Press.
Ruderman, D. B. (1988). *Kabbalah, Magic, and Science: The Cultural
  Universe of a Sixteenth-century Jewish Physician.* Cambridge, MA:
  Harvard University Press.
Russ-Fishbane, E. (2015). *Judaism, Sufism, and the Pietists of
  Medieval Egypt: A Study of Abraham Maimonides and His Times.*
  Oxford: Oxford University Press.
Schafer, P. (1981). *Synopse zur Hekhalot-Literatur.* Tübingen: Mohr
  Siebeck.
— (2011). *The Origins of Jewish Mysticism.* Princeton, NJ: Princeton
  University Press.
Schechter, S. (1908). *Studies in Judaism*, 2nd Series. Philadelphia, PA:
  Jewish Publication Society of America.
Scholem, G. (1946). *Major Trends in Jewish Mysticism.* New York:
  Shocken Books.
— (1973). *Sabbetai Sevi, The Mystical Messiah.* Princeton, PA: Princeton
  University Press.
— (1987). *Origins of the Kabbalah.* (R. Werblowsky, ed., and A. Arjush,
  trans.) Princeton, NJ: Jewish Publication Society.
— (1991). *On the Mystical Shape of the Godhead: Basic Concepts
  in the Kabbalah.* (J. Chipman, ed., and J. Neugroschel, trans.)
  New York: Shocken Books.
— (1996). *On the Kabalah and Its Symbolism.* New York: Shocken
  Books.
— (2015). *Alchemy and Kabbala.* (K. Ottman, trans.) Thompson,
  CT: Spring Publications.

Shahar, S. (1971). Catharism and the Beginnings of the Kabbalah in Languedoc — Elements Common to the Catharic Scriptures and the Book 'Bahir'. *Tarbiz*, 40, 483–507.

Sherwin, B. (1982). *Mystical Theology and Social Dissent: The Life and Works of Judah Loew of Prague.* Oxford: Littman Library of Jewish Civilization.

Soloveitchik, H. (1976). Three Themes in the 'Sefer Hasidim'. *AJS Review*, 1, 311–57.

Stern, E. (2013). *The Genius: Elijah of Vilna and the Making of Modern Judaism.* New Haven, CT: Yale University Press.

Stolzenberg, D. (2004). Four Trees, Some Amulets, and the Seventy-Two Names of God. In P. Findlen, *Athanasius Kircher: The Last Man Who Knew Everything* (pp. 149–70). New York: Routledge.

Swartz, M. D. (2011). Ancient Jewish Mysticism. In F. E. Greenspahn, *Jewish Mysticism and Kabbalah – New Insights and Scholarship* (pp. 33–48). New York: New York University Press.

Thomsett, M. C. (2011). *Heresy in the Roman Catholic Church: A History.* Jefferson, NJ: McFarland & Co.

Tilton, H. (2015). Rosicrucian Manifestos and Early Rosicrucianism. In C. Partridge, *The Occult World* (pp. 128–44). London: Routledge.

Tishby, I., and Lachower, F. (1989). *The Wisdom of the Zohar: An Anthology of Texts.* (D. Goldstein, trans.) Oxford: Littman Library of Jewish Civilization.

Wirszubski, C. (1989). *Pico della Mirandola's Encounter with Jewish Mysticism.* Cambridge, MA: Harvard University Press.

Wolfson, E. R. (2011). Abrahan ben Samuel Abulafia and the Prophetic Kabbalah. In F. E. Greenspahn, *Jewish Mysticism and Kabbalah: New Insights and Scholarship* (pp. 68–90). New York: New York University Press.

Yates, F. A. (1964). *Giordano Bruno and the Hermetic Tradition.* Chicago, IL: University of Chicago Press.

— (1972). *The Rosicrucian Enlightenment.* London: Routledge.

— (1979). *The Occult Philosophy in the Elizabethan Age.* London: Routledge.

Zika, C. (2003). *Exorcising Our Demons: Magic, Witchcraft, and Visual Culture in Early Modern Europe.* Leiden: Brill.

Index

A Note on the Author

Harry Freedman writes about the history of religion and ideas and their relevance to the world today. His previous books include *The Talmud: A Biography* and *The Murderous History of Bible Translations*. Having spent 20 years in rural Devon he now lives in London with his wife Karen. He has 2 grown-up children, two adult step children and an expanding number of grandchildren.

A Note on the Type

The text of this book is set in Adobe Garamond. It is one of several versions of Garamond based on the designs of Claude Garamond. It is thought that Garamond based his font on Bembo, cut in 1495 by Francesco Griffo in collaboration with the Italian printer Aldus Manutius. Garamond types were first used in books printed in Paris around 1532. Many of the present-day versions of this type are based on the Typi Academiae of Jean Jannon cut in Sedan in 1615.

Claude Garamond was born in Paris in 1480. He learned how to cut type from his father and by the age of fifteen he was able to fashion steel punches the size of a pica with great precision. At the age of sixty he was commissioned by King Francis I to design a Greek alphabet, and for this he was given the honourable title of royal type founder. He died in 1561.